THE EVERYTHING® BUDDHISM BOOK 2ND EDITION

Dear Reader,

In 1984 I was at Amherst College with the Dalai Lama for the Inner Science Conference where His Holiness was lecturing on Buddhist psychology and Western thinkers provided commentary. The Dalai Lama's translator took ill and his substitute wasn't up to the task of translating the intricacies of Tibetan Buddhist psychology of mind. The result was hilarious. This is Buddhism in a nutshell; intellect ultimately yields to experience.

Inspired, I went to India after college and found His Holiness in Bodh Gaya giving the Kalachakra Tantra. He also guided us through Shantideva's Guide to the Bodhisattva Way of Life, culminating in taking the bodhisattva vows—"I vow to attain enlightenment for the benefit of all sentient beings."

It is in this spirit, dear reader, that I offer this book. Since 1989, I have been practicing vipassana meditation. I now teach this style of meditation at the Exquisite Mind (*www.exquisitemind.com*) in Burlington, Vermont. Since the time of the Buddha, metaphors have been crucial for teaching the dharma and I compiled many of these into my first book, *Wild Chickens and Petty Tyrants: 108 Metaphors for Mindfulness* (Wisdom). I also write a daily blog on beliefnet, *Mindfulness Matters: Tools for Living Now* (*www.blog.beliefnet.com/mindfulnessmatters*).

Arnie Kozak, PhD

Welcome to the EVERYTHING® Series!

These handy, accessible books give you all you need to tackle a difficult project, gain a new hobby, comprehend a fascinating topic, prepare for an exam, or even brush up on something you learned back in school but have since forgotten.

You can choose to read an *Everything®* book from cover to cover or just pick out the information you want from our four useful boxes: e-questions, e-facts, e-alerts, and e-ssentials.

We give you everything you need to know on the subject, but throw in a lot of fun stuff along the way, too.

We now have more than 400 *Everything®* books in print, spanning such wide-ranging categories as weddings, pregnancy, cooking, music instruction, foreign language, crafts, pets, New Age, and so much more. When you're done reading them all, you can finally say you know *Everything®*!

QUESTION

Answers to common questions

FACT

Important snippets of information

QUOTE

Words of wisdom from experts in the field

ESSENTIAL

Quick handy tips

PUBLISHER Karen Cooper
DIRECTOR OF ACQUISITIONS AND INNOVATION Paula Munier
MANAGING EDITOR, EVERYTHING® SERIES Lisa Laing
COPY CHIEF Casey Ebert
ASSISTANT PRODUCTION EDITOR Jacob Erickson
ACQUISITIONS EDITOR Lisa Laing
ASSOCIATE DEVELOPMENT EDITOR Hillary Thompson
EDITORIAL ASSISTANT Ross Weisman
EVERYTHING® SERIES COVER DESIGNER Erin Alexander
LAYOUT DESIGNERS Colleen Cunningham, Elisabeth Lariviere, Ashley Vierra, Denise Wallace

THE EVERYTHING® BUDDHISM BOOK 2ND EDITION

A complete introduction to the history, traditions, and beliefs of Buddhism, past and present

Arnie Kozak, PhD

Avon, Massachusetts

An Everything® Series Book.
Everything® and everything.com® are registered trademarks of F+W Media, Inc.

Published by Adams Media, a division of F+W Media, Inc.
57 Littlefield Street, Avon, MA 02322 U.S.A.
www.adamsmedia.com

ISBN 10: 1-4405-1028-8
ISBN 13: 978-1-4405-1028-1
eISBN 10: 1-4405-1163-2
eISBN 13: 978-1-4405-1163-9

Printed in the United States of America.

10 9 8 7 6 5 4 3 2 1

Library of Congress Cataloging-in-Publication Data
Kozak, Arnold.
The everything Buddhism book / Arnie Kozak. — 2nd ed.
p. cm.
Includes bibliographical references and index.
ISBN 978-1-4405-1028-1 (alk. paper)
1. Buddhism. I. Title.
BQ4012.S23 2011
294.3—dc22
2010041532

Contents

Dedication

This book is dedicated to the Buddha, Dharma, and Sangha and, in particular, Mu Soeng and the Barre Center for Buddhist Studies, Larry Rosenberg and the Cambridge Insight Meditation Center, and Taihaku Gretchen Priest and the Shao Shan Spiritual Practice Center.

The Top 10 Pearls of Buddhist Wisdom

1. "Everything changes; everything is connected; pay attention."—Jane Hirshfield
2. "Each of you should make himself his island, make himself and no one else his refuge, each of you must make the *dharma* his island, the *dharma* and nothing else his refuge."—The Buddha
3. "Whoever honors his own sect and condemns other sects . . . injures his own more gravely."—King Ashoka
4. "You can search through the entire universe for someone who is more deserving of your love and affection than you are yourself, and that person is not to be found anywhere. You yourself, as much as anybody in the entire universe deserve your love and affection."—The Buddha
5. "Even loss and betrayal bring us awakening."—The Buddha
6. "To live fully is to let go and die with each passing moment, and to be reborn in each new one."—Jack Kornfield
7. "When you paint Spring, do not paint willows, plums, peaches, or apricots, but just paint Spring. To paint willows, plums, peaches, or apricots is to paint willows, plums, peaches, or apricots—it is not yet painting Spring."—Dogen
8. "We are what we think. All that we are arises with our thoughts. With our thoughts, we make our world."—The Buddha
9. "All the happiness there is in the world comes from thinking about others, and all the suffering comes from preoccupation with yourself."—Shantideva
10. "We are human beings who take form through an impetus to joy, interest, and concern."—Arnie Kozak

Introduction

BUDDHISM TRACES ITS ROOTS back to the Buddha, a yogi who lived more than 2,500 years ago in northern India. The Buddha discovered a way to live that radically transformed people's lives, starting with his own. His revolutionary insights have withstood the test of time and his methods can still transform lives as they did in ancient India. The Buddha taught mindfulness, kindness, and compassion. Buddhism, the family of religions that evolved from the Buddha's teachings, is one of the great ethical systems for the benefit of humanity.

While Buddhism may be considered a nontheistic religion, it transcends religious belief into practical experience. You don't believe in Buddhism, you practice Buddhism. In fact, you don't even need to be a "Buddhist" to practice "Buddhism." You just have to sit down and meditate.

At a time when yoga enjoyed widespread popularity, the Buddha was a prodigious yogi. He mastered the yogas of his day and then founded a way that could go beyond all suffering. This way also goes beyond words and needs to be experienced for yourself. The good news is that is available right here, right now.

Jane Hirshfield, in the PBS documentary *The Buddha*, offers an explanation of the Buddha's teachings in seven words: "Everything changes; everything is connected; pay attention." This is a nice condensing of millions of words attributed to the Buddha in the Pali Canon. "Everything changes; everything is connected; pay attention." Got that?!

Buddhism is flourishing in the West. It seems to offer a much-needed antidote to the stresses of modern life. It provides a way to renovate your relationship to uncertainty. It provides a way to renovate your relationship to want. Christians and Jews alike practice aspects of Buddhism while retaining their own traditions and marking their own holidays. From celebrities to the clerk at the gas station convenience store, this vibrant religion is capturing the hearts and minds of many. Buddhism carries within its belly the power to transform individuals, societies, and the world. It is a practice of interior and exterior revolution.

Western soil is changing the face of Buddhism, as did China, Japan, and Tibet in earlier centuries. Buddhism is not a fixed doctrine, but a fluid set of ideas and practices. Wherever you are reading this book right now, chances are there is a Buddhist practice center nearby. After reading this book, you might want to visit one of these centers and try it out for yourself.

Once exotic and Eastern, Buddhism is now a common section at your local Borders or independent bookstore. Hundreds of titles are published each year, many by Wisdom Publications, a nonprofit press devoted to transmission of the dharma—the collected wisdom of the Buddha. Buddhism is also in the news: the Dalia Lama's struggle for Tibet; political unrest in Sri Lanka and Burma; Gross National Happiness in Bhutan.

If you are hounded by a sense of lack, dissatisfaction, or are caught up in a web of suffering, Buddhism has something to offer you. If you are concerned about the state of the world and want to engage in conscious social action, Buddhism has something to offer you. Buddhism has much to offer many, and it may be just what the world needs now to save it from itself.

The Buddha embarked on an adventure to discover his true nature and the true nature of the world. He relied on nothing but his own experiences and invited everyone else to do the same. And now you, too, are invited to have an encounter with the truth and see what Buddhism is all about. It just might surprise you.

CHAPTER 1

The Buddha, the Teachings, and the Community of Practitioners

Buddhism is one of the world's great religions. Behind Christianity, Islam, and Hinduism, it is the fourth most populous religion in the world. And the question might be raised: Is Buddhism a religion at all? What is Buddhism, who was the Buddha, and why is he as relevant today as he was 2,500 years ago? Buddhism promises a path to happiness through the eradication of suffering. Can it do this? This chapter will address these questions.

Religion or Philosophy?

Can you have a religion without god, a supreme being that created the world and intervenes in the lives of his (or her) creatures? Does Buddhism qualify as a religion? Or is Buddhism a philosophical and ethical system for living? It appears that Buddhism can be considered a nontheistic religion, according to Buddhist scholar Damien Keown when considered along seven dimensions common to religion. These seven dimensions include:

1. Practical and Ritual
2. Experiential and Emotional
3. Narrative and Mythic
4. Doctrinal and Philosophical
5. Ethical and Legal
6. Social and Institutional
7. Material

Practical and Ritual

While the ritual elements of Buddhism may seem bare bones compared to the Catholic Church, for example, Buddhism certainly has rites and rituals that are public and private, many of which are associated with monastic life. Different Buddhist traditions place different emphases on ritual.

Experiential and Emotional

The experiential dimension is the most important dimension of Buddhism. The Buddha was the exemplar. He transformed his life not through belief but through experiential practice. And Buddhists follow a similar path. The truth of Buddhism must be experienced. Karen Armstrong notes that the Buddha "confined his researches to his own human nature and always insisted that his experiences—even the supreme truth of Nibbana (*Nirvana*) were entirely natural to humanity."

Narrative and Mythic

Buddhism is not without its myths and legends, including those surrounding the life of the Buddha, which can be read as a parable as well as a biographical account of the historical figure known as Siddhartha Gautama. There are many narrative elements in Buddhism, including the Jataka tales.

Doctrinal and Philosophical

The Buddha chafed at "doctrine" and idle philosophical speculation and sought to teach through direct experience. However, Professor Keown says of doctrine, "if by 'doctrine' we understand the systematic formulation of religious teachings in an intellectually coherent form," then Buddhism qualifies as having doctrine in this sense. For example, there are the Four Noble Truths that are the foundation of the Buddha's teachings.

Ethical and Legal

Buddhism is widely regarded as one of the world's most ethical religions, having incorporated ethics into the foundation of the experiential practices. The central ethic is to "do no harm." Buddhism is predominately a path of peace. For example, the Dalai Lama has consistently advocated peaceful resistance to the Chinese occupation of his country, an occupation that has, by some estimates, claimed a million lives and destroyed 6,000 monasteries.

Social and Institutional

The *sangha* is the community of Buddhist practitioners and it is one of humanity's oldest continuous institutions. Yet the *sangha* is not an institution in the sense that it has a central authority such as the Vatican. It is a diverse collection of people across nations and cultures that practice the Buddha's teachings in diverse ways. Buddhism is also a socially engaged religion seeking to make positive changes in society.

Material

The material dimensions of Buddhism are vast, majestic, and colorful. Buddhists have built breathtaking monasteries, caves, and carvings of the Buddha. King Ashoka left a legacy of iconic structures called *stupas* across India. Buddhist art is colorful and narrative. Buddhists make pilgrimages to holy sites such as the birth and death place of the Buddha and the places where he became enlightened and gave his first sermon.

As you can see, while Buddhism does not have a god and the Buddha is not regarded as a god, it fulfills the other criteria for a religion. You can consider it what you like. You can adopt Buddhism as your religion or you can regard it as a set of experiential practices, such as meditation, that you can integrate with your own religious beliefs. Or, as many do, Buddhism can be approached in an entirely secular manner, as a philosophical system for living, eschewing all rituals, beliefs, and doctrine, just as the Buddha did 2,500 years ago in his search for a way to end suffering. You, just like the Buddha, have the same potential for awakening.

Buddha Versus Buddhism

Throughout this book a distinction will be made between Buddha (the life and teachings of Siddhartha Gautama) and Buddhism (the religious institutions that have developed over the past 2,500 years in many different parts of the world). Not all Buddhism is Buddha as these social organizations have migrated and developed over the centuries.

The first written evidence of the existence of Buddhism is found 400 years after the life of Buddha. King Ashoka of the Mauryan state of Northern India made inscriptions containing references to Buddhism that date from about 269 to 232 B.C.E.

In the West, both Buddha and Buddhism have been an attractive and evergrowing force for both personal growth and social change. You can embrace Buddha without embracing Buddhism. Buddha requires no beliefs, no affiliations and, therefore, no conflict with your own belief system, whether you are devoutly religious or an atheist. Buddha's teachings are universal, transcending time and culture. If you have a mind, then Buddha is relevant to you. Many of the presentations of Buddhism in the West are more Buddha than Buddhism. For example, you will find mindfulness meditation being taught at major medical centers with no Buddhist context or affiliation.

Are You a Buddhist?

How do you become a Buddhist? What does it mean to be a card-carrying Buddhist? Buddhism represents a great diversity of traditions, so there is no one way to become a Buddhist and perhaps, ironically, no need to become a "Buddhist." There is a curious situation in America where many teachers teaching Buddhist meditation would not consider themselves "Buddhist," although they lead lives entirely consistent with the principles and practices of this religion. Buddhism in America has become quite popular and many people might identify themselves as Buddhists.

FACT

According to Russell Chandler, the author of *Racing Toward 2001*, there were an estimated 359 million Buddhists in the world in 2000, with a projected growth rate of 1.7 percent annually. Some estimates have placed this number much higher with over 1 billion Buddhists worldwide, and an increasing number coming from the West. At the dawn of the new millennium, there were approximately 800,000 Buddhists living in the United States.

One prerequisite to identification as a Buddhist would be to take refuge in the Triple Jewel: The Buddha, the *dharma*, and the *sangha*. Buddha is not just the historical person of the Buddha, it is what the Buddha represents—the potential for awakening that you have. Taking refuge in Buddha is not idolatry. Buddhists look to the Buddha as a role model, especially in America (although in Asian contexts it can appear that people are really praying to the Buddha as a god by requesting intercessory prayers). *Dharma* is the body of teachings that the Buddha taught and also the truths that these teachings point to. Sometimes *dharma* is translated as "The Way"—the way to live to get beyond suffering.

Sangha is the community of like-minded practitioners on the same path. It is the people you might practice with at a local meditation gathering in your community, such as a Zen temple, and all the people all over the world stretching back in time 2,500 years. Taking refuge is an initiation into an awakened life. It is like getting on a raft that will carry you across the river of *samsara* (endless suffering).

You can also join a *sangha* by becoming a monk. Monastic initiation is more involved than lay initiation. Many Americans choose to become a monk or a nun in one of these Asian traditions. To do this, you would have to renounce aspects of your life and take on the monastic vows. In the Zen tradition, you would shave your head and devote yourself to a life of service to your Zen master and your *zendo* (Zen temple). There is also lay ordination. Initiation into the Triple Jewel is, perhaps, the closest these diverse traditions have to a universal initiation.

For most religions, becoming a member of that religion requires adopting a particular set of beliefs and a corresponding faith in those beliefs. Buddhism is different in this way. There are some core principles that reflect the teachings of the Buddha and you must be on board with these to be considered a "Buddhist," but these are not articles of faith, like believing in a virgin birth, a creator god, or even an enlightened prophet. They are more practical. Stephen Batchelor suggests there can be "Buddhism without belief" in ideas such as rebirth.

What Makes You Not a Buddhist

Dzongsar Jamyang Khyentse Rinpoche, author of *What Makes You Not a Buddhist*, provides four criteria to consider. To be a Buddhist, one must believe in all four of these tenets or seals. These are: 1) all compounded things are impermanent, 2) all emotions are pain, 3) all things have no inherent existence, and 4) *nirvana* is beyond all concepts.

While these might be considered "beliefs," each is based on direct experience, the kind of experience that can arise from your practice of meditation. If you meditate, you will notice that things are constantly changing—the quality of your breathing, the energy in your body, and the ceaseless flow of thoughts in your mind. All emotions are pain seems harder to accept; after all, joy is not "painful." But this joy won't last (since everything is impermanent) and somewhere in the back of your mind there is the recognition and fear that this experience won't last. Emotions, in this case, might be distinguished from feelings, with emotions being a complex of intense feelings, suffused with thoughts and embedded in a story that eventually has something to do with desire. "All things have no inherent existence" is the teaching on emptiness, and again is less a belief than an experience that arises in meditation. *Nirvana* is beyond all concepts can also be experienced in meditation.

What is *Nirvana*?
Nirvana is not only a grunge rock band from the 1990s, it is a fundamental, and often misunderstood, concept in Buddhism. *Nirvana* is not some blissful place that you go to. *Nirvana* is the cessation of suffering. It literally means "blowing out." What gets blown out is the generation of suffering from the influence of greed, hatred, and delusion.

So if you like being a Buddhist because of the colorful rituals and the exotic association with Asian cultures, the message of compassion and peace, but don't "get" these four seals, Rinpoche suggests you are not a Buddhist in the important sense of being a Buddhist. In other words, to be a Buddhist is to understand Buddhist psychology—to have a direct experience of what the Buddha discovered and that you can discover if you devote yourself to any of the Buddhist meditation practices.

Devotion

While Westerners may be attracted to the more secular forms and practices of Buddhism, in Asia devotion is a common practice. You may find devotion congenial to your needs or not. In America, the Theravada traditions are the least devotional while the Tibetan practices are the most, with Zen somewhere in between. Buddhism has a long tradition of venerating relics and images of the Buddha, even though he was considered a man and not a god. In Tibetan Buddhism there is a pantheon of *buddhas* and *bodhisattvas* available to respond to prayers. According to Professor Kevin Trainor, the Buddha Amitabha is believed to directly intervene during the process of death and rebirth.

In traditional Buddhist cultures, the line between devotion and metaphor becomes blurred. In the West, you may want to see the Buddha as an exemplar to inspire practice. If you bow to the Buddha at a Zen temple, you are not subjugating yourself to a superior being, but bowing to the divinity that resides within yourself. Buddhists take inspiration from the life and work of the Buddha and also honor the Buddha to accumulate merit. Devotion also reflects a sense of gratitude for the teachings of the Buddha and the sacrifices he made to bring those teaching to humanity. You can view him in any way that you like, as a role model or a transcendent being. However you regard him, he was one cool dude!

One *Dharma* or Many?

Buddhism has proliferated in the world by changing and integrating other cultures and religions. As it moved from India eastward, it was influenced by Taoism and Confucianism in China, by Shinto in Japan, and Bon in Tibet. Now Buddhism has arrived in the West. In many cases the traditions from the East have been imported and replicated here, but as Westerners practice and also lead these communities, is a new form of Buddhism emerging? Is there a Western dharma? An American dharma? These are questions that the meditation teacher Joseph Goldstein poses in his book, *One Dharma*. What works to free Asians from suffering may not work for Westerners. At the same time, there is a risk that adapting the teachings to Western soil will dilute them or corrupt them into something else.

The basic teachings of the Buddha provide what is required for a nonsectarian form of Buddhist practice. It's all in the Four Noble Truths, and the core is overcoming suffering and dissatisfaction (*dukkha*) and living with mindfulness and compassion. All *dharmas*, that is, manifestations of Buddhism, share this in common: be mindful, be compassionate. And the poet Jane Hirshfield's seven-word definition of Buddhism may also point towards one *dharma*: "Everything changes; everything is connected; pay attention."

Saints and Teachers

Like most religious traditions, Buddhism has its founders and saints. However, unlike most religious traditions, Buddhism looks to the Buddha as the paradigm for awakening. As a role model, he shows his followers the way to salvation but does not play a direct role in facilitating that salvation. The Buddha's earliest disciples are the closest things to saints. They were all *arhats* ("worthy ones") and included Ananda, Shariptura, Maudgalyayana (Moggalana), and Kashyapa.

Korean Zen master Seung Sahn, founder of the Kwan Um School of Zen, was famous for "Don't Know Mind" that is similar to the "Beginner's Mind" of another famous Zen master Shunryu Suzuki. These pithy sayings reflect an important teaching of the Buddha wherein a lack of intellectualism and arrogance can lead to openness and insight.

Tibetan Buddhists revere *bodhisattvas* who take the form of *tulkus* or *rinpoche*, who are *lamas* who have taken rebirth. His Holiness the Dalai Lama would be the most well known example of a living *tulku*. His status as *lama* indicates that he is a teacher (*lama* translates to "teacher" in Tibetan as *guru* translates to "teacher" in Sanskrit). The purpose of the saint or the teacher is to transmit the *dharma*—just as the Buddha did 2,500 years ago.

Many of the founders of new forms of Buddhism in different countries are also revered as saints, such as Bodhidharma, who brought Buddhism to China and founded Chan, and Dogen, who brought Chan to Japan and founded Zen. In many Buddhist traditions, especially Tibetan and Zen, your relationship with the teacher is an integral component to your spiritual path, and you would expect to have a close relationship with this master to initiate you on the path of the *dharma*, to transmit the teachings, and guide you on this spiritual path. Lineage is therefore extremely important in these traditions, and teacher lineages may stretch back over a thousand years.

The two best known Buddhist masters in the world today are, as already mentioned, His Holiness the Dalai Lama, and the other is Tich Nhat Hanh, a Vietnamese Zen monk who has written extensively, been a peace activist, and has taught throughout the world. These men are revered for their wisdom, compassion, and ability to teach the *dharma* to wide audiences.

Metaphor as Skillful Means

Upaya ("skillful means") is a central Buddhist concept. It refers to a teacher's ability to reach the student and admits a flexibility of approach to teaching Buddhist concepts. The Buddha was able to reach people at all levels of awareness. He was able to tailor his message to the person's experience and he did so through the skillful use of stories, parables, and metaphors. Metaphors run through his teachings as a river runs through the countryside. Skillful means is the ability to make the *dharma* accessible. Modern day examples of *upaya* would be teaching troubled teenagers mindfulness through music, as the meditation teacher Shinzen Young has done. Enlightenment on an iPod? Now that's *upaya*!

The Buddha used metaphors familiar to the world of 2,500 years ago: oxcarts, fire, mountains, rain, streams, bows, and arrows. If the Buddha were teaching today, he would use metaphors from the technological present such as DVDs, e-mail, and pause buttons on remote controls. In his book *Wild Chickens and Petty Tyrants: 108 Metaphors for Mindfulness*, Arnie Kozak presents a collection of traditional and contemporary metaphors.

One traditional parable is the story of Kisa Gotami from the Buddha's time. Having lost her infant son to an illness, she desperately sought the Buddha for his reputed healing abilities. The Buddha listened to her plea and promised to bring her son back to life if she could bring him a mustard seed from a home that had never known death. She eagerly set out on her task but soon realized that death had touched everyone. She returned to the Buddha, having understood the concept of impermanence without his having had to preach. Had he done so at the outset, this teaching would likely have fallen on deaf ears.

The Original Metaphor

Enlightenment is a term closely associated with Buddhism. What happened to the Buddha under the Bodhi Tree is often characterized as enlightenment. This, of course, is a metaphor. When he overcame all of the obstacles and temptations, the "lights" came on, or he became illuminated. Buddhist artwork often depicts Siddhartha with light radiating out in a circle around his dead. But is this the best metaphor? The Buddha said he was *buddho* (meaning "awake," not "illuminated"), and the implications of each metaphor are different. The term "enlightenment" makes this sound like something heavenly and otherworldly.

What about the alternative metaphor of "awakening"? Awakening sounds like something you do everyday, and it is thus more common and more accessible than you might think. Stephen Batchelor suggests these are meaningful differences and that Buddhism is really talking about awakening rather than enlightenment. Throughout this text you will see the terms enlightenment and awakening used interchangeably.

The Axial Age

The Buddha lived and taught in the Axial Age, the period between 800 and 200 B.C.E. According to Karen Armstrong, "The Axial Age marks the beginning of humanity as we now know it. During this period, men and women became conscious of their existence, their own nature, and their limitations in an unprecedented way." This period of humanity gave birth to the philosophies of Confucius, Lao Tzu, Zoroaster, Socrates, and Plato as well as the Hebrew prophets Ezekiel, Zechariah, and Jeremiah. And, of course, the Axial Age was the context in which the Buddha lived and made his mark on the world.

> "A conviction that the world was awry [*dukkha*—filled with grief, pain, sorrow] was fundamental to the spirituality that emerged in the Axial countries. Those who took part in this transformation felt restless—just as Gotama did. They were consumed by a sense of helplessness, were obsessed by their mortality, and felt a profound terror of and alienation from the world."—Karen Armstrong

Advances in agriculture gave rise to food surpluses and the rise of cities bustling with commerce and political power. The Hindu world in which Siddhartha was raised was one of ritual sacrifice. The Vedic worldview consisted of castes and believed that the entire universe was supported by sacrifices. The priest class of Brahmins was integral for the administration of these rituals. A strong belief in the afterlife and a soul that transcended death was part of the worldview Siddhartha lived within. To get to the equivalent of heaven, one had to live a moral life and one's ancestors had to employ Brahmin priests to perform special rituals (*shraddha*). If you were immoral or your family left you in the ritual lurch, your soul might dissolve. In contrast to this, Karen Armstrong notes, "It was by ethics, not magic, that humanity would wake up to itself and its responsibilities, realize its full potential and find release from the darkness that pressed in on all sides."

The Buddha had a vision for political and social change. According to Michael Willis in *Buddhism Illustrated*, "The Buddha's repeated use of agricultural metaphors in his teaching, his acceptance of traders as key patrons, of the monastic community, his insistence on non-violence and his denial of the efficacy of sacrifice can all be read as part of his attempt to provide a new philosophical and religious system for the urban elite of Northern India."

Many concepts associated with Buddhism such as *karma* and *samsara* were imports from Hinduism. The goal for Hindu mystics was to escape rebirth and *samsara* by reuniting one's *atman*, or soul, with Brahman (the creator spirit). This union is the highest form of yoga. This final release is called *moksha.*

Two famous *shramana* (an ascetic who renouces ties with society) teachers were Mahavira, founder of Jainism, and Siddhartha Gautama, founder of Buddhism.

The Buddha was a product of his time and also transcended the received wisdom of Vedic India. He rejected the notion of an everlasting soul and made the radical observation that what is considered self is not a thing but a process, and a process that is ever changing. Suffering results not from living inside of a body (a belief that presumes a duality between body and mind) but from being attached to it. That is, trying to hold onto a solid sense of self when everything is always changing; trying to cling to fleeting pleasures and trying to push away unpleasant experience. He succeeded in discovering a method that could bring an end to suffering, and this method can be reliably reproduced by anyone interested in trying. This method was not about achieving high or rarified states of consciousness but seeing the nature of reality clearly. That clear seeing is what leads to liberation.

Terminology

When reading Buddhist literature, you will see terms that have no easy English translation preserved in either Sanskrit or Pali. Pali and Sanskrit are closely related languages but most of the terms have slight spelling variations in transliteration. Throughout the text the more commonly recognized Sanskrit terms will be used, for example, nirvana, except for selected Pali terms, like vipassana. Here is a table of commonly used terms:

▼ SANSKRIT AND PALI EQUIVALENTS

Sanskrit	Pali	Meaning
Siddhartha Guatama	Siddhattha Gotoma	the Buddha
dharma	dhamma	Teachings, Natural Law
karma	kamma	Action
duhkha	dukkha	Suffering/pervasive dissatisfaction/stress
anitya	anicca	Impermanence
anatman	anatta	No Self/Not Self
nirvana	nibbana	Ultimate state of cessation
dhyanas	jhanas	Meditative states
Vipashyana	Vipassana	Insight Meditation
Sutra	Sutta	Scriptures
Arhat	Arahat	Enlightened One
bikshus	bikkhu	monk
bhikshunis	bhikkunis	nun
samskaras	sankharas	mental conditionings
Tripitaka	Tipitaka	"Three Baskets" of the Pali Canon

CHAPTER 2

The Buddha: History and Legend

The man who would become the Buddha can be seen as a godlike mystic, rational philosopher, psychologist, physician, or social reformer. Buddhist texts contain few references to biographical events from his life. However, historians do agree that he did actually exist and lived a long and prosperous life—he died at eighty years old after teaching for forty-five years, traveling all over India to do so. Although the Buddha's teachings were preserved through oral recitation and first written down hundreds of years after his death, they are considered credible and accurate.

Siddhartha Gautama

Little consensus can be found among scholars on the historical facts of the Buddha's life. This is due in part to the lack of biographical detail he shared in his teachings that later became the Pali Canon. A few key moments in the Buddha's story are known. Up until recently, the year of the Buddha's death was taken to be either 483 or 486 B.C.E. However, new evidence suggests that it might have been as late as 400 B.C.E. His birth would have been 80 years prior to the earlier or later date (either 566 or 563 B.C.E. or as late as 480 B.C.E.). Many of the details of the Buddha's biography come from the poem *Buddhacharita* by Ashvogosa, which was written in the second century C.E.

Myth and Metaphor

The myth of the Buddha is colorful and strains our contemporary scientific view of reality. For example, Siddhartha Guatama was not the first *buddha* nor will he be the last. The Buddhist cosmology does not adhere to a linear sense of time, such that there have been an infinite number of *buddhas* from the past and into the future. Taken literally, such a view would violate the laws of physics that say time only moves in one direction—forward—and that the age of the universe is a finite amount of time. Fortunately, here and in every other place where myth meets reality, a literal belief in traditional ideas does not have to be held to derive benefit from the Buddha's teaching or from the example of his life.

While Siddhartha Gautama is often described as a prince and his parents as Queen Mahamaya and King Suddhodhona, it is more likely that his parents were part of the nobility but not monarchs. His father was a magistrate of a smaller state in the Himalayan foothills. The elevation of the family to the highest royalty may be part of the mythology that has developed around the life of the Buddha.

As with the man himself, the life story of the Buddha can likewise be seen from different perspectives. Taken literally, it speaks of magic, wonder, and prophecy; viewed metaphorically it is a parable of sacrifice in the service of ultimate attainment. Certain elements of the narrative appear to provide drama to the story, but probably little in the way of historical fact. Siddhartha Gautama was born to a noble family in the Himalayan foothills, on the border of northern India and southern Nepal. Siddhartha's mother was Mahamaya, his father Suddhodhana, and he was a blessing to the childless couple as they would now have an heir to rule over the Shakya clan, their small but prosperous region of the kingdom. They named their son Siddhartha, which means "every wish fulfilled."

The Birth of the Buddha

There are many mythologies and stories surrounding the birth of the Buddha. His mother, Mahamaya, dreamt of a white elephant that entered her womb from the right side of her body. According to the legend, Mahamaya experienced a virtually pain-free delivery with the assistance of a tree that bent to offer its branches. The future Buddha exited the womb unbloodied and able to walk and talk. In some accounts, Siddhartha emerged from her right side, avoiding the "pollution" of the birth canal. Sounding much like Muhammad Ali twenty-five centuries later, the infant proclaimed, "I am the king of the world." His mother died a week later.

It is generally agreed upon (with some variation) that when Siddhartha was but days old, his father, Suddhodhana, invited a large group of Brahmins to a feast at the palace so that they could tell the future of the newborn baby. Eight of the Brahmins concurred on the prediction that Siddhartha would either become a great and powerful ruler of all the land or a great spiritual teacher.

What is a Brahmin?

The Brahmins were the priests, the highest class in the hereditary caste system of India. According to the caste system of Hinduism in ancient India, there were four classes of people: Brahmins, rulers and warriors (the Kshatriyas), business people and artisans (the Vaishyas), and finally the unskilled laborers or untouchables (the Shudras).

They warned that if Siddhartha left the palace and saw what the real world was like, he might have an existential crisis and turn towards a spiritual life. If he remained within the cloistered palace walls, he would become a great ruler of the world. One of these Brahmins, Kondanna, was convinced, however, that the young boy would become an enlightened one and warned of four signs that would influence the young Siddhartha and spur him to leave his home and commence a spiritual journey.

The Raising of the Would-Be King

Suddhodhana had no wish for his son to become a spiritual teacher, but dreamed of a son who ruled over the land, the most powerful man as far as the eye could see.

He decided to protect Siddhartha from the possibilities of a hard but spiritual path and vowed to keep him cloistered in the palace, lavishing riches and luxuries beyond imagination on the young boy.

Youth of Luxury and Pleasure

According to the legend, young Siddhartha was surrounded by beautiful things and kept captive within the palace grounds so he would not be subjected to the sicknesses and poverty of the people of the kingdom. Guards were posted all around the palace grounds and Siddhartha was discouraged from leaving and protected from seeing anything distressing. He had everything he could ever want. His life was pleasure and luxury. He grew into a talented athlete, an intelligent and charming young man. His future as a leader of the people seemed secure.

One afternoon, when Siddhartha was eight years old, he sat under the shade of a rose apple tree watching the plowing of the fields as the town prepared for the new crop. He noticed that the plowing had upset the ground and that insects had been harmed in the process. The young boy felt sadness come over him as if he were attached to the insects, as though he had experienced a personal loss. And yet the day was beautiful and the shade of the rose apple tree wonderfully cool. Joy rose up inside him and he experienced a moment of meditative bliss. The compassion and love he felt for the insects took him outside himself and he was momentarily free.

Legend has it that as the day wore on, the shadows moved, except for the rose apple tree, which continued to shield the young Siddhartha.

Since his mother died, Siddhartha was subsequently raised by her sister, Prajapati. She is often called "the Mother of Buddhism" because she played a pivotal role in bringing women into the Buddha's circle. After being denied several times, Prajapati's consistent pleas paid off and Buddha allowed her to start an order of nuns, thus allowing women to enter in the realm of Buddhist practice.

When Siddhartha was sixteen he married the beautiful Yasodhara. Yasodhara was Siddhartha's cousin and considered the loveliest girl in the kingdom. According to legend, he impressed her in a contest by piercing seven trees with one arrow.

At age twenty-nine, Siddhartha's life was as much the life of luxury as it had been before, except his wife was pregnant with their first child, indisposed, and unable to entertain him. She beseeched her husband to find his own diversion, so Siddhartha considered venturing outside the gates of the kingdom after overhearing someone speak of the beauty of the spring in the forest just beyond.

The Four Signs

Siddhartha begged his father to allow him to go beyond the palace walls. Suddhodhana hated to deny his son anything so he quickly tried to ensure that life outside the palace gates was just as perfect as life inside. When Siddhartha wandered outside, everywhere he went he saw happiness, health, and good cheer. Then suddenly an old decrepit man with white hair, withered skin, and a staff to lean on crossed his path. Leaning over to his companion and servant, Chandaka, Siddhartha asked, "What is this?"

Chandaka explained that before them was an old man and told Siddhartha that everyone would age similarly one day. Siddhartha was saddened and shocked by the sight of the old man and wondered how he could continue to enjoy such sights as his garden when such suffering was to come later.

A second trip outside the palace grounds brought the sight of a sick man with oozing sores. Chandaka had to tell him that sickness and pain befalls everyone. At home, the king continued to rain luxury on the prince, hoping to distract him from these disturbing visions and his newfound knowledge. But a third visit outside his sanctuary found him confronting a funeral procession and a corpse. Chandaka explained death to Siddhartha and told him it was inevitable for everyone.

Buddha is also sometimes referred to as *Shakyamuni*, which means "Sage of the Shakya Clan," as he hailed from Shakya.

Siddhartha was overwhelmed. Sickness, old age, and death—how had he missed all this suffering in life? Finally, on another excursion with Chandaka, Siddhartha came upon a yogi in yellow robes with shaven head and an empty bowl. Chandaka explained that this ascetic had renounced all worldly goods and gained peace by doing so. Siddhartha began to think this might be the thing for him. That night the opulence of the palace disturbed him deeply. The four signs had left their mark and the veil of luxury and riches had been removed. The world now seemed a place of suffering and pain. Sudhodhana's plan backfired.

It's hard to imagine how this intelligent young man could get to his thirtieth year without having ever seen the first three of these four signs. Even if he never left the walls of the palace, family members, servants, and priests must have shown signs of illness, aging, and someone was likely to have perished. Viewed as a metaphor for the loss of innocence, the Four Signs are a crucial moment in Siddhartha's story.

Going Forth

Although Siddhartha was married at age sixteen, he did not have his first child until twenty-nine, which was unusual according to the customs of his time. One reason he may not have had his son until then is that he, like most sons of royalty, was away at college in Taxila (in current-day Iran). There is no direct evidence that he was away, but the biographical information about him is unclear. This is a reasonable conclusion and one drawn by Stephen Batchelor in his book *Confession of a Buddhist Atheist.*

After Yasodhara had borne Siddhartha a son, the cycle of birth and death seemed endless and oppressive to Siddhartha—life after life and death after death (or *samsara:* the endless cycle of becoming). Despite his love for his family and the birth of his new baby boy (who he most interestingly named Rahula, which translates to "fetter"), he decided to "go forth" into the world the night his son was born. Legend has it that he snuck out of the palace when everyone fell asleep, including, mysteriously, the palace guards.

His faithful companion Chandaka followed him out into the night, and once outside the palace grounds, he cut off his long beautiful hair, jettisoned his jewels and royal silks, and wore the assembled rags of a wandering holy man. He sent Chandaka back to the palace with the vestiges of his royal life. Siddhartha was now on his way.

This is a remarkable occurrence in the life of this prince. He had been surrounded by all the apparent ingredients for a happy life: he had money, fame, power, love, family, health, and endless entertainment and learning. He was safe, had a promising future, and a beautiful wife and son. Yet even before he saw the Four Signs, he recognized that something was off; all this material comfort could not lead to enduring happiness.

Another incident that propelled him forth happened at the palace after a night of partying with the beautiful consorts. He woke up in the middle of the night to see the beauties sleeping, mouths agape, drooling, and gnashing their teeth. In this moment he recognized the impermanence of all things, especially beauty. "These bodies could be corpses and some day in the future will be," the future Buddha might have thought.

He vowed to live an unfettered existence. Family was not part of the life of a spiritual seeker; he had to go forth alone. The thought of losing his family forever to old age and death must have been a very powerful catalyst for such dramatic change. He was motivated to go forth to find an end to suffering, by whatever means necessary, for the benefit of his family and for all of humanity.

Finding the Way

The forests in the kingdom of Kosala were fertile and green, and housed many seekers of truth called *shramanas*. Siddhartha became one of them.

These ascetics were not seen as beggars and dropouts; to seek a holy life was a worthy cause. The young prince set out to find himself a teacher, and wandered far and wide over the Ganges plain, learning what he could from the available *gurus* (teachers). He spent time with two well-known *gurus* of the time, Alara Kalama and Udraka Ramaputra, and learned everything that these men had to teach.

Siddhartha was a meditation prodigy and quickly reached very high states of meditation (called *dhyanas* or *jhanas* in Pali). However, once he left the profound state of meditative absorption he found himself back in the realm of suffering. He had not gone beyond. So, demurring an invitation to succeed each of these teachers, he continued forth into the forest on his own. He adopted the practice of severe asceticism.

Siddhartha joined up with five ascetics and practiced the principles of asceticism in an effort to achieve enlightenment and discover liberation. One of the Five Ascetics whom Siddhartha spent so much time with was Kondanna, the Brahmin who had predicted his future as a great spiritual teacher. Asceticism was believed to burn up negative *karma* and free one from *samsara*. It was the ascetics' belief that if they suffered enough in this life they could perhaps save themselves in the next. They sought to overcome the desires of the body through the power of the mind. Siddhartha practiced self-denial, mortification, meditation, and yogic exercises, searching for liberation from the ties of the material world. Siddhartha believed that if he could transcend the self he could free himself of the endless cycles of *samsara* and become enlightened—finally free from rebirth.

The Middle Way

As he had demonstrated himself to be a meditation prodigy with Alara Kalama and Udraka Ramaputra, Siddhartha attempted to be an ascetic prodigy, only taking a grain of rice or drinking mud for sustenance each day. Together with his five companions he wore little or no clothing, slept out in the open no matter the weather, starved himself beyond measure, and even ingested his own waste matter. He lay on the most uncomfortable surfaces possible and inflicted severe deprivation on himself, convinced that external suffering would banish the internal suffering forever. He became very ill—his ribs showed through his skin, his hair fell out, and his skin became blotched and shrunken. But still he was plagued with desires and cravings. For years he had been determined to conquer his body and its senses. After seven long years of effort he was close to death.

"Moderate effort over a long time is important, no matter what you are trying to do. One brings failure on oneself by working extremely hard at the beginning, attempting to do too much, and then giving it all up after a short time."—The Dalai Lama

Fortunately, a young girl named Sujata offered him some rice porridge and he took it, breaking his vows of asceticism. When the Five Ascetics saw him partaking of nourishment they grew disgusted with their companion and hurriedly distanced themselves from him. They thought he was returning to the life he had lived before and was leaving the life of a holy seeker.

This was the beginning of his awakening and finding the middle path between the extremes of sensual indulgence and dangerous denial of his physical needs. He recalled his meditation experience under the rose apple tree and realized there was another way to accomplish his goal. With the strength gained from that meal, the emaciated Siddhartha sat beneath a pipal tree and made a new vow: To not get up until he had found what he was looking for.

Awakening

As he nursed himself back to health, Siddhartha became very conscious of his movements in the world and paid close attention to how he reacted to his environment, watching his thoughts as they passed through his mind. He became aware of the movements he made while he ate, slept, and walked. Siddhartha slowly became mindful of his every gesture and thought. Mindfulness is the process of bringing attention to the present moment, away from thoughts of the future or the past or judgments about the present. It's making contact with the lived experience of now. Mindfulness made Siddhartha aware of every craving that passed through him and of how transitory these cravings were. Everything changed: everything came and everything passed.

He began to notice that all things were interrelated. The fruit was attached to the tree that was attached to the earth that received nutrients from the sky when it rained. The earth nourished the insects and animals, which ate the berries that came from the trees that came from the earth that were nourished by the sky. The animals died, the plants died, and so would Siddhartha. Life was filled with interconnectedness and change. And impermanence. Everything that existed would die. He would die, his thoughts would die, and his desires would die. The moment would die, and another would be born in its place.

Whether or not he worried about loss, loss was inevitable as change was inevitable. With change came fear. And with fear came *dukkha*. This word has no direct equivalent in English. It is most commonly translated as "suffering," like the kind of suffering that Siddhartha saw outside the palace—sickness, old age, and death. *Dukkha* also refers to something more thoroughgoing and can also be translated as "pervasive dissatisfaction" or a sense of things "being off center," "out of kilter," or "awry." Sometimes it is translated as "stress."

FACT

Siddhartha is known by many names, including: Siddhartha Gautama (in Pali his name is Siddhattha Gotoma), his birth and family name; Shakyamuni, Sage of the Shakya Clan; Buddha, the Fully Awakened One; and Tathagata, the Thus-Perfected One or the One Who Has Found the Truth.

The pipal tree—the tree under which Buddha sat—comes from the Asiatic fig tree, and became known as Bodhi Tree, the tree of "awakening." One sacred bodhi tree in Sri Lanka is thought to be 2,200 years old! Today, a descendant of the original Bodhi Tree sits just where Buddha sat approximately 2,500 years ago. Followers of Buddhism visit the tree and meditate, hoping to achieve an enlightened mind just like Buddha.

Enlightenment

As he sat under the Bodhi Tree, meditating and watching his thoughts come and go, his mind started to break free of the constraints of his ego. He entered each moment fully present as his thoughts dropped away.

The discovery under the pipal tree is usually described as enlightenment—his final illumination and transcendence of suffering. That moment has also been described as "awakening," and in fact, *Buddha* translates into "an awakened one." Enlightenment and awakening provide different images. Enlightenment suggests turning the lights on while awakening suggests coming out of sleep. Enlightenment conveys something esoteric while awakening suggests something rather ordinary, something you do every day.

Mara Gives His Best Shot

During his time under the tree, the Buddha's arch nemesis, Mara, appeared. Mara can be seen as a metaphor for desire; he marshals armies of beautiful women and alluring visions to distract Siddhartha from his path. Undeterred, Siddhartha persisted with his meditation, transforming Mara's forces into flowers that rained petals down upon his head. Mara's final ploy was to show Siddhartha a vision of himself, the one called "Siddhartha." But this self, too, Siddhartha realized is not unchanging, not real, not worth clinging to. Striking a now famous pose, the soon-to-be Buddha reached down with his right hand to touch the earth as witness to his awakening—to his seeing through the illusions provided by Mara. Mara, having used all the tricks in his bag, gave up.

"Only when faced with the activity of enemies can you learn real inner strength. From this viewpoint, even enemies are teachers of inner strength, courage, and determination."—The Dalai Lama

Siddhartha continued to meditate through the night, and according to the scriptures, he first experienced all of his past lives, and then finally experienced what is known as dependent origination—the "causally conditioned nature of reality." Rebirth was a common belief in Siddhartha's time, so the first two insights are not original or particularly relevant to the power of his later teachings. However, the insight of dependent origination *is* original to him and crucial to his teachings. Dependent origination is the recognition that every moment is conditioned by a previous one, that things unfold in an interconnected chain of becoming.

The Buddha

The legend says that after his time under the pipal tree, Siddhartha had radically changed. When he encountered other people they could sense this change. Soon after the Buddha attained enlightenment, he walked by a man, a fellow traveler. The man was struck by the Buddha's unusual radiance and peaceful demeanor.

"My friend, what are you?" he asked the Buddha. "Are you a god?"

"No," answered the Buddha.

"Are you some kind of magician?"

"No," the Buddha answered again.

"Are you a man?"

"No."

"Well, my friend, then what are you?"

The Buddha replied, "I am buddho." ("awake")

And so the name stuck and Siddhartha became the *Buddha*. Siddhartha often referred to himself as the *Tathagatha*, one who had "gone thus." At first, he was ambivalent about his discovery and feared that people would not understand it. It took some time and deliberation for him to make the decision to commence his teaching career, a career that would last forty-five years. His first students were his old emaciated ascetic friends and the first lesson he taught was The Four Noble Truths. This first sermon in the deer park at Isipatana (or Sarnaht) is often referred to as the first turning of the wheel of *dharma*. In some sense, if all you knew about Buddhism was the Four Noble Truths, you would have enough wisdom to attain your own enlightenment. Buddhism has emerged to incorporate many other teachings, but the Four Noble Truths remain at its heart.

CHAPTER 3

The Buddha's Teachings: The Four Noble Truths

The Buddha's teachings were passed down orally until the first written record of the Buddha's teachings appeared hundreds of years after his life. It is believed that the teachings available today are an accurate representation of what the Buddha taught 2,500 years ago. From the time he rose from his seat under the Bodhi Tree, to the time of his death forty-five years later, the Buddha taught everyone he came in contact with—the *sangha* grew from a handful of ascetics to Kings and multitudes.

The First Sermon: The *Dharma* Wheel Turns

The Buddha was in the Deer Park near Sarnath, outside of Varanasi, preparing to give his first sermon to his first disciples, the Five Ascetics who had shunned Siddhartha when he took the rice porridge from Sujata. When they saw him subsequently they couldn't help being impressed with his radiant countenance and thought he might be on to something, so they agreed to hear his teachings. This is the moment that set what is known as the *Dharma Wheel* turning and was eventually to lead the five *bhikkus* (Buddhist monks) toward their own enlightenment.

When ascetics met each other walking on the road, they would ask, "Whose *dharma* do you follow?" *Dharma* refers to teachings as well as the truths those teachings point to. It can also be translated as "natural law." And within Buddhism it can refer specifically to the collected body of teachings attributed to the Buddha.

But the Buddha had no texts to read from, no theories or theologies to offer his listeners. What he had was his own practical experience. On the one hand, he had the indulgence of palace life, and on the other hand, he had the deprivation of asceticism, neither of which led to enduring happiness. Under the Bodhi Tree he discovered the Middle Way and presented this discovery as the Four Noble Truths. He had discovered a *method* for ending suffering, not a *theory*. He did not teach dogma. The experience of awakening was available to anyone who was willing to sit down and give it a try. Students did not have to accept anything on faith; in fact, the Buddha insisted they not do so.

The Doctor Is In

The Buddha's first teaching was the Four Noble Truths. These Four Noble Truths can be thought of as a medical metaphor. The Buddha often considered himself to be a physician, more so than the founder of a religion, and as a doctor he offered medicine to heal the illness of the human condition.

As a physician, he provided a diagnosis for the human condition (First Noble Truth), an etiology (cause for the condition; Second Noble Truth), prognosis (Third Noble Truth), and prescription for the treatment (Fourth Noble Truth). *Dharma*—the truth reflected in these teachings—is the medicine. The Four Noble Truths can take you all the way to enlightenment. His teaching was radical and he was concerned people may not be open to or understand his message.

Although the Buddha was teaching from his practical experience and not some abstract doctrine, he feared the *dharma* might be difficult to understand, so he used metaphors and images to help his disciples connect with the truth of his teachings, a truth they could test for themselves. He preached then and throughout his long illustrious career "the cause of suffering and the end of suffering" (and not as often misportrayed, "life is suffering"). His teaching was revolutionary and asked people to experience things that ran counter to custom and even to common sense (for example, that the typical sense of self was an illusion).

Teachings as Vehicle, Not Destination

The Buddha offered a metaphor: His teachings were a raft to carry the seeker across the river of *samsara*. Once to the other side, he cautioned them to discard the raft. Truth had to be personal, and they should not keep carrying the raft on their back in case it might be useful again some day. The teachings carried on your back in this way are at risk for becoming dogma, and the Buddha wished to avoid that. Any truth must be experienced firsthand and not taken on the authority of a teacher, including himself.

The Four Noble Truths

The Buddha's teachings were a pathway to letting go of suffering, freeing oneself from pain. The Buddha knew the only way was the Middle Way. He knew that excessive pleasure (a life built on sensual delight) or excessive pain (such as the life of an ascetic) led to continual suffering and not to release from that suffering. And so in the first sermon there at the Deer Park, the Buddha spoke of the Four Noble Truths and the path to *nirvana*. He presented his truths as a program of action and not just ideas to consider.

THE FOUR NOBLE TRUTHS ARE AS FOLLOWS:

1. The Truth of Suffering (*Dukkha*)
2. The Truth of the Cause of Suffering
3. The Truth of the Cessation of Suffering
4. The Truth of the Path That Leads to the Cessation of Suffering

Back to the Buddha's medical prescription: The sickness is *dukkha* that infects every moment of existence. The cause of the *dukkha* is craving or desire. The prognosis is good. While much of suffering is self-inflicted, there is a way out of this mess and that place is *nirvana*. The way to realize *nirvana* is the Noble Eightfold Path. Following the Path is the way to healing and recovery of sanity.

The First Noble Truth: The Truth of Suffering

According to Buddhist scholar Damien Keown, the Buddha said, "What, O Monks, is the Noble Truth of Suffering? Birth is suffering, sickness is suffering, old age is suffering, death is suffering. Pain, grief, sorrow, lamentation, and despair are suffering. Association with what is unpleasant is suffering, disassociation from what is pleasant is suffering. Not to get what one wants is suffering."

Dukkha is most often translated as suffering and certainly it refers to suffering. The world that the Buddha lived in was a world that knew warfare, great poverty, and disease. Life expectancy was short and infant and child mortality was great. One could not progress spiritually if the truth of this suffering and one's own mortality remains denied. By extension, the suffering of others cannot be denied either.

But *dukkha* goes beyond these obvious forms of suffering of aging, sickness, and death. It also refers to a pervasive dissatisfaction that colors every moment of life. The Buddha described this aspect of *dukkha* by the very choice of *dukkha* as the term. "Du" of *dukkha* means "bad," and "ka" means "wheel." The Buddha invoked the metaphor of a bad wheel to capture the essence of *dukkha*. It is more than suffering. It describes an oxcart whose wheel is off its axle, biasing every movement of the cart, a wheel that is broken and out of true, or a wheel that is missing a chunk. That bumpy dissatisfaction or sense that things are not right captures the more important aspect of *dukkha*. Buddhism is notorious for the statement, "Life is suffering." But this is misrepresentation and a caricature of the importance of *dukkha* and paints a bleak picture. However, the notion of *dukkha* as pervasive dissatisfaction suggests that much unhappiness is self-inflicted. It comes from misapprehending the nature of reality and the self. Still sounds like bad news, right?

> "This is the direct path for the purification of beings, for the surmounting of sorrow and lamentation, for the disappearance of pain and grief, for the attainment of the true way, for the realization of Nibbana."—Buddha

Well, think about it this way. If *dukkha* is self-inflicted, there is a way out of this misery, and it is to this possibility that the remainder of the Four Noble Truths point.

This sense of being "off" can even show up in pleasant experiences because of a nagging awareness that they will change; you can't have your cake and eat it, too. *Dukkha* is like a background radiation that permeates every experience, even the joyous ones. Even if you are free from illness and enjoy wealth and power, like Siddhartha, you may find that something is missing; you may feel a sense of lack. Happiness is vulnerable when it is dependent upon external events going a certain way. If your sense of contentment is contingent upon things you cannot control, such as the opinions and behaviors of others, then you are vulnerable to *dukkha*. For example, you may be looking forward to an evening out with your partner. You enjoy a fantasy of how the evening will go, what you will order, how you will feel engaged in brilliant conversation. These fantasies make you happy and fill you with a sense of expectation. They also make you vulnerable. Suddenly the phone rings and your partner must beg out of the plans, because of too much work at the office. If you remain attached to the fantasy, you may now feel let down, even angry. The happiness-producing fantasy was contingent upon things going a certain way, and when they didn't, there was no more happiness.

The Three Marks of Existence

Dukkha is the first of the three marks of existence. *Dukkha* is descriptive; it's the diagnosis. The second two marks are the culprits; they are part of the diagnosis. *Anicca* is best translated as "impermanence." Things are constantly changing. If you don't appreciate this, you suffer because you are not in touch with the actual nature of reality. Stephen Batchelor put it eloquently when he said, "It's transitory, it's impermanent, it's constantly moving on, it's unpredictable, every moment is an opening to another possibility. Nothing stands still, nothing is fixed, there is no kind of ultimate ground that doesn't move, that is unconditioned. Everything is within this extraordinary rhythm and flow of life itself."

Do I need to sequester myself away from the world—like a monk would—in order to realize enlightenment?
The Buddha believed the Path was for everyone and no matter who you are you can realize *nirvana*. Sometimes the most challenging practice takes place in the outside world, as you are forced to work harder when confronted with the many distractions of daily life. Enlightenment may be easier in a monastery, but is available anywhere.

Anatta is the next culprit, and while not difficult to translate, it is difficult for the Western mind to grasp. It means "no self" or "not self." *Anatta* suggests that what appears to be "me" is not something solid, enduring, or stable. Whatever this "me" is is also subject to *anicca*. It's always changing from one moment to the next and only gives the appearance of solidity. According to many religions, there is an everlasting identity known as the soul. The soul outlives the body and the mind and continues after earthly life is over. The Buddha rejects the idea of an eternal soul. Whatever this self appears to be it is not solid and is always changing. On the one hand, this may strike you as a frightening proposition. On the other hand, the Buddha's path is one of personal salvation through your own efforts. The Buddha's teachings are also pragmatic and don't require belief in concepts such as an afterlife. The marks of impermanence and no-self will be explored further in the Second Noble Truth.

Self is a process just like everything else. And furthermore, what you take to be yourself is a metaphor for identity in that this moment is based upon previous similar moments from the past or future similar moments from an anticipated future. This process of comparison gives rise to a solid self or an ego that is more like a thing than a process. A lot of energy is invested into this ego self. It must be identified and protected; self-esteem must be enhanced and it is often the subject of obsession. Think of all the energy you will have once you give up all that protection for something that doesn't really exist. As the poet Wei Wu Wei noted,

Why are you unhappy?

Because 99.9 per cent

Of everything you think,

And of everything you do,

Is for yourself—And there isn't one.

The Three Poisons

The Three Poisons (*kleshas*) are greed (craving, desire, thirst), hatred (aversion, aggression), and delusion (ignorance). The unawakened mind is inextricably intertwined in these three poisons. They arise out of misunderstanding the three marks of *dukkha*, *anicca*, and *anatta* and, in turn, greed, hatred, and delusion are the primary causes of *dukkha*. In going through the process of awakening, you greatly reduce your involvement with these poisons, and it is by reducing these poisons that you can progress toward the awakened mind.

Each of these concepts is intimately bound up with one another. This is the beauty of the Buddha's teaching and it points to a profound understanding of psychology and behavior. It's very likely that your day is filled with a variety of desires and aversions—things you want and don't want. These can be material things, sensory things, or emotional experiences. It's also very likely that you will attribute a sense of permanence to something that is not and fall into the trap of the enduring self or ego (at least once!).

The three poisons are a ubiquitous threat, and the Buddha's teaching offers antidotes for each of the poisons. For greed he suggests generosity (*dana*). For hatred he suggests loving friendliness (*metta*) and compassion (*karuna*). For delusion he suggests the possibility of waking up to a more accurate experience of reality.

The Five Aggregates

In order to understand the nature of the self, the Buddha broke down the individual into five groups, or five aggregates of attachment, in his second sermon at the Deer Park.

The five aggregates he named are as follows:

1. The aggregate of matter (eye, ear, nose, throat, hand, etc.)
2. The aggregate of feelings and sensations (sight, sound, smell, taste, thought, form)
3. The aggregate of perception
4. The aggregate of volitions or mental formations
5. The aggregate of consciousness (response)

Each aggregate is subject to change. Your body changes constantly. If you are over forty, you know this more than most. In fact, most cells of your body change every seven years and, in fact, every atom in your body changes over about once every year. Every atom! From a physical standpoint there is nothing in you today that was in you a year ago. So, what persists? Feelings and sensations change constantly as well. Your ideas change. Your volitions change as well—volitions can be thought of as your intentions or the basis for your actions.

Volitional action changes as well. What you intend to do today will have an effect on what you do tomorrow. Or the intent with which you live your life today will affect your life tomorrow. And finally, you have consciousness (or response), which also changes constantly. You hear something with your ear and become conscious of the sound with your mind. You decide to act on the sound you hear. Your responses continually change.

Since you cannot act on that which you do not experience (you do not act on a sound you do not hear), you'll find that the fifth aggregate, consciousness, depends on all the other aggregates for its existence. The action or response you make based on the intention you had based on your perception of your senses from your body is *solely* dependent on each of the preceding phenomena. This is the Buddha's teaching of *dependent origination*.

Take a simple example: You pass by a pizzeria and your *nose* (body) twitches as you *smell* (sensation) the scent of fresh tomatoes and cheese. You *think* (perception), "Wow, a piece of pizza would sure taste good." Your senses are aroused and you decide *(volition)* to go in to buy yourself a slice. You enter the pizzeria and put some money on the counter *(response)*. Suddenly, a dog passes by the window of the pizza place. You *see* the dog and *think* how you should hurry home to walk your own poor dog, who has been alone since seven o'clock that morning. You *head out* the door toward home. You can see here that you move from sensory experience to perception to volition to response all day long—the aggregates of attachment in action.

The person you call "me" is made up of these five aggregates and nothing more. These aggregates are constantly changing. Therefore, the person you call "me" constantly changes as well. There is no fixed "me" or "I." There is no permanent self, nothing to grab on to. The only way out of this endless cycle is to see that the perception of a fixed self is an illusion that you are attached to. Letting go of this attachment is to liberate yourself from suffering.

These five aggregates together comprise *duhkha,* or suffering. If you think of a river, you will notice that the river is constantly changing. You cannot see one part of the river and stop to examine it and find it as fixed. Just like the river, you are ever changing.

The Second Noble Truth: The Cause of Suffering Is Desire

In the Buddha's words, "This, O Monks, is the Truth of the arising of Suffering. It is this thirst (*tanha*) or craving which gives rise to rebirth, which is bound up with the passionate delight and which seeks fresh pleasure now here and now there in the form of (1) thirst for sensual pleasure, (2) thirst for existence, and (3) thirst for non-existence."

The Second Noble Truth can be summed up in one word—*desire*—and is known as the truth of arising (of suffering). Desire is like an overflowing river carrying you away to *samsara*. A traditional myth provides a metaphor for the relationship to desire. According to the myth, the first beings were nonmaterial entities whose lives were long and blissful until they tasted a sweet substance. That taste created the craving for more tastes and eventually through this process of increasing desire they became solid and differentiated into the creatures humans are today. This metaphor suggests that desire, or thirst as it is sometimes called, weighs you down.

In the Buddha's Fire Sermon, he warned, "Monks, everything is burning. And what is burning? Monks, the eye is burning, visual consciousness is burning, visible forms are burning…Burning with what? Burning with the fire of desire, the fire of aversion, the fire of delusion." In other words, the three poisons. And so the warning goes through the five senses and concludes with an invitation towards detachment as a path to liberation. You suffer because you reach out for certain things, push other things away, and generally neglect to appreciate that everything is changing constantly (*anicca*). The Buddha's admonition should not be interpreted as a condemnation of the senses, but rather a call to examine your relationship to your senses. Are they pushing you around, leading you into trouble, becoming an excessive preoccupation? Here again, the call is to the Middle Way, neither indulging in nor avoiding sensory experiences.

The Source of Desire

Desire comes from sensation and sensation is caused by contact with something that gives rise to the sensation. The cycle of suffering and desire carry on infinitely. For instance, you feel a gnawing sense of lack (the sensation) and see an ad for a powerful new car (the contact that forces the sensation or, in this case, exaggerates the sensation) that you believe will change your life forever. Your self-esteem, the ad, and the possible purchase of the car are causal, relational, and interdependent (the purchase is based on the sight of the ad that you saw when you were feeling bad about yourself). As you probably already know, such retail therapy does not lead to enduring happiness.

But the *most* direct cause of suffering is wanting something—desire. This desire is not limited to material objects, though they can certainly cause much suffering. Who doesn't want a beautiful body, a nice home, a new pair of shoes? But wanting, desiring, also extends to having a serene disposition, your candidate of choice in office, a healthy life, a well-behaved dog, and attachment to ideals, ideas, and opinions.

Clouding the Truth

The desire that you have for so many things keeps you from seeing things as they are. Taken to an extreme, desire can lead to addiction to substances such as drugs or food. Everyone is addicted to some degree to thoughts of "me" and "mine." All this craving leads to pain. Have you ever felt a sense of lack and tried to fill it with things and experiences? Has it helped? Probably not. This is the truth of the arising of suffering. Desire keeps you trapped, going nowhere, like a hamster on an exercise wheel (but at least the hamster is getting some exercise).

The Third Noble Truth: Suffering Can End!

The Buddha said, "This, O Monks, is the Truth of Cessation of Suffering (*nirodha*). It is the utter cessation of that craving (*tanha*), the withdrawal from it, the renouncing of it, the rejection of it, liberation from it, non-attachment to it."

Nirvana literally means "cooling by blowing" or "blowing out." What blows out? Adherence to the three poisons (*kleshas*): greed, hatred, and delusion. It's like putting that fire out that the Buddha spoke of in the Second Noble Truth. This is the prognosis. The misery can stop if life can be approached with wisdom (*prajna*) instead of desire. It's hard to get to this realization without some meditation. By doing so, you examine the moment-by-moment changing nature of experience. When you do this, you see into the three marks, or reality, and are no longer fooled by them. These marks, again, are *dukkha* (suffering; pervasive dissatisfaction), *anicca* (impermanence), and *anatta* (no-self). Short of buddhahood, you might be able to have a peek at this experience from time to time in meditation. These peeks are reminiscent of the peak experiences discussed by Abraham Maslow and other psychologists. They are a glimpse. According to Buddhist scholar Todd Lewis, *nirvana* can be understood as "an impersonal state that transcends individuality" and as "eternal, tranquil, pure, and deathless...and the only permanent reality in the cosmos." Nagarjuna, the second-century philosopher (and second most influential person in the history of Buddhism after the Buddha), added to the definitional mystique of *nirvana* when he said, "There is not the merest difference between *samsara* and *nirvana*." What he means by this is that *nirvana* is beyond all conditions, beyond all categories, and cannot be grasped by the conceptual mind. It goes beyond intellect and must be experienced for yourself to be understood.

Advanced meditation provides the opportunity to burn up past *karma* or the conditionings that you have experienced. It is akin to untying knots that have accumulated in your mind over a lifetime of experiences. Each knot that is untied, each conditioning that is deconditioned, every bit of *karma* that is burned up moves you closer to awakening. Taken to its ultimate realization you will reach *samyaksambodhi*—perfect and complete enlightenment. Language begins to fail in its ability to capture this experience, so you'll have to sit down and experience it for yourself. Bliss is one of the words that approximates the experience, and in the Japanese Zen tradition, it has been called *satori*. Whatever it is called, it can be tasted through meditation.

The Fourth Noble Truth: The Way

To get to *nirvana*, you must traverse the Noble Eightfold Path. This path can be divided into three sections: morality (*sila*; right speech, right action, right livelihood); meditation (*samadhi*; right effort, right mindfulness, right concentration); and wisdom and insight (*prajna*; right view, right thought). This is an entirely self-sufficient path. No outside intercessor is required to reach this salvation. Indeed the gauntlet is thrown down for you to work out your own salvation.

Buddhism is religion in action rather than belief. It is also practical rather than intellectual, as is reflected in the metaphor the Buddha used of the man shot by an arrow. Humanity is like the man, wounded by an arrow, and the arrow is *dukkha*. Intellectual pursuits over practical application would be akin to hesitating to withdraw the arrow before you find out what kind of wood it was made out of, who shot the arrow, and at what angle the arrow entered your body. What matters most in that moment is getting medical help—the healing *dharma* found through meditation, not philosophical speculation.

"This, O Monks, is the Truth of the Path which leads to the cessation of suffering. It is this Noble Eightfold Path, which consists of (1) Right View, (2) Right Resolve, (3) Right Speech, (4) Right Action, (5) Right Livelihood, (6) Right Effort, (7) Right Mindfulness, (8) Right Meditation."—The Truth of the Path (Magga)

The fifth-century Buddhist teacher Buddhoghosa calls morality and meditation the two "legs" upon which wisdom leading to liberation stand. Morality is the foundation for meditation and meditation is the foundation for wisdom. Each builds on the other and you can't get to wisdom without the other two.

This is known as "the Middle Way." It does not promote excessive sensual pleasure or excessive self-denial. It is a moderate path that avoids extremes. The Eightfold Path is a plan of action for realizing *nirvana*. The Noble Eightfold Path will be covered in detail in the following chapter.

The Basics

The Four Noble Truths are the basic teachings of the Buddha. They embody action and have the potential to guide you toward a radical transformation. These teachings revolutionized the spiritual and later political landscape of ancient India. These simple truths are not abstractions. Each one is testable through your own experience. To work through the Four Noble Truths, you recognize, realize experience, and practice. These are the actions for enlightened living. The Four Noble Truths are a wake-up call to how your life is being encumbered with self-inflicted misery, and offers a way out of this misery.

CHAPTER 4

The Noble Eightfold Path

The Middle Way, or the Noble Eightfold Path, is the roadmap for Buddhist living. There are three sections of the Path that contain the eight "right" or "wise" ways to be, and each section is a platform for the next in a continuous process. Morality is the foundation for meditation, meditation is the foundation for wisdom, wisdom is the foundation for morality, and so forth. Each of the eight aspects supports and interacts with the other. As the name implies, they are folded into one another as a field manual for a meaningful spiritual life.

The Noble Eighfold Path

1. Right Speech
2. Right Action
3. Right Livelihood
4. Right Effort
5. Right Mindfulness
6. Right Concentration
7. Right View
8. Right Resolve

What is meant by the word *right*? The Buddha uses the word *right* in the way we would say something is appropriate. You could just as well substitute *wise* for *right.* So if you look at the list above, you will see that the Buddha is not prescribing or proscribing specific actions because appropriate action depends on context. Even the moral foundations are not commandments for behavior. Instead, these right or wise approaches stem from directly experiencing which actions lead to happiness and which actions lead to misery. The goal is to transcend dualistic notions of right and wrong. Remember, the Buddha said, "I preach suffering and the end of suffering."

The Three Divisions of the Path

The Eightfold Path can be divided into three different categories. The Pali for each category appears in parentheses after the word to which it corresponds. They are as follows.

1. Morality (*sila*)
2. Meditation (*samadhi*)
3. Wisdom (*prajna*)

All the steps in the Noble Eightfold Path fall into one of these categories. Morality includes numbers one, two, and three: right speech, right action, and right livelihood. Meditation is made up of the middle three steps (four, five, and six): right effort, mindfulness, and concentration. Finally, Wisdom is comprised of numbers seven and eight: right view and right resolve.

These may appear in different orders and in different descriptions. The order isn't critical because the process is not linear; each part of the Path interacts with every other part.

Wisdom, Morality, and Meditation

Wisdom is made of right view and right resolve, and these two can be considered the hardest practices to master on the Eightfold Path. Wisdom is gained through the practical experiences and insights that you have as a direct result of meditation practice. It is not gained only through intellect, reading texts, or through rituals.

Morality or ethical conduct is comprised of right speech, right action, and right livelihood. All three of these elements have as their core a spirit of lovingkindness and compassion. Morality in Buddhist practice comes from a compassionate heart and mind and is expressed through the things you say, the things you do, and the occupations you choose. Finally, meditation consists of your mental disciplines of right effort, right mindfulness, and right concentration.

Practicing

The eight steps are not meant to be done sequentially but are to be practiced all the time, simultaneously, each and every one. Every day is an opportunity to practice. The Middle Way is a program of action. You can picture these steps as spokes of a wheel. In order for this Dharma Wheel to turn, all the spokes must be in good working order. Once you have understood what each step means, and have undertaken an attempt to practice the steps in your daily life, the Dharma Wheel starts rolling and you are headed down the path toward a happier life.

Right Speech

Speech is a powerful force and can be used for good or for harm. To practice right speech, you must speak the truth and avoid unnecessary communications such as gossip. While you might not always be certain of the right thing to say, you probably know the *wrong* things to say. Here are some of the examples of speech you might want to avoid when practicing right speech:

- Lies
- Slander
- Cursing or abusive language
- Raising one's voice unnecessarily
- Harsh words
- Speaking too much (rattling on)
- Gossip
- Creating enmity

Think before you speak and try to restrain your tongue because these actions can lead to suffering for yourself and those around you.

Right Action

Right action can be understood through the directive: "Do no harm," at least not intentionally. Where do you draw the line? Is eating animals causing harm? Is wearing animal products causing harm? In the time of the Buddha, monks would eat whatever was placed in their begging bowls unless it was intentionally killed for them. The Dalai Lama eats meat for medical reasons. Does eating plants cause harm? In the Mahayana schools there is more emphasis on vegetarianism to minimize the risk of harm. The Theravada monastic code does not prohibit the consumption of meat. Right action is similar to right speech. Your actions should be harmonious with your environment, leading to peace rather than ill will. Do nothing that will cause harm to others. Obviously harmful acts include the following:

- Stealing
- Taking of life, human and otherwise
- Destruction of person or property or peacefulness
- Overindulging

Right action also includes sexual responsibility, such as not commiting adultery. It also includes being mindful of your intake of alcohol and recreational drugs.

Right Livelihood

What do you do for a living? Right livelihood means to avoid harm through your work in the world. The monks in the Buddha's time addressed this issue by taking vows of poverty. Monks then and now renounce material possessions, except for a robe, a begging bowl, and few other items. Does this suggest that to pursue the Noble Eightfold Path you should renounce the material world? Just as with sensory perceptions of the body, the goal is not renunciation, but rather a lack of attachment. There is no prohibition against the accumulation of wealth or of having luxurious possessions. It all depends on the relationship you have to these things. In fact, in the traditional view, great wealth may be a sign of good *karma*. Whatever the status of your *karma*, material wealth provides an opportunity to help others through generosity.

"The Eightfold Path is thus a path of self-transformation: an intellectual, emotional, and moral restructuring in which a person is reoriented from selfish, limited objectives towards a horizon of possibilities and opportunities for fulfillment."—Buddhist scholar Damien Keown

Right livelihood asks you to look at your choices for work and decide if what you are doing to put food on the table is causing harm to anyone or anything else. Even more than not doing harm, right livelihood goes a step further and encourages you to do work that is helpful to others. It requests that you live an honorable life. Occupations a Buddhist might want to avoid include but are not limited to the following:

- Arms dealer
- Drug dealer
- Working with intoxicants and poisons
- Butcher
- Executioner

In today's world, right livelihood can cause some confusion. You want to occupy yourself with activities that promote harmlessness and peace and cause no injury to others. Is being a bartender practicing right livelihood? That is up to you. How does your vocation affect your meditation practice? Is it helping or hindering? Can you practice harmlessness and drill oil? Can you work with nuclear weapons and maintain serenity for yourself and others? Right livelihood asks that you examine your occupation. Can you spend your work time, energy, and effort practicing peacefulness and kindness in the world?

It should also be noted that the Buddha considered no war a just war. Therefore, a profession in the military would not be considered right livelihood. Acts of violence were clearly against the Buddha's teaching.

Right Effort

The next three disciplines are all mental disciplines and directly relate to meditation practices.

All this practice takes quite a bit of effort, so now you need to make sure you are using the appropriate amount of effort, somewhere in between the extremes of laziness and overdoing it. Right effort also means getting rid of improper attitudes and thoughts. When unproductive or unsavory thoughts arise, you must expend the necessary level of effort to return your attention to what is happening in the present moment.

Remember how the Buddha expended great effort to realize enlightenment. He sat through the armies of Mara and did not move until he had accomplished what he set out to accomplish. You can think of Buddha sitting serenely when you are feeling restless during meditation to renew your resolve. To benefit from the Buddha's teachings, effort must be expended. There is no such thing as a free lunch in the universe.

Right Mindfulness

Right mindfulness requires a foundation of right concentration. While practicing mindfulness meditation, or vipassana, you will have a direct experience of the three marks of existence. By paying attention to, for instance, the rising and falling of your breathing or the arising and fading away of sensations in the body, you will have a direct experience of impermanence (*anicca*). When you see how your mind engages with painful stories or identifies with themes of loss or deprivation, you have a direct experience of suffering (*dukkha*).

When you practice and the mind gets concentrated and stays with the moment-to-moment phenomenological energies of being alive, you have a direct experience of no-self (*anatta*)—if it is all energy, who is it that is meditating? You have an experience of awareness without identification with me and mine. This meditation practice can help you to weaken the bonds of attachment that keep you in *samsara* and to simultaneously promote wisdom—clear seeing into the actual nature of things. Meditation provides a crucible to experience the chain of causality or what the Buddha called dependent origination in action. You can see for yourself how the mind and its usual habits generate desire and ignorance.

Right mindfulness has to do with living your life in the moment and being mindful of everything you do. When you eat, eat. When you wash the dishes, wash the dishes. When you read, read. When you are driving the car, pay attention to driving the car (what a concept!).

Right mindfulness asks you to retrieve your attention from the future, especially if that future-oriented attention takes the form of worry. Right mindfulness asks you to retrieve your attention from the past, especially if that past-oriented attention takes the form of regret. Once retrieved, bring your attention back to the present moment and notice with interest what is happening.

The Buddha was practicing right mindfulness when he was observing his thoughts, his sensations, his bodily functions, and his mind. The key to mindfulness is not to judge the contents of your mental experience as good or bad, wanted or unwanted, right or wrong. Right mindfulness and right effort go hand in hand. Without right effort there wouldn't be mindfulness, since mindfulness takes an appropriate degree of effort. Without mindfulness, effort would be futile.

Buddhists love lists. There are the Three Jewels, Three Poisons, Four Noble Truths, Four Foundations of Mindfulenss, Four Immeasurables, Five Aggregates, Five Hindrances, Five Precepts, Eightfold Noble Path, the 108 defilements, and many more!

When you are mindful of your thoughts and actions, ethical conduct becomes possible in everyday life. This also connects to wisdom as well. From your direct experience, you will start to notice which actions are skillful and lead to happiness and which actions are unskillful and lead to misery. This process is empirical, that is, you can test it out in real time, moment-by-moment. Again, it's not about following some pre-ordained code of conduct but realizing what works and what doesn't.

Right Concentration

As mentioned earlier, progress along the Path requires meditation. The mind must be your ally and not your enemy. The Buddha did not invent meditation; such techniques were being practiced in his day and for thousands of years before his time. As you may recall, the Buddha was a meditation prodigy, falling into a meditative state spontaneously under the rose apple tree when he was eight-years-old and was the star pupil of his Hindu ascetic teachers Alara Kalama and Udraka Ramaputra. Under their tutelage he attained profound states of *samahdi* (concentration).

These trance-like states, while quite profound, always left him back in *samsara* once he was done meditating. The other risk of this one-pointed intensive meditation is that it could become addictive, promoting subtle craving for more and more sublime experiences. In a sense these trance states provided an escape from reality, not liberation from it. While concentration is an important foundation for training the mind, it was not the ultimate solution he was seeking. The Noble Eightfold Path includes right mindfulness and right effort in addition to right concentration. Mindfulness was the method that most directly spoke to the impermanence of things and helped the Buddha to realize his awakening.

Right concentration is an important foundation for right mindfulness. It is by practicing the appropriate forms of concentration that you make mindfulness more available. One technique used in meditation for right concentration is concentration on the breath.

For example, you can pay attention to your breathing, noticing the sensations of the inhalation and the exhalation. When attention is pulled away by thoughts, images, or emotions, you bring your attention back to the sensations of breathing happening now. When attention is pulled into the future or starts dragging the past along, you disengage from those fantasies and memories and return attention to this sensation of the breath happening now.

This type of meditation is called one-pointed meditation, because you are focused on one point and keep coming back to that point. By practicing right concentration you can come to mindfulness of the moment. Right concentration supports right mindfulness. Together with right effort they form the third element of the Eightfold Path, known as *samadhi* (meditation).

Right View

Right view means to have a total comprehension of the Four Noble Truths. Right resolve means a detachment from hatred (and cruelty). These factors are unique to the Buddha's teachings. The culmination of these views, based on morality and meditation, is the experience of *prajna* (wisdom or insight into the ultimate reality of things).

The Buddhist scholar Todd Lewis puts it succinctly about *prajna*: "a faculty that enables one unfailingly to see reality clearly amid the constant flow of human experience." This kind of seeing is existential (aware of the finite limits on life) without becoming morbid. This insight shows you the preciousness of life and the pervasiveness of suffering, not only for yourself but also for everyone. This naturally leads to a feeling of compassion (*karuna*) for all beings and a wish to help them arises.

What did the Buddha mean by right view? Right view is the ability to experience things beyond conditioned experience. It removes the biasing filters of past experience and allows you to experience reality closer to the way it actually is. It requires letting go of preconceptions, judgments, and reactivity developed over a lifetime of habit. Meditation (and its constituents: right effort, concentration, and mindfulness) will help you to identify your preconceptions, judgments, and reactivity, and to see how they are active in your experience.

Right view is *getting* The Four Noble Truths. That is, understanding *dukkha*, the causes of *dukkha*, how to stop it, and how to engage in a lifestyle that will address it. The goal is to live life well without causing harm to yourself or others. The goal is to experience things as they are without adding any preconditions, biases, or distortions. It is to find a natural happiness that is always available but obscured from your gaze in the way the sun is always there but sometimes obscured by clouds. Being in the moment is practicing right view.

The Eight Hooks

In the *Pathamalokadhamma Sutta*, the Buddha said,

Among humans, these things, namely,

Gain, loss, status, disrepute, blame, praise, pleasure, and pain

Naturally are impermanent, uncertain, and liable to change,

The wise, ever mindful, understand these things,

And contemplate them as always shifting and changing

Thus, delightful things cannot oppress their minds,

They have no reaction to disagreeable things,

They have abandoned all liking and disliking (for worldly concerns).

Further, they know the path of nirvana, dust-free and without sorrow,

They have reached the other shore of existence and know this correctly.

The Buddha warns about the eight worldly things to avoid. These four pairs of opposites are reflected in the above *sutra*.

- Taking delight in money, material possessions; feeling distress when separated from these things
- Taking delight in praise and things that boost the ego; feeling distress when receiving criticism or disapproval
- Taking delight in maintaining a good reputation or personal image; feeling distress when image and reputation are diminished
- Taking delight when making contact with pleasurable things; feeling distress when making contact with unpleasurable things

What does the Buddha mean here? These are eight hooks for the mind and are thusly eight attitudes that make you vulnerable to *dukkha*. The Buddha is not encouraging you to become zombie-like with no self-preserving instincts. Rather, he is cautioning against basing your self-worth, happiness, and well-being on their occurrence.

In other words, beware of contingent self-worth. All things mentioned here are either not in your direct control (that is, it is something someone else does to us) or they cannot be controlled because they are always changing (that is, the fundamental truth of impermanence). He is not saying don't enjoy things, but he is saying that enjoyment might be a double-edged sword if not tempered by the wisdom of impermanence. He is saying don't take yourself so seriously. He is saying don't invest so much energy into self-protection. Don't base your self-worth on what other people think of you. In fact, spend less time on figuring out your self-worth and more time on paying attention to your experience (and while you're at it, why not focus on helping others, or at least not doing harm to others).

"It is very interesting and important to note here that thoughts of selfless detachment, love, and nonviolence are grouped on the side of wisdom. This clearly shows that true wisdom is endowed with these noble qualities, and that all thought of selfish desire, ill-will, hatred, and violence are the result of a lack of wisdom . . ."—Walpola Rahula

Gain, loss, status, disrepute, blame, praise, pleasure, and pain are eight hooks to avoid, and they may beset you constantly. Inevitably you may succumb to them on a regular basis. Alternatively, each moment is an opportunity to recognize the hook and to disentangle yourself from its barbed grasp. Mindfulness practice helps you to disentangle. To be mindful is to see how you are hooked and allowing fear to overtake you. You can see how your sense of content has become contingent. You can breathe into this moment with interest and a commitment to get off the hook or put your energy towards solving the problem in a practical matter. If the problem can't be solved right away, you can breathe through the uncertainty.

Right Resolve

Right resolve involves intentions. The spirit in which you approach everything—a spirit of kindness, compassion, and harmlessness to your fellow beings—is essential to right resolve. The goal is to move away from the ego-related concerns of "me" and "mine," towards a lifestyle of service where your motivations are not ego driven but more selfless.

A Noble Process

The Noble Eightfold path is a process. Don't worry about getting it perfectly at every moment. Do not expect that you will automatically wake up one morning with a wonderful loving feeling toward everyone that you express through tireless works of selflessness. It took many years to become conditioned the way you are and it will take some time to make changes. The Path provides the methods to accomplish this.

Everything you need to awaken is included in the Four Noble Truths. The insights and methods provide a toolbox to tackle a lifetime of conditioning. This conditioning afflicts everyone and keeps you behind a veil of illusion. One of the biggest illusions is the illusion of separation. That is, "me" as being separate from "you," and not just people—everything. The traditional belief, now supported by quantum physics, is that there is an interconnection amongst everything. And what we experience as solid objects is really mostly empty space.

If you know that everything is interconnected, you will behave differently in the world. Not only is everything interconnected, it is also in flux—constantly changing. Wisdom invites you to recognize this and to enjoy the ride. Reality is a process, not a collection of things. The world (including your body) is a ceaseless dance of energy and matter, interdependent and impersonal. It only becomes personal through the process of attachment and identification through language—"me and mine." The process of the Four Noble Truths can give you a direct experience of this truth. When interdependence is experienced, compassion for others and the earth arises naturally.

CHAPTER 5

The Buddha's Ethics

At their core, the Buddha's teachings are a prescription for ethical conduct in the world. By cultivating wisdom you minimize harm to yourself and the people and planet around you. By embracing meditation, you find a path to find peace in the midst of everyday chaos and a world riddled with uncertainty. Ethical conduct is a foundation for meditation and wisdom, but this is not morality for the sake of morality or social control. You act in the ways described in this chapter because you *know* that it leads to greater happiness.

The Five Precepts and Ten Unwholesome Actions

The moral precepts (*sila*) overlap to some extent with the Ten Commandments (don't lie, steal, or kill), and embody the Golden Rule (do unto others what you would have others do unto you). Translating *sila* as morality might create confusion; ethics might be a better choice for this term. The basis for practice and the path to awakening are these ethical precepts. They are done not out of some sense of moral purity but out of necessity.

The Five Precepts are:

- Do not destroy life.
- Do not steal.
- Do not commit sexual misconduct.
- Do not lie.
- Do not become intoxicated.

It's hard to kill someone in the morning and meditate with concentration and mindfulness in the afternoon. The fallout from unwholesome actions interferes with the mind's ability to train itself. In addition to the five *silas*, the Buddha also cautioned against another five unwholesome actions, making for a list of ten. This action list of ten things to avoid can be grouped into things *not* to do with your body (don't kill, steal, harm with sexuality), speech (don't lie, don't be harsh with words, don't gossip, and don't engage in frivolous speech), and mind (don't get lost in desire, don't get lost in hatred, don't get lost in wrong resolve).

According to Donald S. Lopez Jr., in *The Story of Buddhism*, when a vow is taken, from the Buddhist perspective, it takes on a subtle physical form in the body itself and remains so until death or until the vow is broken. As long as the vow is in the body, the person accumulates merit for it.

In many traditions, taking vows means to commit yourself to the practice of the five *silas* (not to kill, steal, lie, sexual misconduct, and intoxication). The ten unwholesome actions will be presented within the context of the five precepts. American Buddhist teacher Joseph Goldstein likens the ethical precepts to a warning sign on the beach: "Danger, Strong Undertow." The Buddha is the lifeguard who has put up this warning sign. The precepts are a template for living an awakened life.

Do Not Destroy Life

Every living thing seeks its own survival and a version of its own happiness. This precept asks you to consider this in your actions. It's an invitation to revere life. Don't do things that cause harm to others. This is the practice of *ahimsa* ("not harming"). Don't kill, maim, or assault. If you recognize that all life is interconnected, this makes intuitive sense. Buddhists who believe in rebirth make the point that the being you harm may have been your mother in a previous lifetime. It also makes sense not to harm because the mind state that accompanies harming will be harmful to you as well. It's a lose-lose proposition.

In regard to fellow humans, the guidelines are fairly clear, but when it comes to the animal kingdom, the considerations become more complex. Is it okay to kill a mosquito? What about one that may be carrying malaria? Can you protect yourself from a dangerous animal? What about insects and worms harmed in plowing fields? Remember Siddhartha's distress at seeing the plowed fields and the harm this caused its inhabitants? As with all the precepts, intention is essential. To deliberately harm is different than inadvertently harming because it is accompanied by a different mind state, and would therefore have different *karmic* consequences.

The Buddha taught that all sentient beings possess *buddha-nature* and are considered fundamentally good. *Buddha-nature* is the potential to awaken and achieve enlightened mind. Buddha believed that all people have *buddha-nature*, no matter what they have done or how they look on the outside.

But it gets complicated. What if you hunt for deer? This is intentional taking of life to be sure, but in certain areas of the United States deer populations are so dense that many deer get killed on the highways, also causing damage to cars and people. So which action causes less harm? What about native first people, such as the Inuit, whose lifestyle is supported through reverential hunting of animals and using them for food, warmth, and tools? Are these people prevented from awakening? Certainly not, and what you can conclude from this is that there are no "rules" and you should not be attached to rules (that's what really keeps you from awakening).

It would be impossible to go through life without harming another living thing, however hard you try. This precept invites you to take care with respect to life, letting kindness and compassion take the lead in your actions. It cautions against perpetuating the Three Poisons through your actions, especially hatred, aggression, and violence.

To accomplish this you may have to be more thoughtful in how you conduct your life and consider how many animal products you encounter on a daily basis in your clothing, food, and other things. There may be relative levels of harm to consider, such as eating beef raised on a factory farm living in huge crowds, eating corn, and taking antibiotics versus one raised on a rolling Vermont hillside eating grass. That cow, at least, enjoyed a happy life before it became your dinner.

More dilemmas can be found in contemporary issues such as assisted suicide, abortion, and the death penalty. Here again, absolute rules cannot be formulated and you must use your self-knowledge and wisdom to discern appropriate action. Arguments can be made on either side of each issue, and there is no central Buddhist authority, like the Vatican, to issue policy.

Do Not Steal

The second precept advises you to not take what is not freely given from another. This does not just include stealing tangible objects, but intangibles as well, such as ideas or time. It invites you to develop a sense of generosity toward others and respect of others' property.

Generosity

The things you have can reinforce the illusory sense of a solid self, bring considerations of "me" and "mine" into the mind. This is clearly the case when things are taken that are not freely given, but also the case when there is a lack of generosity. A lack of generosity reinforces the illusory sense of separation from others. This precept also points to the poison of greed. Greed could motivate you to take what is not yours. But it's not just stealing that is considered here. It's having more than your fair share. Westerners are privileged relative to much of the rest of the world. And even here in the West, some are more privileged than others. Many children in the United States don't get enough to eat, and yet dining at all-you-can-eat buffets is a popular and inexpensive form of entertainment whose sole purpose is to nurture the poison of greed.

According to the World Bank, the richest 20 percent of the world's population consume 76.6 percent of its resources. The poorest 20 percent consume 1.5 percent. The richest consume 45 percent of all meat and fish while the poorest only consume 5 percent. The richest consume 58 percent of energy and the poorest 4 percent. Wealthy industrialized nations spend billions on cosmetics, perfume, entertainment, drugs and alcohol, and military spending. This spending is orders of magnitude greater than what is spent on basic education, water, sanitation, health, and nutrition for those in need around the world.

You may have seen a bumper sticker years ago that read, "Live simply so that others can simply live." Here again is a reminder to walk the Middle Path between the extremes of indulgence and deprivation. This is not an invitation to give away all your possessions. Rather, it is an invitation to consider the impact of your actions in the material world and how they affect yourself and others. The Middle Way is compatible with financial security. After all, the Buddha had to ensure the material needs of the *sangha*, and did so by garnering the support of kings and laypersons that provided parks, temples, food, and other material support for those dedicated to the Noble Eightfold Path.

Do Not Commit Sexual Misconduct

The third precept is sexual respect for yourself and others. Sex is a powerful force. Sex is a force for creation and a force for great harm when abused.

Spiritual communities are not immune from sexual misconduct, as the scandals within the Catholic Church have recently shown, and even Buddhist communities have succumbed to sexual improprieties. This precept invites you to consider the power of sexuality and to use it mindfully with respect and responsibility for yourself and others. This precept is certainly a caution to avoid the obvious forms of sexual misconduct, and often refers to adultery just as the Ten Commandments do. However, it is broader. Don't do anything that can use the powerful force of sexuality in a way that harms.

Despite its puritanical origins, the United States is a highly sexualized culture. Sex is everywhere: in advertising, on television, in videos, and movies. Pornography is a multi-billion dollar industry. Sex addiction is a growing clinical problem. Sex is everywhere and, like Buddha confronting the temptations of Mara, you will be challenged to be mindful in this arena on a daily basis. Sex taps directly into the poison of desire. If you seek lasting fulfillment from a transitory phenomenon like sex, it is bound to bring frustration. The Buddha taught that lasting happiness couldn't be found by pursuing desire in relentless fashion.

As with all aspects of the Middle Way, this precept is not an admonition towards prudery or even modesty. As with all the precepts, it is an invitation to be awake in the area of sexuality, an area that is challenging to be awake in because it is a deeply rooted biological drive compounded by media-based cultural conditionings. This precept is also an invitation to foster selfless loving in your intimate relationships along with harmony, safety, and enjoyment.

Do Not Lie

Like sexuality, speech is a potent force in the world and can be the source of great harm if not done with awareness, integrity, and honesty. The Buddha likened the tongue to an axe. Words can harm others; words can harm you, even your own words towards yourself. This precept includes the four unwholesome actions of lying, speaking harshly, gossiping, and being frivolous.

This precept is much like the right speech of the Eightfold Path. Do not lie, slander, be dishonest in any way, speak with insincerity, promote falsehood, misrepresent information, or gossip maliciously. Do not be indifferent to the truth in any situation with any event that arises. Be truthful in everything you do and bring love and kindness into your environment.

The Buddha told his followers about the five courses of speech. Speech may be "timely or untimely, true or untrue, gentle or harsh, connected with good or with harm, or spoken with a mind of loving-kindness or with a mind of inner hate." Obviously, he felt the skillful member of the five pairs to be the first.

Words are powerful, and the invitation here is to be mindful and intentional about how you use your words. In addition to not lying, you are encouraged to avoid words (including your own private thoughts) that are harsh, critical, angry, or belligerent. The Buddha also encouraged his followers not to gossip because of the harm it can cause.

American Buddhist teacher Jack Kornfield tells a story of making a commitment to not talk for a period of time about anything that was not about his direct experience (that is, gossiping about people he knew). He found, remarkably, that he had little to say!

The final consideration for speech is to make your speech meaningful and to avoid engaging in frivolous or useless talk. The ability to speak is such a wonderful capacity and one that may get taken for granted. If you remained silent instead of engaging in gossip and frivolous speech, how quiet would things get? The natural opening from these cautions is being receptive. When your mind is not entangled in lying, criticizing, gossiping, and wasting its time on frivolous talk, you could then enjoy a space for listening (and hopefully you'll be hearing the right speech of the person you are talking to!).

Do Not Become Intoxicated

This precept has a range of interpretations. On one end, there is strict prohibition against any intoxicating substance, even a single drink of alcohol. Some teachers include caffeine and tobacco as well. On the other end, the prohibition is against ingesting sufficient substances to induce intoxication and thereby impairment. In other words, it's hard to meditate with any skill if you are drunk. Think about the terms for intoxication.

First, there is "intoxication" itself, which means "to poison," Then there are the colloquial terms for intoxication: *smashed, hammered, wrecked, polluted, wasted*, and *annihilated.* None of these seem conducive to exploring your inner experience with accuracy. There is a tradition to drink sake to celebrate the New Year in Zen temples in Japan. "Happy sake," if you will. As with all the precepts, your approach can be empirical—based on your own experience—rather than following *rules.* You will find that being mindful of what you put into your body will support your progress along the path. The Buddha cautioned, "do everything in moderation, including moderation"—don't become attached to rules for the sake of having rules. This is just another attachment, another prison to encumber your freedom.

Media, food, and entertainment may be other forms of "intoxication." This precept is a caution to be mindful of all forms of consumption and to see if they are contributing to suffering or providing you with a temporary release with a subsequent crash back into suffering. This precept brings the poison of greed back into focus. Why do you consume? Can you consume mindfully? Do you have to consume so much?

The ethical precepts provide a foundation for mindful living that promote awakening, compassion, and wisdom. You do or don't do the behaviors described above not to be a "good girl" or a "good boy," but because you recognize the value in doing so. It's wise to act in these ways and you'll know this from your direct experience. Acting without harming makes sense and promotes your practice. It also makes the world around you a better place.

The Five Hindrances

The actions sanctioned in the precepts can be seen as hindrances to practice and living an awakened life. In addition to the five precepts and the ten unwholesome actions, the Buddha also discussed the Five Hindrances to spiritual progress:

1. Doubt
2. Desire
3. Ill Will
4. Restlessness and Compunction
5. Sloth and Torpor

As you practice mindfulness and meditation, you will become aware of each of the Five Hindrances arising in your mind. You will doubt that what you are doing is meaningful and worthwhile. Don't you have a million other better things to do? What is so important about just sitting here? All manner of desire, including sexual fantasies, will come up to distract from your object meditation. You will deal with anger, hatred, and ill will as you dwell on the people and situations in your life. Restlessness and compunction will arise, and you'll want to get off the meditation cushion. Sloth and torpor will make you sleepy and make you want to watch television, rather than examine your own mind.

Overcoming Hindrances

Each of these hindrances is something to work through. They can actually be looked at as gifts that further progress along the Path. Right effort is needed to counteract them. You must exert effort to cut through these resistances, just as the Buddha sat through Mara's assaults under the Bodhi Tree. Don't take them personally.

It is important not to become entangled in the hindrances. Don't overidentify with them. Everyone goes through them. See if you can observe these feelings and watch them arise and watch them pass. As Ayya Khema said in *When the Iron Eagle Flies*, "Cessation of suffering is not due to the fact that suffering stops. It is due to the fact that the one who suffers ceases to exist."

The Four Immeasurables

Buddhism makes goodness an explicit virtue and aspiration. Goodness is embodied in what are known as the *Brahma Viharas*, or the Limitless Abodes, or the Four Immeasurables. These include lovingkindness or loving friendliness, compassion, sympathetic joy, and equanimity, and together they comprise what might be considered emotional intelligence.

While the Buddha did not place extreme emphasis on these qualities, he felt they arose naturally when one realized the Four Noble Truths. These qualities are, in a sense, process outcomes of living a Buddhist life. When you realize the causes of suffering and seek to overcome them, these qualities are able to come through. Each of them has at its core a lack of self-preoccupation. When you can give up your obsessive preoccupation with

"I, me, and mine," there is a lot of energy left over to devote to others in the form of lovingkindness, compassion, and rejoicing in their good fortunes. When there is no longer a self to protect, equanimity shows up in its place and you are able to confront any situation with an even and unperturbed mind. Each of these qualities has a "near enemy," a quality that seems like it but is not, and a "far enemy" that is its opposite.

Lovingkindness (*Metta*)

Lovingkindess or loving friendliness is an attitude of beneficence towards all beings, including yourself. The Buddha said, "You can search through the entire universe for someone who is more deserving of your love and affection than you are yourself, and that person is not to be found anywhere. You yourself, as much as anybody in the entire universe deserve your love and affection." In lovingkindness, you seek to generate feelings of safety, peace, well-being, and freedom for yourself, loved ones, strangers, and even your enemies. The near enemy to lovingkindness is an affection that is motivated by selfishness. The far enemy of lovingkindness is enmity.

Compassion (*Karuna*)

Karuna is an ability to bear witness to suffering without fear. It is to be empathetic with a quality of openness, spaciousness, and stillness. Compassion requires the courage to see what is present and a willingness to hold it in your heart. It is a form of non-judgmental care of yourself and others. When you are fully present with another you are in a compassionate posture. The meditation teacher Sharon Salzberg noted, "The simple act of being completely present to another person is truly an act of love." The near enemy of compassion is pity or sympathy. The far enemy of compassion is cruelty.

Sympathetic Joy (*Mudita*)

Mudita requires you to relinquish judgment and comparison and rejoice in the success and happiness of others. *Mudita* is an antidote to jealousy, envy, craving, and resentment, all of which are the far enemies of *mudita*. *Mudita* is non-selfish, non-attached optimism. *Mudita* balances *karuna* by preventing brooding; *karuna* balances *mudita* by avoiding sentimentality or ignorant optimism. The near enemy to *mudita* would be exuberance, an excited state of mind that overlays a sense of attachment or feeling of deprivation.

Equanimity (*Uppekha*)

Upekkha is usually translated as "equanimity" and this captures an important aspect of this state: a calm, tranquil mind in the face of any circumstance, even the most challenging ones. *Upekkha* can also be translated as "interest," and this interest is how you get to be tranquil in the midst of a painful situation. When you are interested in something, you are paying more attention to it than to your painful story about it. Equanimity brings a wise acceptance to every situation. Indifference is the near enemy of equanimity. It's not just dissociating from unpleasantness that gets you there, it's clear seeing. Being attached through craving and clinging is the far enemy of equanimity.

More Precepts

The Five Precepts previously outlined apply to laypeople practicing Buddhism. However, there are other precepts that apply to monks only, or *bhikkus*. A more rigorous set of ethics applies to those practicing a monastic life, and the number of precepts a monastic might vow to undertake varies from one Buddhist tradition to another. Here, however, are five additional precepts that are traditionally taken by monks entering monastic life:

1. Do not take food from noon to the next morning (except lemon water).
2. Do not adorn the body with anything other than the monk's robe.
3. Do not participate in or watch public entertainments.
4. Do not use comfortable beds.
5. Do not use money.

These additional precepts are designed to separate monks from life outside the monastery. Feasting, comfort, financial freedom, personal style, and entertainment are all restricted. These restrictions serve to focus the attention of each monk on the task at hand: the search for enlightenment through practice. These additional precepts are designed to limit the distractions that monks have to deal with so they can devote their exclusive energy toward awakening.

Each of these additional precepts serves to widen the gap between the monk's life and the life of the laypeople in his community. Though monks are encouraged to live among the population in order to better serve them, their focus is on meditation, mindfulness, the acquisition of wisdom, and the practice of the precepts. A monk's life is dedicated to selflessness. Each of the additional precepts a monk might undertake emphasizes the abandonment of self-identification and the practice of selflessness.

CHAPTER 6

The Buddhist Community

Community, or the *sangha*, is an integral part of Buddhist practice. In fact, it is one of the Triple Jewels, along with *buddha* and the *dharma*. As in other great religious traditions, community plays an essential role in keeping the practitioner on the right path, supported by others who share similar beliefs and interests. In Buddhism, each member of the community helps other members to continue on the Noble Eightfold Path.

The Three Jewels

You might call yourself a Buddhist if you practice the Five Precepts and if you take refuge in the Three Jewels. But what is meant by the Three Jewels of Buddhism? The Three Jewels are the basic components of Buddhist practice. The Three Jewels of Buddhism are:

- The *buddha*
- The *dharma*
- The *sangha*

Buddha means the Awakened One, the Enlightened One. For the *buddha* jewel you take *buddha* as your refuge. But it's not the person of the Buddha that is sought for refuge; rather, it is the possibility for awakening. The Buddha taught that everyone has *buddha-nature*, that is, the capacity to awaken. You are *buddha*, and it is to this realization that refuge is taken.

Dharma has multiple meanings. *Dharma* is the collection of the Buddha's teachings. In the Buddha's time wandering ascetics would meet each other and ask, "Whose *dharma* do you follow?" They would then provide the name of their teacher. The Buddha was unique in that he did not follow another teacher's *dharma* but had figured things out for himself under the pipal tree. *Dharma* also refers to the deeper truths that the Buddha's teachings point to. It refers to the truth of *dukkha* and the possibility of *nirvana*. *Dharma* is also translated as "natural law": seeing clearly into the reality of things.

Equally important is the community, the *sangha*. The early *sangha* was comprised of the Buddha and his followers. This included his former five ascetic friends and the proliferation of people that followed, including common people and kings. People joined the community through their wish to end suffering and upon hearing the wisdom of the Buddha. You could become monastic or be part of the community as a lay practitioner. 2,500 years later, these choices are still available, and the *sangha* is one of humanity's oldest continuous institutions.

Yet, it is not a formal community. It has no central authority, holds no annual conference, and has no membership roster. It is a loosely collected group of like-minded individuals who practice living the Four Noble Truths and other Buddhist teachings, practices, and rituals that have developed over the centuries. The *sangha* is the worldwide collection of Buddhist practitioners as well as the small group of people with whom you meet to meditate together on a regular basis in your community. Even individuals who practice on their own are part of the *sangha*.

"When we say, 'I take refuge in the Buddha,' we should also understand that 'The Buddha takes refuge in me,' because without the second part the first part is not complete. The Buddha needs us for awakening, understanding, and love to be real things and not just concepts. They must be real things that have real effects on life. Whenever I say, 'I take refuge in the Buddha,' I hear 'Buddha takes refuge in me.'"—Thich Nhat Hanh, *Being Peace*

Taking refuge in the Buddha does not mean that you are hidden and protected by a great and powerful force. It means to align yourself with the Buddha and strive to become a *buddha* yourself. Similarly, you can take refuge with the *dharma* by aligning yourself with the teachings. Likewise, you can take refuge in the *sangha*. The *sangha* is not just about membership or social support. It's more than being a card-carrying Buddhist. The *sangha* provides support for your practice. Each member of the *sangha* supports each other. To sit in meditation with a group provides a different experience. It gets you to sit up straighter and put more effort into your practice. And it also provides something intangible, something ineffable and powerful. The *sangha* is the glue that keeps everything together.

Monks and Nuns

The Triple Jewel can be pursued at different levels. In the East, there is a long tradition of monastic orders, or monks (*bikkhu*) and nuns (*bhikkunis*). To become a monk or nun is to devote yourself to spiritual life. A child is old enough to become a monk when he can "scare the crows away," which usually means about seven or eight years old. The Buddha accepted his son Rahula into the sangha when he was only seven years old. Seeing the grief this caused Rahala's grandfather Sudhodhona, the Buddha made a subsequent rule about the minimum age for *bikkhus* entering the *sangha*. In the Buddha's time, monks upon joining the *sangha* were told the four things they could always use for the four basic necessities of life: the foot of a tree for accommodation, robes made of rags for clothing, food offered as alms, and fermented cow's urine for medicine. If you become ordained in the Zen or Tibetan Buddhist traditions today, the basic necessities have been updated! But life would remain simple. A monk in the Buddha's time was allowed eight possessions: three robes, a water strainer, a begging bowl, a needle, razor, and a belt. Monks and nuns are expected to shave their heads and live a life of celibacy.

Why do Buddhist monks have to be celibate?
On the point of celibacy, it is not clear whether the Buddha recommended this, as was the custom of the day, or as means to limit the material resources the *sangha* would require (it takes more food to support families than solitary monks). It is not clear that the Buddha's teaching or the *dharma* require celibacy. Householders (as lay practitioners are called in India) have been known to reach enlightenment too, although the demands of daily life will make this more challenging.

Monasteries can be quite elaborate and large social institutions. For example, the Abhayagiri monastery in fifth-century Sri Lanka had 5,000 monks. Prior to China's invasion of Tibet in 1959, the Drepung monastery housed 10,000 monks. These monks need quarters, meals, and a place to worship. Many Asian monasteries nurture a pipal tree (or the Bodhi Tree), the tree under which Siddhartha reached his great awakening.

The First Jewel: The Buddha

The Buddha was both a man and a symbol. When you take refuge in the Buddha, you bow in respect to what this man accomplished in his lifetime. When you take refuge in the Buddha, you also bow to what he represents—your awakened nature. The Buddha's example can be a raft that carries you across the river of *samsara*. He can show you a path, but he cannot walk it for you. In this way, Buddha is neither a god nor a saint. "Role model" may be a better way to think of the Buddha.

Some people, especially in traditional Buddhist cultures, may look to Buddha as a source of salvation. In Tibet he is referred to as Lord Buddha. In the West, however, he is more the hero of an epic story of sacrifice and deliverance from greed, hatred, and delusion. He had everything, then nothing before finding the Middle Way. Through his voluminous teaching over a long career, he has left a detailed path that any interested party can follow. He left a repertoire of methods that can lead to liberation. He was a great yogi and represents the potential for radical transformation, from a life of suffering to a life of liberation.

Lasting Legacy

In the *Razor's Edge*, W. Somerset Maugham tells the story of Larry Daryl, a modern-day Buddha-like figure who sacrificed wealth and privilege to find a spiritual truth. Maugham says, "He's not famous. It may be that when his life at last comes to end he will leave no greater trace of his sojourn on this earth than a stone thrown in a river leaves on the surface of the water. Yet it may be the way of life he has chosen for himself may have an ever growing influence over his fellow men so that long after his death, perhaps, it may be realized that there lived in this age, a very remarkable creature."

The Buddha *is* famous, of course, and he was a "very remarkable creature" whose sacrifices, insights, and lessons provide a way for every human being to attain a meaningful and lasting happiness, free from suffering. The Buddha might have dwelled in obscurity like Larry Daryl, yet he decided to share his insights with anyone willing to listen. By doing so, he revolutionized humanity and the potential for transformation, compassion, and happiness.

Buddha-nature—the *buddha* within everyone—is not created but rather revealed. It is present now, but perhaps obscured by your stories of desire and aversion. *Buddha-nature* is not made; it is not a destination. It is here right now. The Buddha showed humanity this potential.

Practicing the Buddhist path will help to make this *buddha-nature* accessible and clear. You will go through similar trials as the Buddha did if you commit yourself to these practices. This path is challenging; but anything worthwhile is. When you are struggling to keep yourself on the cushion, you can imagine the Buddha confronting the temptations of Mara, sitting steadfast and resolute. This image can inspire you to keep sitting.

If Siddhartha could do it, you can do it! This is what it means to take refuge in the Buddha.

FACT

The fat and happy "Buddha" you've seen in Chinese restaurants is not Siddhartha Gautama, Shakyamuni Buddha. He is Budai in China or Hotei in Japan. He is often depicted smiling and laughing. He is more of a folklore figure, but is often mistaken for the historical Buddha.

The Buddha does not ask you to believe in him or to pray to him. Any peace of mind that comes to you comes from your own effort and not divine intervention. He shows you a path that you are free to take all on your own. *Buddha* is empirical, meaning subject to experimentation and also referring to the information coming from your own experience. There is no blind allegiance; there is only practice. It's as if all Buddhists are from the state of Missouri with its state proclamation: "Show me!"

See for yourself: You, too, can take refuge in the Buddha.

Living Buddha

Bearing in mind the Buddha's caution to avoid people claiming to be "enlightened," taking refuge in the Buddha can also mean finding an appropriate teacher. You might know of a Buddhist who is qualified to teach you the *dharma* in your community or at special *dharma* centers around the country. Find yourself a teacher who embodies the teachings of the Buddha. When you find a living Buddha, you witness the compassion and lovingkindness that is possible.

The Second Jewel: The *Dharma*

The second of the Three Jewels is the *dharma*. The *dharma* is the entire collection of Buddhist scripture and thought, including all modern Buddhist teachings, as well as the traditional, original teachings, such as the *sutras* in the Pali Canon. The *dharma* is all the spoken word and written text passed down through the generations.

Today there are many sources for the *dharma*: books, DVDs, MP3s, streaming Internet video and recorded *dharma* talks. There are also practice centers and monasteries. The proliferation of Buddhism in the West in conjunction with modern communication technologies has created an unprecedented availability of the *dharma*.

There are two types of *dharma*: that which can be read or heard—transmitted from person to person—and that which is realized. *Realized dharma* is *dharma* experienced through the practice of the Four Noble Truths—the realization of the Truth, or awakening.

The *dharma* surrounds you. Any experience can awaken you to the *dharma*. Have you ever found yourself sitting outside, enjoying the wonders of a beautiful day? Suddenly you hear a bird call out and its call is pure and sweet and fills you with joy. You lose yourself completely in that moment, just listening to the sounds of the bird. The bird is the *dharma*; the bird teaches you something about awakening. In that moment your story of "me" disappears and you awaken to a reality that takes over where stories stop. Anything can be the *dharma*: a bird, a work of art, a cup of coffee, a dog barking, the rain, even difficult experiences are *dharma*. Every experience holds the possibility of revealing some truth.

Roshi is a title given to a Zen master, under whom a student must study if she hopes to reach enlightened mind. In Japanese it means "venerable master."

Zen master Suzuki Roshi said that it is difficult to keep our mind pure. In Japan, there is a phrase, *shoshin*, which means "beginner's mind." In Buddhism, the aspiration is always to keep this beginner's mind, this openness and readiness. Suzuki said, "In the beginner's mind there are many possibilities; in the expert's mind there are few." Do not take the *dharma* as an absolute, definable, and fixed reality. It changes just as everything changes. Be open to what you experience and avoid preconceived notions, especially those that apply to being on a spiritual path. As you journey on the path toward enlightened mind, let go of what you learn on the way and keep your mind fresh and clean.

The Third Jewel: The Sangha

The Buddha's first followers were his five former ascetic colleagues. Soon, he went from teaching men who were already renunciants to lay people. A wealthy young man named Yashas became a follower and attained enlightenment under the Buddha's tutelage. Yashas' father also became a follower but as a lay practitioner (*upsaka*). Lay followers did not follow monastic rules, but practiced the teaching by taking the Triple Refuge: *buddha*, *dharma*, *sangha*. Yashas' mother also took refuge in the Triple Jewel and became the first female lay follower. In the days before Facebook, Buddha's teaching caught on. Through the social networking means available in the sixth century B.C.E., friends of Yashas came, and friends of friends. Word spread. The Buddha sent the first sixty enlightened ones out to spread the teachings. Noted Buddhist scholar Kevin Trainor cites the Buddha saying, "Travel forth, monks, for the benefit of the many, for the happiness of the many, out of compassion for the world, for the well-being, benefit, and happiness of gods and humans."

Can the average person attain enlightenment?
Vacchagotta approached the Buddha and asked him if there were lay followers practicing the Buddha's principles who achieved "high spiritual states." The Buddha told Vacchagotta that yes, there were "not one or two, not a hundred or two hundred or five hundred but many more" who did.

Despite the Buddha's repudiation of the caste system, not everyone was welcome in the *sangha*. If you were a debtor, a criminal, runaway slave, or other person shunned by society, you were not welcome. The Buddha likely made such rules mindful of not offending his wealthy patrons upon whose generosity the *sangha* depended. In this way, he was a skilled politician and not detached from the practical realities of life. The *sangha* depended upon the patronage of kings and the wealthy. To this end accommodations were made. The most controversial issue where the Buddha did depart from social norms was allowing women to be ordained as nuns (*bikkhunis*). It took some repeated pleading, however, from his Aunt Prajapati.

The Buddha's main hangout was in the Jeta Grove where he and the *sangha* spent nineteen rainy seasons (outside of the ancient city of Shravasti). The Jeta Grove was donated by Anathapindaka, who bought the spread from Prince Jeta. Jeta drove a hard bargain and Anathapindaka had to cover the ground with coins to secure it for the *sangha*. With all that coin, Jeta built quite a country retreat for the monks. This compound, with its combination of land and rich benefactors, served as a model for Buddhism spreading throughout Asia. The monasteries that emerged from these auspicious beginnings also served as cultural institutions. A central component of the monastery was the *dharma* hall and the library.

The Buddha and the *sangha* wandered around much of what is today Northern India. During the three-month monsoons, they would take refuge in special places built by wealthy patrons, like the Jeta Grove. They also did not want to travel during the rainy season for fear of injuring life that may be out during the rains, such as worms.

Monastery (*vihara*) life consisted of meditation, initiation rituals, study, and recitation of what later became the Pali Canon. Two traditions emerged: the forest refuge where monks could do intensive meditation practice, and the village monastery where they served the local community through education, rituals, and also did their own practice. In some places, monks retreated to caves. Charismatic leaders led many of these communities.

Contract with the Community

Lay practitioners were known as *upasaka* (males) and *upasikas* (females). A lay practitioner becomes so by formally reciting the Triple Refuge and committing to the five precepts in a ceremony with other members of the community. In traditional Buddhist societies (for example, Sri Lanka), there is little emphasis on meditation and more emphasis on generosity (*dana*) and morality (*sila*).

The most basic act of *dana* is a food offering to wandering monks. Or, as in Sri Lanka, women will take prepared food to the monastery for the monks. In Tibet, generosity may take the form of the "tea offering," where money is donated so that all the monks can have yak butter tea. The laity can also "sponsor" the recitation of mantras or *sutras*. Money, clothing, flowers, and incense may also be given.

Generosity is an important part of spiritual practice. To give is to overcome ego-based attachment to things. It also helps to foster a sense of interconnectedness. According to the Jataka tales, that recount the "past lives" of the Buddha, the Buddha made a generous offering of himself to a hungry tigress so that she could sustain the strength to feed her young. Such selfless acts also generate merit *(punya)* for the lay practitioner, and the generation of merit is a primary motivation in Asian cultures.

On special occasions the lay community will adopt additional precepts such as not eating anything other than lemon water after lunch; no dancing, singing, music, ornamenting the body with perfumes, garlands, etc.; or not sleeping in high and luxurious beds (monks already partake of these restrictions). In Asia, the focus for the laity is on right conduct/action rather than on the meditative disciplines, and also visiting holy pilgrimage sites. In Tibet, prostrations and turning prayer wheels are central practices for the lay practitioner.

Strength in Numbers

The monastic setting certainly provides a place for individuals willing to devote their entire life to their spiritual development and to the service of all. However, it is not realistic for everyone. Still, there is power in numbers. What you find difficult alone, you might find easier with the strength of numbers behind you. The world around you may not be on the same spiritual page as you are, and this may be an obstacle. You may feel overwhelmed by others who are leading an unreflected life and are caught up in the suffering of greed, hatred, and delusion. Having a group that supports your commitment, that encourages you to proceed against what at times can seem to be overwhelming odds, can make all the difference between staying on the Path or falling off.

"We take refuge in the Buddha because Buddha is our great teacher...We take refuge in the law, in the *Dharma*, because it is good medicine...We take refuge in the Buddha's community, or *sangha*, because it is composed of excellent friends..."—Dainin Katagiri

As you sit to do your meditation, perhaps you start wondering *why* you are sitting on a cushion when you could be watching *Law and Order.* Perhaps work beckons or the house needs cleaning. Without a *sangha* to keep you on track, over time the voices in your head that discourage you from your practice may get louder and louder until they crowd out that little voice inside yourself that urges you onward. The *sangha* can help bring you back to the path and hold you there. The *sangha* can be a powerful force of encouragement.

Generosity

Dana (donation) is a key Buddhist practice throughout the world. Giving generates a sense of generosity that is an antidote to the poison of greed. Giving also helps the practitioner to cultivate a sense of compassion for others and to overcome selfishness and the notion of an enduring self.

There would be no Buddhism today without the generosity of kings, merchants, and common people at the time of the Buddha and beyond. Giving results in merit, but the giving cannot be calculated solely to attain merit; giving should be done with serene joy.

Merit can also be transferred to others, such that your generous acts could be offered for the benefit of all humanity. In Tibet, for instance, family members of the deceased will offer merit to assist in a favorable rebirth. Even kings took this seriously. For example, Sri Lankan kings would keep "merit books" of all their good deeds and have these read back to them on their deathbeds to put their minds at ease.

According to Professor Trainor, King Sirisanghabodhi reflects the epitome of generosity. This fourth century C.E. Sri Lankan king abdicated his throne when his treasurer mounted a coup against him. He became a wandering monk, much like Siddhartha did when he left the palace. Paranoid, the new king worried about Sirisanghabodhi's popularity and placed a bounty on his head. One day, a poor man shared his meal with Sirisanghabodhi and told him about the bounty on his head. The former king rejoiced upon hearing this news, and asked the poor man to take his head as a reward for his generosity and to fulfill his own sense of perfection of generosity. After the poor man hesitated, Sirisanghabodhi cut off his own head!

Finding the Three Jewels Today

How can you find refuge in the Three Jewels today? If you are interested in Buddhism, where can you find a teacher to provide the guidance you will need, and a group to support you? There are many Buddhist communities all over the world today.

Buddhism in Your Neighborhood

Buddhism is found the world over. In the United States, there are approximately 3 to 4 million proclaimed Buddhists, out of a total population of approximately 300 million people. There are somewhere between 500 and 800 Buddhist centers in the United States. (See Appendix D for a list of Buddhist centers near you.) Visit a few centers if you can and sit with a few different groups. Buddhists live in Australia, South Africa, Hungary, Poland, Russia, Italy, the Netherlands…they're everywhere!

If there is no Buddhist center in your vicinity, you can always look online for sitting groups within a reasonable distance of your home. You can do a Google search for "Buddhist sitting groups" in your area. You may find sectarian Buddhist centers, such as Zen temples and Tibetan Buddhist centers (for example, Shambhala), and you may find nonsectarian, *vipassana*-based centers or sitting groups. You can also find online Buddhist communities.

You can read the latest issue of the *Inquiring Mind*, a free *dharma* journal that may be distributed near you that provides an updated list of retreats and sitting groups. There's a vast array of information out there on Buddhism in all its forms, such as the Buddhist magazines *Tricycle, Buddhadharma,* and *Shambhala Sun.* You can also read blogs such as *Mindfulness Matters: Tools for Living Now* on *www.Beliefnet.com* that has helpful links and discussion about a variety of Buddhist topics.

Your phone book, local newspaper, and free weekly are also good sources of information. Look under Religious Organizations or Churches. Sometimes community bulletin boards are good sources of information. You could also get some like-minded friends together and start your own sitting group.

You can find a teacher at a center or through members of your sitting group. If you find an established *sangha* in your area, you will most likely find a teacher comes along with the *sangha.*

CHAPTER 7

Karma and Worldview

Karma is one of the fundamental concepts of Buddhism. A good grasp of the meaning and implications of *karma* will help you to appreciate the liberating potential of the Buddha's teachings. *Karma* is about responsibility—taking it and understanding how one thing affects another. This chapter will look at common misconceptions about *karma*, and how *karma* serves as the ethical core of Buddhist practice. This chapter will also examine the Buddhist worldview through the realms of desire, form, and formlessness, and the wheel of life.

Popular Misconceptions of *Karma*

Karma means "deed" or "action" in Sanskrit. However, *action* is not substituted for *karma*, as *karma* carries much more weight than the simple understanding found in action. *Karma* is one of the most popular and perhaps least understood concepts in Buddhism. *Karmic* actions can be behaviors as well as thoughts and emotions.

There are multiple ways to consider *karma*. One way is "local" *karma*; actions in the present (including mental actions) have an impact on future experiences. Another is "remote" *karma*; actions performed in this lifetime have an impact on future rebirths. Remote *karma*, of course, depends on the idea of rebirth, which may be an alien idea to many people in the Western world. From a scientific perspective, there is no evidence for rebirth. However, your own direct experience can reveal the working of local *karma*. What you think now will affect how you feel later. What you do now will bear fruit at some future point in time. This is different from a universal balance, that is, "you reap what you sow," which is a common misconception of *karma*.

Consider local *karma* like this: You can't kill someone in the morning and then have a peaceful meditation in the afternoon. Here are some of the most common misconceptions about *karma*.

Misconception: *Karma* Is Retaliation from an Outside Force

How many times have you heard someone say, "She has bad *karma*," referring to someone who has had a run of bad luck. In the West, *karma* has often been interpreted as equal to the principle of "an eye for an eye"—the retaliatory principle that you are punished with the same punishment you inflict on another. However, this is a misconception and misunderstanding of the Buddhist meaning of *karma*. According to the Buddha's teaching, you are not made to pay for past mistakes, nor are you rewarded for your past good deeds—but you *are*, in fact, what you *do* or intend to do. More to the point, *karma* is the process by which your actions shape your life.

Since the Buddha did not acknowledge the presence of a theistic power, *karma* would not be associated with an external, objective judge. In the words of Shantideva (an eighth-century Buddhist teacher), "Suffering is a consequence of one's own action, not a retribution inflicted by an external power...We are the authors of our own destiny; and being the authors, we are ultimately...free."

Misconception: *Karma* Involves All Actions

Karma only involves intentional actions. Therefore, if you were to step accidentally on a spider, you would not invoke *karma*. You unintentionally stepped on the spider. There was no intent to hurt the spider.

However, if you decide beforehand that you are going to kill the damn spider that is living in the garage and stomp on him with malice aforethought, you will experience the *karmic* ramification of an action that is laced with hatred and aversion (remember, one of Three Poisons). If you understand *karma* as one moment conditioning future moments, you can see the interdependent chain of cause and effect. When your mind is clouded by aggression, this will generate particular effects. When your mind is occupied by peace, this will generate its own particular effects. This effect will be on your own mind moments and on your behavior that, in turn, affects others.

"It is mental volition, O monks, that I call *karma*. Having willed, one acts through body, speech or mind."—The Buddha

It might be helpful to set aside notions of "good" and "bad" *karma* because this distinction just creates confusion and reinforces misconceptions. Instead, think of skillful and unskillful actions. When remembering that actions include behavior and also mental actions (thoughts, feelings, and images that you intentionally engage with and nurture), you will discover that certain actions lead to beneficial results, that is, you feel good and others around you feel good.

If you walk down the street smiling, you will feel good and others around you will feel good. This is acting skillfully ("good *karma*"). You will also discover that certain other actions lead to harmful results, that is, you feel bad and others around you feel bad. If you yell and criticize and kick the dog, you will be lost in feeling bad, later experience regret, and adversely impact those around you. This is acting unskillfully ("bad *karma*"). Acting from the

Three Poisons of greed, hatred, and delusion is unskillful, while acting from their opposites—generosity, kindness, and wisdom—is skillful.

Karma as the Ethical Center

In Buddhism, actions matter. And therefore *karma* serves as an ethical compass for your life. *Karma* is not a complicated concept. It is as simple as this: What you do, what you say, and what you feel will have an effect.

Effects of Actions

You can taste the effects of some types of *karma* right away, but other *karmic* actions will bear fruit at some point in the future. *Karma* points to the realization that everything is interconnected in some way.

But your actions have much greater effect than one day's span. *Karma* is a process of constant change. If you do skillful acts now you can change your later *karma*. For Buddhists, the belief in *karma* is a guiding moral compass. However, do not worry or obsess on past actions. Take care of your life today. Live in the moment and change the present. Thereby you can change the future as well.

Traditionally, Buddhists would undertake their lives in a way to maximize their skillful *karma* by generating merit. They do this by donating food to begging Buddhist monks, donating money to the monastery, and doing good deeds. If you live your life in accordance with the Buddhist teachings and moral principles, you will automatically be on the way towards generating merit and limiting unskillful or destructive *karma*.

Whatever the ultimate truth of *karma* and rebirth, it can't hurt to live a good life that seeks to limit harming others and seeks to be less selfish and more generous (in fact, research suggests generous people are happier). Another important consideration about *karma* is that not all suffering is the result of *karma*. Local conditions such as temperature and internal conditions such as a virus have nothing to do with your *karma*. It is only through deep wisdom (*prajna*) that you would be able to know which bits of suffering are due to past *karma* and which are due to local conditions. Uncertainty winds up being the order of the day.

Karma and Rebirth

In the traditional Buddhist view, moving between this life and rebirth is not a random act, but is determined by the actions in your current life. In this manner, you would be the heir to your own actions. As Peter Harvey says in *An Introduction to Buddhism*, if you commit acts of hatred—violent acts, such as murder, rape, incest, or bodily harm—you will be reborn into a life in hell. Here again the question arises whether this hell is meant literally or metaphorically. Unskillful or unwholesome actions of hatred and aggression leave one in a state that is very much like hell. You are trapped in a hot place of emotion with no hope for escape. You are blinded by rage, and out of control. That sounds like hell.

On the night of the Buddha's enlightenment he is said to have remembered 100,000 past lives. How is such a statement to be interpreted? How critical is a belief in rebirth to the early teachings of the Buddha? The cultural milieu of ancient India during the Buddha's time involved a vast and colorful universe of gods and goddesses. The Buddha speaks of gods and *devas* in his sermons, but he did not see them as godlike in the common sense of gods. These gods were trapped in *samsara* just as humans.

Rebirth is a fertile metaphor. It is not necessary to believe in rebirth to be a Western Buddhist or to derive benefit from the Buddha's teachings. On the one hand, as a metaphor, rebirth is a potent concept about the cycles of experience that occur right here and now. On the other hand, Tibetan Buddhists take the concept of rebirth literally and base much of the culture, beliefs, and rituals on this possibility.

Whether metaphor or actual, "rebirth" occurs in every moment during *this* lifetime. When you breathe, your breath goes through a cycle of birth and death. As you move through life, you go through cycles of thought and emotion; everything is constantly changing. This is the cycle of becoming and when characterized by greed, hatred, and delusion, leads to never-ending cycles of suffering. The goal of Buddhist practice is to become liberated from these cycles of becoming that infiltrate every moment of life.

You may be wondering, if there is no self and no soul, what is it that takes rebirth? How can *karmic* fruits be carried into a next life? The personality of "me" and "mine" does not persist, but the mental energy or *samskaras* are what Buddhists would say persist in the form of impersonal consciousness. That energy is what, for instance, the Tibetan Buddhists believe takes rebirth.

However, if human birth is considered be "precious" and rare, you might be wondering what the universe was doing for billions of years before human beings evolved? The idea that human life is precious seems a bit humanocentric, given the vast expanse of geological time where humanity is but a blink, unless this notion of linear time is dispensed. Again, the issue is whether you can derive benefit from the Buddha's teaching without having to take these ideas literally. The answer is a resounding yes.

How long is Buddhist time?
The Buddha is said to have remembered ninety-one *kalpas* of time. A *kalpa* is an enormous amount of time. For example, if there was a mountain that reached many miles into the sky, and that mountain was made of pure granite, and once every 100 years that mountain was stroked with a silk cloth held in the mouth of a bird, then a *kalpa* would be the time it took to wear the mountain away to nothing.

However, the notion of rebirth may be congenial to you. The Buddhist notion of rebirth is different than other concepts of reincarnation that you may be familiar with. Since there is no personal essence, "you" cannot experience rebirth. Something carries forward but it is not your personality or "soul." You can think of it like a candle flame. One candle flame can light another candle. The flame "passes" to the next but has a unique identity. Within the system of birth and rebirth, there were considered to be many worlds and many ways in which one could be reborn—*endless* worlds and *endless* ways to be reborn.

Whether conceived of actual rebirths or rebirth into the next moment, these cycles involved not only human births. A person was not necessarily born as a human in every lifetime. There are also animals, spirits, gods, titans, and the inhabitants of hell. The early Buddhists rejected the Hindu caste system, so in rebirth it was possible to move from a god to a human, an animal to a god. There was no safety in reaching a higher life form. Every life form was subject to death and therefore rebirth. Most Buddhists in the Western world would take these realms and forms as being metaphorical or mythical.

The Three Realms

According to Buddhist cosmology, there are three realms—or types—of existence: the Realm of Desire, the Realm of Form, and the Realm of No-Form. These realms can be understood as the fruits of meditative experiences or the *jhanas* (meditative states). There are eight *jhanas* corresponding to the three realms. If you are in the realm of desire, you have not yet reached the first meditative state. The realm of form corresponds to meditative states one to four, and the realm of no-form corresponds to the highest meditative states (five through eight).

The realm of desire will be explored in detail below. It includes the Wheel of Life and is a potent metaphor for *karma*, suffering, and the motivation to get beyond The Three Poisons of greed, hatred, and delusion to the liberation of *nirvana*.

The Realm of Form

The realm of form (*rupa)* and its corresponding meditative states can be understood through the metaphor of the "higher gods." These meditative states correspond to contact with the form of the body and are the basis for *vipassana* meditation. They can also refer to forms of meditation that involve visualization.

The Form *jhanas* are:

- Rapture and Pleasure Born of Seclusion
- Rapture and Pleasure Born of Concentration
- Equanimity and Mindfulness with Pleasant Abiding
- Equanimity and Mindfulness, Neither Pleasure Nor Pain

Thanissaro Bikkhu presents the *jhanas* in *The Paradox of Becoming*. The Buddha said, "Then quiet secluded from sensuality, secluded from unskillful mental quality, he enters and remains in the first *jhana*: rapture and pleasure born of seclusion, accompanied by directed thought and evaluation." The first *jhana* provides the foundation for the next. The Buddha said, "Rapture and pleasure born of concentration, unification of awareness free from directed thought and evaluation—internal assurance." The second *jhana* gives way to the third, "Then with the fading of rapture, he remains equanimous, mindful, and alert, and senses pleasure with the body. Equanimous and mindful, he has a pleasant abiding." He goes on to describe the fourth *jhana*, "Then with the abandoning of pleasure and pain, he enters and remains in purity of equanimity and mindfulness, neither pleasure nor pain. He sits permeating the body with a pure, bright awareness."

The Realm of No-Form

To reach the highest *jhanas* is to reach the realm of no-form (*arupa*). Recall, however, from Siddhartha's story that he had attained the highest *jhanas* while meditating with his teachers Alara Kalama and Udraka Ramaputra. Once he came out of these rarified and sublime states he found himself right back into *samsara*. So even though these states are delightful, they do not represent liberation. *Nirvana* is not a state of meditation, but a release from all conditioned and constructed existence.

These meditative states are based on profound concentration, and the Buddha described these states as, "the complete transcending of perceptions of form, with the disappearance of perceptions of resistance." The practitioner will experience "infinite space" and will then transcend infinite space into "infinite consciousness." And from infinite consciousness the practitioner will transcend into the "dimension of nothingness." But you're not done yet! This dimension of nothingness itself is transcended, and the practitioner will experience the dimension of "neither perception or non-perception." These states correspond to the *jhana*s five through eight.

The Formless *jhana*s are:

- Infinite Space
- Infinite Consciousness
- Nothingness
- Neither Perception Nor Non-Perception

The Realm of Desire

Within the Realm of Desire there are six categories into which you can be born in any given moment. These realms comprise a circle; one is not "higher" than the other. These represent states, momentary and more permanent, that you may find yourself in at any given moment. Psychoanalyst and Buddhist practitioner Mark Epstein presents the traditional Buddhist Wheel of Life as a model for the neurotic mind. Each of the six realms depicted in this model can be understood as a state that you will experience at some point, perhaps many points in your life. In the very center of the wheel, at the hub of the wheel, are three animals representing the three poisons (*kleshas*):

- Greed or desire is represented by the rooster
- Hatred or anger is represented by the snake
- Delusion or ignorance is represented by the pig

The six realms are:

- The God Realm
- The Human Realm
- The Realm of Jealous Gods (Titans)
- The Animal Realm
- The Realm of Hungry Ghosts
- The Hell Realm

Whether or not you end up as a god or a hungry ghost largely depends on your *karma*, your intentions and actions. *Nirvana* is beyond these realms and is thus the attractive appeal of awakening, enlightenment, or liberation.

According to John Snelling in *The Buddhist Handbook*, the most fortunate age to be born in is termed a *Bhadra Kalpa*. During a Bhadra Kalpa, at least 1,000 Buddhas will be born (over the course of 320,000,000 years). Each Buddha will discover the *dharma*, and teach it for anywhere from 500 to 1,500 years, until a dark age sets in and the teaching is lost. Humanity is currently in a *Bhadra Kalpa* now.

The Realm of Desire is named so because it is the realm in which beings perceive objects through their senses and experience desirability or undesirability. Desire is the root of suffering, and there is much suffering in the Realm of Desire. The Realms of Form and No-Form are not subject to the same experiences.

The God Realm

According to Mark Epstein, the God Realm is "inhabited by beings with subtle bodies, not prone to illness, who delight in music and dance and exist in extended version of what has come to be called peak experiences, in which the participant dissolves into the experience of pleasure, merging with the beloved and temporarily eradicating the ego boundaries." In other words, this is a state that feels good but is temporary. There may be twenty-six "mansions" in the god realm, but there is a tendency to become complacent here. If life were all pleasure and bliss, where would the motivation for transcendence come from? This realm also tends to be rather self-absorbed (no *bodhisattvas* here), and suffering persists, albeit in a subtle way.

Realm of Jealous Gods (Titans)

According again to Dr. Epstein, the jealous gods "represent the energy needed to overcome a frustration, change a situation, or make contact with a new experience." This is the realm of ego, mastery, and striving. For example, the jealous gods can overtake your meditation practice in an ego-driven way, and this remains a pitfall. Striving cannot be overcome with striving. In other words, you can get caught in the trap of desiring more and more pleasurable meditation experiences. You may have had a taste of one of the *jhanas* and now your mind is fixated on having that experience again. Sometimes the jealous gods are portrayed as titans, warrior demons *(asuras)*, which have taken their human traits and used them in the pursuit of power. They are always in foul temper, always causing trouble for someone, and do not symbolize rest or peace.

Animal Realm

In the animal realm, you are caught up in desire and instinct, especially sexuality and the pleasures of the senses. It is a realm without awareness and states that are probably all too familiar to you. Animals are trapped in ignorance, and have no way of getting out of their instinct-driven behaviors.

The animal realm is pure desire and tinged with the suffering that comes with desire.

> "Never forget how swiftly this life will be over, like a flash of summer lightning or the wave of a hand. Now that you have the opportunity to practice *dharma*, do not waste a single moment on anything else."—Dilgo Khyentse Rinpoche

The traditional Buddhist view is that animals do not have sufficient awareness to generate good *karma* (due to the lack of conscious intentionality). "Does a dog have *Buddha-nature*?" is a question that divides Buddhists. Again, metaphorically, the animal, like the state of passion, is probably quite familiar to you.

Realm of Hungry Ghosts

The forth realm is restless spirits (*pretas*). Hungry ghosts are the most interesting form of *preta*. The hungry ghost has a pinhole mouth and a huge stomach and is therefore never satisfied. Adequate amounts of food can never pass through their small mouths and the narrow necks, and when it does, immense pain is experienced. This can be seen as a metaphor for greed that takes the form of excessive desire.

For instance, if you try to find happiness through having material things, this can become a futile pursuit. The more you have the more you want. That is like being a hungry ghost. A materialistic guru once said, "To become one with everything you need to have one of everything." But can this really provide happiness? Research suggests that material wealth beyond a certain point of providing for basic needs does not lead to happiness. If taken literally, if you are not generous in this lifetime you may be reborn as a hungry ghost. Fortunately, traditional Buddhists set out food from their meals to "feed" hungry ghosts. Some Buddhist festivals in Asia aim to take care of the hungry ghosts who are suffering as a result of their bad *karma*.

There is an episode of *South Park* that features one of its eight-year-old characters, Cartman, pacing in front of a game store awaiting the release of the new Wii. Unfortunately for him (and everyone around him), the Wii won't be released for another three weeks. Cartman grunts, "Come on...Come on...How much longer?" He bemoans his fate, "Time is slowing down. It's like waiting for Christmas, times a thousand." Cartman is a hungry ghost!

Hell Realm

Fear, even to the point of paranoia, can characterize the hell realm. It's not the place you want to be. Early Buddhists, just like everyone else, had vivid imaginations when it came to suffering and torture. Metaphorically, you could be endlessly cut up, burned, frozen, eaten, beaten, or tortured in any number of ways, only to die and wake up and do it all over again. Some areas of hell contain abominable nightmares, unbearable sensory experiences, and horrible visions. The denizens of hell symbolize hatred, and the pervasive self-inflicted anxiety of *dukkha*. There are as many as ten hells in the Realm of Desire, and the inhabitants must make their way through all in order to escape the anguish and suffering. There are realms where you may be hot (eight of those) or cold (also eight of those), or where you may be lacerated, or eaten alive. Take your pick!

The third realm is the demon (*asura*), a state dominated by anger. In Asia, however, these demons may not be regarded metaphorically. Evil spirits can wreak havoc or cause mischief.

Human Realm

The human form, on the other hand, is a very desirable realm to inhabit. It could be said to be the center of everything in the Buddhist cosmos. It is within the human form that you have your only chance for enlightenment and escape from *samsara*. In any given moment you can be in any of the realms, depending upon your actions and intentions. One way to think about *samsara* is the endless cycling between these realms of experience. The human realm contains the seed of its own awakening.

Although humans still have some very negative traits, they are free from the extreme negativities of life as a hungry ghost, animal, or hell-being. Humans have the capacity to do right and wrong; it is therefore in the human realm that positive or negative actions are performed. This is state where your *karma* gets played out. Buddhists who take rebirth literally see the human realm as the only realm that can influence its future rebirth.

Dependent Origination

Dependent origination is the most original and radical of the Buddha's teachings. It describes the process that perpetuates the suffering and pervasive dissatisfaction of *dukkha*. Noah Levine provides an example of the process of dependent origination in his book *Against the Stream*. The twelve steps include: (1) *ignorance* that leads to (2) *mental formations* (that is, thoughts, emotions, images) that lead to (3) *consciousness* that requires (4) *material form* (that is, something to be conscious of) that has (5) *six senses* (the basic five plus another sense of mind) that create stimuli that generate (6) *contact* that gives rise to sense impressions that generate (7) *feelings* (that are either pleasant, unpleasant, or neutral) that generate (8) *craving* (that seeks to either keep or push away the feeling) that leads to (9) *grasping* (or pushing away) that produces (10) *becoming* (which means to identify with the experience; to take it personally) that leads to (11) *birth* (taking form around the grasping) that leads to (12) *suffering* or pervasive dissatisfaction.

Consider an example. You are walking down the street on automatic pilot lost in some story about the future or the past (ignorance). You see a bar and think to yourself, "I'd really enjoy a beer" (mental formation). You make a decision to go into the bar and plan to order a beer (consciousness). You walk into the bar (material form). Inside the bar your senses make contact with the visual array of bottles at the bar, the smells, and sounds, and imagine which of the many beers you will order (six senses). The beers look good and you also notice the whiskey selection (contact). This contact gives rise to a pleasant feeling of expectation (feelings). You decide to order a boot-size beer with a whiskey chaser (craving). You drink that one and then another despite knowing that you've probably had enough (grasping). You regret having drunk so much and wish you hadn't gone into the bar at all (becoming). You castigate yourself for your weakness; you call yourself a "loser" (birth). You feel sick to your stomach (suffering).

Levine sums it up: "dependent origination is the downstream current of life. Without intentional mind training (that is, meditation) we just float along, addicted to our habitual reaction." It's the process of *karma* in action. One mind moment leads to the next. Behavior, thoughts, and feelings all affect each other in a ceaseless process. And if you are not mindful, the process will lead to suffering. Being mindful gives you the opportunity to break the cycle of becoming, break out of *samsara*, and avoid suffering.

Making Sense of the Cosmos

Again, it is unclear whether the Buddha "believed" in these concepts or just used them as part of the vernacular of the time and as metaphors for his teachings. Whether the realms and *devas* are to be considered real or metaphorical, they provide a colorful element to Buddhism.

To contrast Buddhism in its more secularized form, consider this quote from Professor Kevin Trainor describing worship of the god Kataragama in Sri Lanka: "Worshippers seek the god's favor by engaging in various austere physical practices, including rolling in scorching sand, piercing their cheeks, tongue, and other body parts with skewers or hooks, and walking across burning coals." This type of worship that has emerged more recently might be explained by the growing population's need for immediate emotional gratification from a god-like figure, rather than "the ideals of sensual and emotional restraint that have traditionally characterized Sri Lankan Buddhism."

CHAPTER 8

Buddhism in India: Life after Buddha

The Buddha traveled all around India spreading the teachings and showing his followers how they could awaken. The *sangha* grew until thousands were practicing the Four Noble Truths. This chapter looks at the end of Buddha's life, and how the *sangha* grew and spread throughout India and beyond. These beginnings, supported by great kings, helped to establish what is now called Buddhism, one of the world's major religions.

The Buddha's Final Days

The Buddha lived to be eighty years old. It was a time of unrest in India and the king of Magadha, Ajatasattu, had planned an offensive against the republics to the east of his kingdom, determined to wipe them out. Buddha had decided to avoid the carnage and headed north to the margins of the Ganges basin. As death approached and the Buddha prepared to leave this world, he lived a life of increasing solitude, searching out places of quiet and peace. He was ill and was intent on making sure the *sangha* knew everything they needed to know before he departed this world.

A Simple Life

It might be easy to imagine the Buddha surrounded by riches and adored by many, much as some religious leaders are today. However, the Buddha remained a mendicant monk, and he frequently lived outside, among the mango groves, begging food for his meals. He also spent a lot of time in the palace of his childhood friend, the now King Pasenadi of Kosola. He and the *sangha* also dwelled in structures built specifically for them to spend the rainy seasons, the three-month monsoon that visits India each year.

His demise was particularly upsetting to his long-time companion, Ananda. Ananda wanted to know who would take over for the Buddha, who would be the next in line to continue the teachings. But the Buddha knew that no one needed to take over. Each person would be a "light unto himself." By practicing the principles the Buddha had set forth, each could become self-reliant and work toward awakening. The *sangha* did not need an authority figure. The Buddha had taught them all they needed to know.

Final Days

The Buddha was growing weak and tired. He was ready to let go of his life. It can be inferred that he made a conscious decision to die when he ate some tainted pork, but did not allow others who had received the offering to do so.

He reminded the *sangha* that he had only taught them things he himself had experienced and had taken nothing on the word of another. He told them to do the same. They should practice the disciplines he had taught them and should always, most important of all, live for others with loving-kindness and compassion for the entire world.

The Buddha partook of his last meal, a meal of spoiled meat given to him by a blacksmith named Chunda. Chunda placed the meat into the Buddha's alms bowl, and out of gratitude the Buddha ate it. The Buddha insisted that no one else present eat the meat he ingested, and he made them dispose of it after he was finished. In order that Chunda not feel responsible for the Buddha's illness and impending death, the Buddha called Chunda to his side and told him how grateful he was for the meal.

FACT

Reclining Buddha statues represent the Buddha on his deathbed. His final words were, "Each of you should make himself his island, make himself and no one else his refuge, each of you must make the *dharma* his island, the *dharma* and nothing else his refuge" Some of these statues are quite large and beautiful, such as the Manuha Paya in Burma from the ninth century.

The Buddha became ill with food poisoning and traveled on to his eventual death site, Kushinigar. He then asked the *sangha* if they had any questions for him, if there was anything yet they did not understand. Right up until the end of his human life, the Buddha served others and thought only of what the *sangha* needed. But no one came forth to ask any questions.

The Buddha then asked if perhaps they were not asking questions for which they needed answers out of reverence for him. If this was the case, he said, they could ask their questions through a friend. When still no one came forth the Buddha knew they were well-versed in his teachings and, as Karen Armstrong tells us in *Buddha*, he uttered his last words: "All individual things pass away. Seek your liberation with diligence."

The Buddha died after teaching the *dharma* for forty-five years. Crowds gathered around the great sage to witness his passing and hear his last words. It is said he died with a smile on his face.

The Buddha was cremated according to custom and his remains were distributed amongst his followers along with other relics and enshrined in *stupas*. You can still visit some of these relics in India today. While the Buddha did not present himself as the founder of a religion, his relics and pilgrimage sights have been treated as holy for the past two thousand years.

The Buddha's ashes were then delivered to eight different *stupas* as holy relics. These *stupas* would later become the object of much devotion. In India, Tibet, and Southeast Asian countries, *stupas* are usually dome-shaped with a center spire. In China, Korea, and Japan they became multi-tiered structures known as pagodas. They have traditionally been regarded as places of peace, sending out pacifying energies into their surroundings.

The Followers

The Buddha had taught his students well. His emphasis on self-reliance left the *sangha* in good shape. However, differences of interpretation and later conflicts would emerge. He had left behind his teachings, the *dharma*, and the *sangha* knew the *dharma* would guide them if they followed it.

FACT

When it came to the code of monastic rules (*vinaya*) the Buddha told the *sangha* to just follow the major rules. Unfortunately, he did not specify which ones were major and minor and later conflicts arose over the interpretation of the monastic rules.

However, shortly after the Buddha's death, one of the newly ordained *bhikkus*, Subhadda, rebelled. He suggested that now that the Buddha was gone—the one who oppressed them by telling them how to do this, how to do that—they had the freedom to do whatever they desired. They had the freedom to choose.

One of the Buddha's greatest students, the Venerable Mahakassapa, became very upset at Subhadda's statement. He decided that a council should be called to recite aloud all of the Buddha's teachings. He knew well that if they did not establish the Buddha's teachings soon, it would not take long for all to be corrupted and lost.

The Buddhist Councils

According the modern-day edition of the Pali Canon, over the past 2,500 years there have been six *dhamma* (*dharma* in Sanskrit) councils (*dhamma-*

sangitas) or "dhamma recitations." The process was as follows: "the basic teaching of the Buddha were first recited by an elder monk and then chanted after him in chorus by the whole assembly. The recitation was considered to be authentic when it was unanimously approved by all of the monks in attendance." The recitations were not committed to written words until the Fourth Council some 500 years after the Buddha's death.

The First Council: The Council at Rajagriha

Three months after the Buddha's death, 500 senior monks (*arhats*) gathered together at Rajagriha in what has come to be known as the First Council. Rajagriha was the capital of Magadha, which was one of the four great kingdoms (in addtition to Kosala, Vansa, and Avanti) in ancient India. Their hope was that they would be able to establish the Buddhist canon and create the definite teachings of the Buddha.

Ananda and Upali each took on a special task at the council. Ananda, as the longtime companion of the Buddha, was responsible for the recitation of the Buddha's teachings. It was felt that since he had spent so many years by the Buddha's side, he would have heard the teachings most frequently. Upali was given the task of setting forth the rules of discipline for the *sangha* (*vinaya*).

Arhat means "worthy one" in Sanskrit. An *arhat* is one who has attained enlightened mind and is free of desires and cravings. An *arhat* has nothing more to learn and has absorbed all of the Buddha's teachings.

Each of the *arhats* recited the teachings, examining the words to ensure they were accurate. They recited them over and over again, and each repetition was checked to make sure they all agreed that it was correct. The First Council lasted seven months.

The members of the council carried the memorized teachings away with them to all parts of the country, wherever disciples of the Buddha were to be found. Thus, the oral tradition of passing on the Buddha's teaching was established and remained exclusively so for many hundreds of years and actually continues to this day.

The Second Council: The Council at Vesali

One hundred years later, the Second Council took place to settle disagreements regarding the monastic rules. This council was held at Vaishali and 700 *arhats* attended. The Elders of the council felt that certain members of the *sangha* were taking some of the Ten Precepts too lightly and that there was a general slackening of discipline.

A group of monks put forth a series of changes in the precepts, making them more lax than they had been previously. For example, they felt it was acceptable for the members of the *sangha* to accept money, and debated the need for the precept that forbade them to use money.

The assembly of monks thereby discussed the validity of the Ten Precepts. The dissenting monks, the Vajjians, were outvoted. They refused to give in, however, and seceded from the group of the council of Elders. Thus, Buddhism was divided into two schools of thought: Theravada and Mahayana. The Elders belonged to the Theravada school; Vajjian monks split off to create the Mahayana school that differed in the interpretation of the precepts and philosophy.

King Ashoka and the Third Council: The Council at Pataliputra

The Third Council convened in 326 B.C.E. with 1,000 monks working for nine months. The need for this council arose as debate was being carried on about both the *dharma* and the precepts. At this time, King Ashoka was ruling a vast empire in India, created by his grandfather Chadragupta Maurya in the wake of Alexander the Great. He had taken the throne in a bloody war and was a ruthless leader with many violent triumphs to his credit. But during the eighth year of his rule, after a particularly gruesome battle at Kalinga, King Ashoka became shaken by the bloodbath—upward of 100,000 people are said to have been slaughtered—and it set the stage for his powerful personal transformation.

King Ashoka was largely responsible for the spread of Buddhism beyond India's borders and its emergence as one of the world's great religions. He sent emissaries as far as Greece to the west and China to the east. He practiced tolerance and respect for other religious disciplines, promoted peace instead of war, and established schools, hospitals, and orphanages for his people. He was living proof that it is possible to rule a great nation with kindness and open-mindedness, promoting peace and goodwill.

Ashoka ran into a monk who told the mighty king that he could use his power for good instead of evil. The monk was a Buddhist. Ashoka soon exchanged his sword for the *dharma*.

He stopped hunting and fighting, and started meditating and doing humanitarian work. Instead of soldiers he had missionary monks, who spread the *dharma* wherever they could, reaching out past the boundaries of India and into the neighboring nations. He built 84,000 *stupas* and thousands of monasteries throughout the land. King Ashoka inscribed his new beliefs on rocks that can be found throughout India, Nepal, Pakistan, and Afghanistan.

These inscriptions would come to be known as the Edicts of King Ashoka and included such promises as moderate spending, proper schooling for children, medical treatments for everyone, promotion of proper behavior. He promised to practice the *dharma* until the end of time, to always be available—no matter what he was doing—for the affairs of his people; he promoted respect for everyone and all religions.

Because he practiced such spiritual generosity, many less-devoted practitioners entered the Buddhist practice and the purity of the practice was diluted. Ashoka sought to weed out these weak links from the monasteries he had created and called a new council with the genuine, steadfast monks who were left.

At the Third Council, the teachings were reviewed and a new, purified collection was set forth. Nine missions of *arhats* were sent out to spread the *dharma* into different areas of India and across its vast borders into other countries.

Ashoka became a role model for other kings throughout Asia, such as King Devanampiyatissa in Sri Lanka, who was converted to Buddhism by Ashoka's son, Mahinda. Another great king/convert was Menander I (Milinda in Pali). He is the subject of one of the earliest preserved texts outside the Pali Canon, dated from the second century B.C.E. In this text he interrogates the monk Nagasena on a variety of doctrinal issues. The king eventually gave up his thrown to become a Buddhist monk. More recently, King Kirti Sri Rajasahna, who ruled the Kandayan kingdom in Sri Lanka before the British conquered it, helped to revive Buddhism by importing monks from Thailand and patronizing Buddhist temples and art. He did so, even though his personal religion was Hinduism.

The Fourth Council: One North One South

There were two Fourth Councils. One is believed to have taken place in Sri Lanka in 29 B.C.E. with 500 monks writing down the orally transmitted teachings for the first time. Another council is said to have been held in India in the first century C.E. This council was led by Kanishka, ruler of what is today Pakistan and northern India. King Kanishka loved the teachings of the Buddha and often had *bhikkus* teach him the *dharma*.

He soon found that they were not in accord on the teaching of the *dharma*, and he was very distressed over the differences he heard. At the advice of another, he convened a council to sort out the differences. Five hundred monks compiled a new canon at the Fourth Council.

This was the start of the Mahayana scriptural canon: the collection of Mahayana teachings. Theravada Buddhists, however, do not recognize this council.

In the Theravada tradition, a Fifth Council took place in Mandalay, Burma, in 1871. 2,400 monks labored for five months inscribing the *Tipitaka* ("Three Baskets") onto marble slabs. The sixth council took place in Rangoon in 1954, with 2,500 monks from all the Theravada countries.

The Eighteen Schools

During the time of the Second Council, Buddhism started to splinter into different schools of thought. Then, as the *dharma* spread to other countries and cultures at the time of King Ashoka, different traditions arose. There arose the Hinayana and the Mahayana traditions. Hinayana was the tradition that spread under King Ashoka.

Hinayana refers to a group of eighteen Buddhist schools, of which only one is currently in existence, Theravada. Mayahana Buddhists, who called their tradition "the Great Vehicle," named the other traditions of Buddhism Hinayana—meaning "Little Vehicle"—which is not considered a favorable term by many Buddhists. Today you would not use the word Hinayana to refer to the Theravada tradition of Buddhism.

The Pali Canon

A complete copy of the Canon, in original Pali as well as its English translations, is housed in the 4,000-volume library at the Barre Center for Buddhist Studies, in Barre, Massachusetts. The Canon occupies an entire bookshelf, standing two and a half by eight feet tall, comprised of 140 volumes on six and one-half shelves. These volumes contain approximately 30,000 pages of text.

One version of the Canon in the original Pali language has been published by the Pali Text Society in England; the other is published by the Vipassana Research Institute in India. These gray and maroon volumes with their Sanskrit-looking characters (Pali and Sanskrit are closely related) are embossed with gilded letters. These volumes represent the teachings of the Buddha. They are known as the *pitakas* ("baskets"). The Pali Canon was written down on palm leaves at the Fourth Council and was thus passed down intact to future generations of scholars and the *sangha*.

Pali is the language that the Buddha spoke. The Canon consists of the three "baskets." The *Vinaya* (monastic code of discipline), which covers daily practices to how to maintain harmony among the monks and nuns. The *Suttas* (the popular discourses) contains the collection of the central teachings of Theravada Buddhism, including all the Jataka tales, the *Dhammapada*, and various discourses. There are more than 10,000 discourses.

The discourses typically start with, "Thus I have heard…" to emphasize the direct link to the Buddha. Also noted are the location and the audience the Buddha was addressing. The *sutta* (*sutra*) section of the Pali canon includes the Digha Nikaya (Long Discourses), Maijhima Nikaya (Medium-Length Discourses), Samyutta Nikaya (Connected Discourses), Anguttara Nikaya (Numbered Discourses), and Khuddaka Nikaya (Small Texts).

The *Abhidhamma* is "a compendium of profound teachings elucidating the functioning and interrelationships of mind, mental factors, matter, and the phenomenon transcending these." In Pali, *abhi* means "ultimate," so *Abhidharma* meant the "ultimate truth," or ultimate teachings. The *Abhidharma* can be thought of as a view of the world from the perspective of ultimate enlightenment.

The *Pratimoksha* (Pali, *Patimokkha*) ceremony is based on the monastic code of the Pali Canon (*vinaya*). Twice each month, monks gather to reaffirm their commitment to the monastic code of conduct.

The *Pitaka* was the written down version of the oral tradition that persisted at the time of the Buddha and in the years after his death. Recitation of the canon persisted even after it was written down and continues to this day. Contemporary Burmese master Mahathera Vicittasarabhivamsa can recite the *Tipitaka* from memory. Over the centuries, the Pali Canon has been preserved in Burma, Sri Lanka, Thailand, and Cambodia, and the versions that emerged in these different countries are meaningfully the same, attesting to the validity of their contents.

Mahayana Scriptures

The Mahayana Buddhists had their own scriptures, which were written in Sanskrit. These texts included:

1. The *Sutras* (the words of the Buddha): including the Heart *Sutra*, the Lotus *Sutra*, and the Diamond *Sutra*. (Perfection of Wisdom *Sutras*)
2. *Shastras:* the commentary on the *sutras*.
3. *Tantras:* mystical texts.

As Mahayana Buddhism grew, new texts were added. The Mahayana asserts that emptiness (similar to *anatta* or "no self") permeates everything and that the earlier texts were not explicit enough on this point, a criticism

of the *Abhidharma*. The Mahayana asserts that nothing is fixed; everything is empty, including *nirvana*. *Nirvana* is not a thing that can be attained. All concepts can lead to attachment and thus become a pitfall preventing you from experiencing *prajnaparamita* ("perfection of wisdom"). The Mahayana *sutras* explore such themes as emptiness.

The Lotus *Sutra* is another prominent Mahayana text that was very influential in China. The oldest surviving copy was translated in 286 C.E. The Lotus *Sutra*, in contrast to the Heart *Sutra*, is a long discourse with about twenty-eight chapters. According to Professor Mark Blum, the Lotus *Sutra* covers three themes:

- A universal path to liberation
- The eternal nature of the Buddha
- Pragmatism represented by the bodhisattva

The Parable of the Burning House appears in the Lotus *Sutra*. Children are playing in a burning house and they don't heed their father's warning to escape because they are so enthralled with the game they are playing. Their attachment to the game represents the dangerous attachment to greed and desire. The father entices them out with a promise of better entertainment, and then gives them jewels and bells. These represent the *dharma*.

ESSENTIAL

The second most influential person in the history of Buddhism is Nagarjuna (the Buddha being the first). He founded the *Madhyamika* ("School of the Middle Way"). He cautioned that dualistic ways of perceiving are limiting and took the Buddha's notion of dependent origination (that is, nothing exists except in relationship to something else, and thus everything is interconnected) to its logical conclusion whereby the difference between *nirvana* and *samsara* disappears.

From the Buddha's death until the third century B.C.E., Buddhism spread across many nations and took on different forms and traditions. It spread from India to Sri Lanka, Burma, Cambodia, Laos, Thailand, China, Japan, Korea, Mongolia, Nepal, Russia, Tibet, and Vietnam. Thanks to the great reformed leader King Ashoka, Buddhism became one of the greatest religions of the world, and the teachings were passed down so that they can be practiced today.

Eighteen different schools came out of the Second and Third Councils as practitioners differed on matters of philosophy, with one surviving today as the Theravada. Today there are different traditions of Buddhism, just as there were in the past. In fact, the three major surviving traditions within Buddhism can be considered related but distinct religions: Theravada, Mahayana (for example, Zen), and Vajrayana (for example, Tibetan Buddhism).

CHAPTER 9

The Three Vehicles

There are three different vehicles, or schools, of Buddhist teachings, and virtually all sects of Buddhism fall into one of these three schools. As discussed, Theravada and Mahayana Buddhism grew out of the early councils as differences arose in practice and philosophy. The three schools of Buddhism are Theravada, Mahayana, and Vajrayana. These vehicles, while overlapping, can be considered distinct religions. Half of the world's population resides in countries where Buddhism was once a dominant force.

The Diversification of Buddhism

There is no one Buddhism, no essential Buddhism that can be taken apart from its tradition. In fact, the term "Buddhism" is a relatively recent invention, first being coined by scholars in the eighteenth and nineteenth centuries. Prior to this Buddhists were called "followers of the Buddha." Western interest in Buddhism began when archeologist W. C. Peppe unearthed a soapstone urn with the inscription, "a receptacle of relics of the Blessed Buddha of the Sakyas."

The first serious Buddhist scholarship appeared in 1844 by Eugen Burnouf who observed that religious traditions far flung across Asia came from a common source in India and concluded they were a "family of religions each with its own integrity." According to contemporary Buddhist scholars Robinson, Johnson, and Thanissaro, it might be better to think of "Buddhist religions" rather than a single Buddhist religion. These are the Three Vehicles.

Buddhism is not based on one central text, such as the Bible, Koran, or Torah. In fact, there was nothing written at all for 400 years, as the teachings were passed down through oral recitation. So over the years, a multitude of guidelines for practice came into being and Buddhism became diversified.

There are three *vehicles* of Buddhism, meaning three schools of Buddhist thought. The word *vehicle* comes from the Sanskrit word *vada*, meaning "ferryboat." Think of the image of the river crosser and his raft; these vehicles can ferry you across the river of *samsara* to *nirvana*.

There is no one authority on Buddhism—there is no pope, no president, no leader of the Buddhist people. There is no central office, no definitive source. Buddhism is alive in many forms, with many voices today. Within the three vehicles there are Tibetan Buddhism, Zen Buddhism, Pure Land, Yogacara, and more. But all these forms can fit within the three vehicles, and some would agree that they could even fit within the two main vehicles—Theravada and Mahayana.

Theravada Versus Mahayana

Mahayana Buddhism emerged as a reaction to early Buddhist orthodoxies in the first century, although the term "Mahayana" does not appear until the sixth century C.E. Mahayana took root in northern India and made its way east and north to Tibet, Mongolia, China, and Japan. Mahayana diverges philosophically with Theravada and claims to be based on texts attributable to the Buddha that are not in the Pali Canon and were not discovered until centuries after the death of the Buddha.

According to Buddhist scholar Mark Blum, in the Mahayana, "faith in the power, omniscience, and eternal spiritual assistance of the Buddha assumed a new sense of importance and Buddhism now took on a decidedly more devotional form." The Buddha was now a cosmic being. If a form of Buddhism that feels more religious is congenial to you, you will find the Mahayana forms such as Chan, Zen, Tibetan, and Pureland Buddhism more interesting.

On the one hand, Mahayana offers the possibility of becoming a *buddha* to everyone, and on the other hand elevates the Buddha from a compassionate teacher to a celestial guru. Such "buddha realms" or "pure lands" may be taken literally or metaphorically to represent certain states of being. Devotion to your teacher is also a key feature of Mahayana traditions such as Zen and Vajrayana, where your teacher is seen as the living embodiment of Buddha, providing you with the opportunity to become *buddha* too. Consequently, there is more emphasis on lineage.

The Mahayana placed more emphasis on the *bodhisattva* and deemphasized the historical Buddha and also the Four Noble Truths. The Buddha became more of a god than a man. But the Mahayana didn't invent the *bodhisattva* concept. The Jataka tales speak of the Buddha's past lives and that presumes the idea of the *bodhisattva*. What is a *bodhisattva*? A *bodhisattva* vows to attain enlightenment for the benefit of all sentient beings. It's an explicit commitment towards awakening with an added dimension, predicated on the idea of rebirth, to keep taking a human life to be of benefit to others.

To accomplish this formidable goal the *bodhisattva* must undertake six (or ten) *paramitas* (perfections). The six *paramitas* are generosity, morality, patience, vigor, meditation, and wisdom. The expanded list of ten *paramitas* includes in addition to the six: skillful means, conviction, strength, and knowledge. The *bodhisattva* also pursed the five *margas* (paths) and the ten *bhumis* (grounds or stages of spiritual attainment).

The ten *bhumis* are: joy, purity, brightness, radiance, difficult to conquer, facing *nirvana*, far-going, immovable, spiritual intelligence, and *dharma* cloud. There is a belief that supernatural powers emerge as one progresses on this *bodhisattva* path. At advanced stages a *bodhisattva* can appear anywhere at will and appear simultaneously. Imagine what that could do for your multitasking efforts!

Before the Mahayana, enlightenment was not discussed in the explicit selfless terms of the *bodhisattva*. Instead, there was the path of discipline (*shravakayana*) and the solitary *buddha* (*pratyekabuddha*). The Mahayanists looked down upon this approach as inferior (*hina*); and you'll see Theravada referred to as Hinayana Buddhism versus Mahayana (great vehicle). Such comparisons seem inherently anti-Buddhist. While the *bodhisattva* path is seen as complete and perfect buddhahood (*samyaksambuddha*), there seems to be nothing inferior in the earlier approaches merely because the attainment of buddhahood for the benefit of all was not explicitly emphasized. This would be like saying the Buddha didn't get it right. It appears that he was silent on the issue rather than encouraging a selfish form of enlightenment.

Theravada

Theravada Buddhism can be traced all the way back to the First Council, shortly after Buddha's death. Theravada Buddhists claim that they have adhered to the Buddha's original teachings and are, therefore, the purist form of Buddhism. They established the Pali Canon, the teachings that were passed down orally for 400 years. The Pali language is still used as the primary language for the texts of Theravada Buddhists millennia later.

The Theravada ("Doctrine of Elders") is the sole surviving school of Buddhism from the early days of Buddhism. It traces it roots back to the Buddha himself and his closest disciples. It is also known as southern Buddhism because this is where it has flourished over the centuries: Sri Lanka, Thailand, Burma, Cambodia, and Laos. Theravada keeps its ties close to the life of the Buddha and the Pali Canon (unlike Mahayana, which has introduced new texts and concepts).

Theravada Buddhism in America

The Theravada forms that have made their way to America, especially, are more "Buddha" than "Buddhism." That is, they preserve the essential practices the Buddha developed and taught and most closely resemble his path to awakening. Notably, meditation is central to the Theravada traditions taught in America, where interested parties can learn meditation through a traditional ten-day silent meditation retreat. Here you can engage in the core Buddhist practice of *vipassana* without having to engage with any rites or rituals or take any monastic vows. It's more of a bare bones practice of Buddha and can be found in the teachings of S. N. Goenka from Burma who founded the Vipassana Meditation Society, which has centers in the U.S. and all around the world. There are also teachings founded on the Thai Forest tradition with its main practice center, the Insight Meditation Society in Barre, Massachusetts, its sister non-residential center Cambridge Insight Meditation Center, and the Spirit Rock Center in California.

Mahayana

Mahayana Buddhism is the vehicle most familiar to Americans in the form of Zen. Mahayana has been around since the Second Council, but Mahayana can also argue a direct descent to the Buddha's teachings. Mahayana Buddhists believe they split off from the Theravada tradition in order to reform the teachings and take them back to a purer form the Buddha had originally taught, although the Mahayana *sutras* such as the Perfection of Wisdom and Heart *Sutra* are not directly attributed to the Buddha.

Manjushri is the *bodhisattva* of wisdom—he symbolizes the wisdom one needs in order to seek the truth. In artworks depicting Manjushri, he is often portrayed with one hand holding a sword, which is needed to cut through illusion to the heart of wisdom. In the other hand he holds the sacred text of wisdom, the Prajna-Paramita *Sutra*.

If you think Buddhism lacks prophecies, think again. Buddhist scholar Mark Blum describes the Mahayana belief in the "Period of the Final Law." This period of dark decline for humanity (know, as *mofa* in Chinese and *mappo* in Japanese) had come about somewhere between the sixth and eleventh centuries because too much time had elapsed since the death of the Buddha, and fewer and fewer people understood his teaching. "This final period could last up to ten thousand years and all sorts of dire consequences were described, such as increased corruption, conflict, and even a shortening of human life. But the end of this age was unambiguously marked by the advent of a new *buddha* Maitreya, who will usher in a new era of peace and enlightenment."

Emptiness

The cardinal emphasis of Mahayana is on *shunyata*, often translated as "emptiness" or "the void." The Buddha's early teachings discuss the emptiness of self (*anatman*, *anatta*) and in the Mahayana this concept is expanded to everything.

Shunyata is, perhaps, the most confusing and mystical of the Buddhist concepts and the most difficult for the Western mind to grasp. Truth goes beyond dualistic distinctions and thus "emptiness is form" and "form is emptiness." Huh? This is a departure from the earlier concepts presented in the Abhidharma that did not hold to this notion of emptiness.

These distinctions can get you bogged down in subtle philosophical arguments. Is the world real? And what does it mean to be real? To further clarify things (or complicate things), things can be seen as conventionally real, but there is an ultimate reality that underlies what is perceived. Confused yet?

In Mahayana tradition, when one wakes up one realizes that the *whole world* is emptiness, that emptiness is not just the self but all things, and form and emptiness are the same thing, indistinguishable from one another. Or as stated in the Heart *Sutra*: "Form is emptiness, emptiness is form." It is hard to grasp this conceptually. The best way is to practice meditation and experience it for yourself.

Like the self, everything has the quality of space and energy and change.

Further Explanations

Stephen Batchelor tries to cut through this confusion by going back to basics. According to Bachelor, the Buddha's original teachings did not make these distinctions between relative and ultimate reality (which themselves are at risk for creating a duality). Things are constantly changing, he taught, and he cautioned his followers not to cling to anything. Everything that occurs does so in dependence upon something else (the doctrine of dependent origination).

But is there really a duality here? Conventional reality is necessary so that you know your name and know how to find your way home. Ultimate reality refers to something else. When you meditate you will experience these conventional things in a different way—this is where language breaks down—such that some deeper or more ultimate sense of things will be experienced.

Reaching Enlightenment

It's hard to describe in language and has to be experienced for yourself. When all these concepts cease to function, you have reached enlightenment. When you go beyond dualistic categories such as self and world, you are liberated. This is what all Buddhists strive for. The aim is to get beyond all your preconceived notions of reality, including those about yourself. Beware! You can become attached to the concept of emptiness itself, and through the back door you will once again be trapped in the world of concepts and miss out on liberation. Don't worry though. Of course in the next moment you'll have another chance!

Vipassana practice plays a more central role in the Theravada than in the Mahayana where *vipashyana* (Sanskrit for *vipassana*; Mahayana *sutras* were written in Sanskrit and they therefore use the Sanskrit version of terms over the Pali. That is, *dharma* instead of *dhamma*, *nirvana* instead of *nibbana*) is combined with elaborate imagery, chanting, and other practices that developed in the centuries after the Buddha. In the Mahayana, *prajna* (wisdom) may be represented by Manjushri, who yields a sword that cuts through delusion and desire.

Ox-Herding Pictures

The Mahayana Path is captured in the traditional sequence of painting in the Chan and Zen traditions. The ox, an animal sacred in India, represents *buddha-nature*, and the boy in the illustrations represents the self.

- "Seeking the Ox." Here you are lost in *samsara*, but having been exposed to the teaching of the Buddha, you are pulled towards a higher truth.
- "Finding the Tracks." Here you engage with listening to teachings and finding the path.
- "First Glimpse of the Ox." Meditation practice provides the vehicle to start realizing a taste of *prajna* (wisdom).
- "Catching the Ox." Comes when you have a deeper grasping of the *kleshas* or three poisons (greed, hatred, and delusion), and the limitations that come with regarding the self as a solid object worthy of protection (*anatta*).
- "Taming the Ox." This occurs when you start to have peeks at the peak experience of *satori.*
- "Riding the Ox Home." When you have a complete experience of *satori.*
- "Both Ox and Self Forgotten." This comes when you can now experience life with the freedom that *satori* provides.
- "Both Ox and Self Forgotten." Here you go beyond even the concepts of *dharma* and the tradition you studied within. The Buddha likened this to the raft that carries you across the river of *samsara*, once you've reached the other side you don't keep carrying the raft.
- "Returning to the Source." From this place you realize that the entire natural world is the embodiment of enlightenment.
- "Entering the market with Helping Hands." This makes the *bodhisattva* path explicit. Having gotten to this place you now work for the betterment of everyone else.

Bodhisattvas

Much as the Theravada student strives to become an *arhat*—a spiritually enlightened individual—so the Mahayana student strives to become a *bodhisattva*. A *bodhisattva* is a person who has already attained enlightenment, or is ready to attain enlightenment but puts off his own final enlightenment in order to re-enter the cycle of *samsara* and save all sentient beings. A *bodhisattva* is the ultimate in compassion, and Mahayana Buddhists believe that enlightenment can be attained not only by striving individually but also by helping others to achieve enlightenment as well.

Every *bodhisattva* resolves to realize the Four Great Vows:

1. Sentient beings are numberless; I vow to save them.
2. Desires are inexhaustible; I vow to put an end to them.
3. The dharmas are boundless; I vow to master them.
4. The Buddha Way is unattainable; I vow to attain it.

Bodhisattvas willingly seek to be reborn into the endless cycle of *samsara* so that they can constantly help others toward their own enlightened state. They need wisdom so that they can discern how to help others toward *nirvana*. *Bodhisattva's* employ compassion and love for all beings. They use *upaya* (skillful means) to accomplish their aim of benefiting all sentient beings.

Inherent within skillful means is wisdom—the ability to discern how to help each sentient being toward enlightenment. Wisdom heart is referred to as *bodhicitta*—the quality that allows them to be open to the suffering of others. Therefore, someone who desires to become a *bodhisattva* will develop and then generate *bodhicitta*. As you can see from the concept of the *bodhisattva*, Mahayana traditions rely more explicitly on concepts of rebirth, whether taken literally or metaphorically.

In addition to generating *bodhicitta*, the *bodhisattva* also strives for the Six Perfections:

1. Concentration (meditation)
2. Giving
3. Morality
4. Patience
5. Persistence
6. Wisdom

Without the explicit commitment to rebirth for the benefit of all sentient beings, Mahayanists looked down upon Theravada practitioners and called them *shravakas* ("listeners"). Being an *arhat* (an enlightened one) is not enough; one must strive to become a *buddha*. Without that commitment, Theravada appears to honor the letter of practice ("well, the Buddha didn't say I had to take rebirth") versus the spirit of the practice—a wish to benefit everyone. If one does not believe in rebirth, this distinction becomes moot, but in the Buddha's day these were very much living arguments.

Since there haven't been any more *buddhas* in the past 2,500 years, the argument likewise seems moot. A *bodhisattva* can also be understood as a future Buddha. If you take the *bodhisattva* vows, you undertake the arduous journey towards not just enlightenment but *buddhahood*. Good luck! The *bodhisattva* trucks in compassion and wisdom, and these virtues are more explicitly pursued and codified in the Mahayana traditions.

Three Bodies (*Trikayas*)

Mahayanas believe that *buddha-nature* appears in three different forms. These bodies are the forms that the Buddha or *buddha-nature* take. This is known as the Three Body Doctrine of compassion. As elsewhere, these bodies can be interpreted symbolically as well as literally. The three forms are:

- *Nirmanakaya* (emanation body) refers to the historical Buddha as he embodied the truth of the *dharma* in a perfected form. This is reflected in the story of Vakkali, who called for the Buddha when he was sick. The Buddha told him, "What good is the sight of this putrid body to you? Vakkali, the one who sees the *dharma* sees me; the one who sees me, sees the *dharma*." The Buddha and the *dharma* are one in the same (and you will often see this conjunction: *buddhadharma*).
- *Sambhogakaya* (bliss body) is the idealized form of the Buddha. This "body" of the Buddha is not limited to its physical form and, in traditional thought, would occupy different realms or represent different states of consciousness. This body is experienced through intensive meditation.
- *Dharmakaya* (truth body). According to Buddhist scholar John Peacock, the "*Dharmakaya* is synonymous with ultimate truth and is seen as being totally transcendent and unchanging." The *Dharmakaya*

refers to the approximation the human mind can sometimes make with reality. This body is enlightenment.

Differences Between the Two Main Schools

Another difference between Mahayana and Theravada Buddhism is the scriptures that each tradition claims. The Pali canon is the library of teachings claimed by Theravada Buddhists and was the first known collection of Buddhist literature. In addition to the Pali canon, the Mahayana Buddhists have an extensive collection of scriptures written in Sanskrit that contain the Buddha's words and more, as translations and additions were made over the years.

Theravada Buddhists do not generally discuss *bodhisattvas*, but they do believe in Maitreya. Maitreya is believed to be the future Buddha, the Buddha who will appear after the present Buddha is long gone and the teachings have been forgotten. Theravada Buddhists believe Maitreya is currently a celestial *bodhisattva*, and will appear on Earth as the new Buddha in future years.

Some well-known schools of the Mahayana tradition of Buddhism are Madhyamika, Yogacara, Pure Land, and Zen Buddhism. Pure Land and Zen Buddhism are covered in later chapters.

Vajrayana

Vajrayana Buddhism developed out of the Mahayana school of teachings sometime between the third and seventh centuries B.C.E. It is said that the Buddha practiced this esoteric tradition, but because of its advanced and special nature, it didn't evolve into common practice. Vajrayana Buddhists believe the Buddha taught these practices through special texts, called *tantras*, but the *tantras* themselves didn't come to light until the seventh century.

Vajrayana Buddhists believe their teachings can be directly linked to the Buddha and that *they* practice the purest form of Buddhism. Vajrayana is found predominately in Tibet, a remote country surrounded by the Himalayan Mountains and isolated from the rest of the world. Tibetan Buddhism emerged when Mahayana Buddhism reached Tibet and it became intertwined with the native Bön folk religion.

Padmasambhava, a Buddhist monk who arrived in Tibet from India, is considered one of the founders of Vajrayana Buddhism and is credited with developing many of the practices present today.

Tibet absorbed Buddhism into its culture wholeheartedly. According to Jack Maguire in *Essential Buddhism,* "No other country in history has absorbed this religion so thoroughly and, in turn, invested it with so much native character or so much cultural power. As Vajrayana grew increasingly influential in Tibet, so did the monastery as the focus of daily life, a position it retained until the mid-twentieth century...Over time, the monasteries assumed complete political control of the country, giving Tibet a singularly sacred form of government for centuries."

Vajrayana relies heavily on symbol and ritual, more so than other forms of Buddhism. It invokes magical deities belonging to a cosmic monastery. The practices in Vajrayana Buddhism are special and complex. The teachings are designed to bring the student to enlightenment in this lifetime; therefore, the practices are intense, subtle, and difficult, and enlightenment presumably occurs more quickly than with other forms of practice. The student of the *tantric* practices has a teacher, called a *guru* (an enlightened teacher is a *lama*). The practices are often kept secret between the student and teacher, which adds to the mystery around the tradition.

The practices of Vajrayana revolve around a spiritual "toolbox" that contains such items as: *mandalas*, *mantras*, *yidam*, *mudras*, and *vajras*.

Mandalas

Mandalas are maps of the spiritual world. They are usually represented in artwork as a symbolic pattern. The pattern is usually in the form of a circle with intricate designs within. The patterns are representative of the sacred place where the Buddha or deities abide. They are used for contemplation and meditation and are designed to guide the process of spiritual awakening.

Mantras

Mantras are mystical incantations whose repetitions contain the potential for spiritual connection. By repeating a *mantra* you can clear the mind and purify speech. The most famous *mantra* in Vajrayana is *Om mani padme hum* (roughly translates to "Hail to the Jewel in the Lotus"). Viewing the written *mantra* is also just as powerful as the incantation. You can also spin the written form of the *mantra* around in a prayer wheel, which is believed to have the same beneficial properties as chanting and viewing the written form.

What and who is a Dalai Lama?
The Dalai Lama is considered to be the present incarnation of the *bodhisattva* Avalokiteshvara. The third great leader of the Geluk lineage of Tibetan Buddhism was given the title Dalai Lama ("Ocean of Wisdom") and was deemed to be the physical manifestation of the compassionate *bodhisattva*. The present-day Dalai Lama is the fourteenth Dalai Lama.

Prayer wheels, also called *Mani* wheels by the Tibetans, are mechanical devices for dispersing spiritual blessings. Prayer wheels look like two wheels with an axle in between them. Paper with the *mantra* printed on it many times over is rolled around an axle of the wheel in a protective container. Tibetan Buddhists will circumambulate a *stupa* that contains dozens or even hundreds of these prayer wheels, chanting, "Om mani padme hum" and spinning the wheels as they walk by. Some wheels are portable, with a handle, and some are much larger and stationary.

Yidam

Yidam are meditational deities. Tibetan art colorfully represents a multitude of spiritual deities, both male and female. They are considered to be different manifestations of the Buddha. Some of the *yidam* are actually wrathful deities. *Tantric* masters subdue these demons to subordinate them to the service of the Buddha.

Mudra

A *mudra* is the formation your hands take when meditating. The formation is deeply symbolic and often relates to a particular deity. A common *mudra* is the cosmic *mudra*:

The dominant hand is held palm up on your lap. The other hand is placed on top of the dominant hand so that the knuckles of both hands overlap. The thumbs touch lightly so that you are forming a circle.

Vajra

Vajra is a Sanskrit term meaning "thunderbolt." It is *dorje* in Tibetan and can be translated as "diamond" or "adamantine," referring to its indestructible qualities of emptiness. *Vajras* are symbolic, ritual objects such as a bell or dagger used in the manifold Tibetan ceremonies, rites, and rituals.

Vajrayana Practice

The student in Vajrayana Buddhism is called the *chela.* The *chela* is initiated into his practice by his *guru.* The *chela* is given a *mandala* of his prescribed *yidam.* Practice can be arduous. For example, in one practice you would undertake 100,000 prostrations and numerous repetitions of *mantras.*

CHAPTER 10

The Spread of Buddhism

Buddhist practice spread quickly within India as the Buddha and his disciples traveled around the country introducing the *dharma* to the population. The power of his message and the proof of its value were evident as thousands joined the *sangha*. "Followers of the Buddha" were soon to be found beyond the borders of India in Sri Lanka, Southeast Asia, and beyond. Eventually, what is now called "Buddhism" spread to China, Korea, Japan, and Tibet.

Sri Lanka

Remember that monks were mendicants—they had few possessions. They traveled by foot, begging for food, mingling amongst the native people while performing compassionate acts to further themselves along the path toward enlightenment. As they traveled they spread the message of the Buddha's teachings and convinced people—through example rather than self-promotion—that the Path was a good way to live. Their passage through south Asia was one way in which Buddhism started to spread across the continent.

King Ashoka Sends His Son

Also recall that King Ashoka was another primary reason for the spread and growth of Buddhism. Ashoka was the great Buddhist missionary. Powerful and respected, Ashoka was able to attract people to the Buddha's teaching through his missions and architectural monuments throughout his kingdom.

King Ashoka had cast his eye toward the south and decided to send his son, the monk Mahinda, to the beautiful tropical island Sri Lanka as a missionary. Mahinda was well received by King Devanampiyatissa, the king of Sri Lanka, and they held many enthusiastic and energetic conversations about the religion that had so completely changed Ashoka.

After its glory days under King Ashoka, Buddhism in India took a downturn. The Islamic Mongol invasions and the resurgence and strengthening of Hinduism (in part due to a repopularization after incorporating elements of Buddhism) were to take a toll on the influence of Buddhism. By the thirteenth century C.E., Buddhism was substantially weakened in India and all but disappeared. Fortunately, it was to take a stronghold in other parts of the world, a thriving that continues to the modern era.

Captivated by such engaging exchanges, the native king asked Mahinda to bring a branch of the Bodhi Tree to Sri Lanka so they could have their own symbol of enlightenment. And so Mahinda sent for his sister, Sanghamitta, who soon left India for Sri Lanka, bearing the gift her brother had requested. A grateful King Devanampiyatissa planted the branch on the grounds of the Mahavihara—the first and largest monastery built in the city of Anuradhapura. To this day there are Bodhi trees in Sri Lanka considered to be relatives to the original branch brought over by Sanghamitta.

Sri Lanka embraced Buddhism and shortly it was thriving in the small nation. Sometime around 100 B.C.E., during the Fourth Council held in Sri Lanka, the Pali scriptures were written down on palm leaves.

Sri Lanka Nurtures Buddhism

Some 400 years later, in the fifth century C.E., a Buddhist monk by the name of Buddhaghosa left India for the beautiful island. Buddhaghosa wrote a detailed examination of the *Tipitaka*, a commentary on the Pali texts, called *Visuddhimagga* (Path to Purity). It is still widely read today and is considered the great treatise of Theravada Buddhism. In Pali, *Buddhaghosa* means "Voice of Enlightenment." He was also known as The Great Translator.

Mahinda had so much success with Buddhism in Sri Lanka that 500 women asked if they could join the order. When Mahinda's sister, Sanghamitta, arrived, she founded the first order of Buddhist nuns in Sri Lanka. These nuns were known as *bhikkunis*.

During the fourth century C.E., the Buddha's tooth was brought to Sri Lanka with great fanfare. To this day there is a celebration centered on the Buddha's tooth. It is preserved in the city of Kandy in the Temple of the Tooth Relic. Daily rituals revolve around the venerated tooth; it is a much revered and celebrated artifact.

Buddhism was eventually challenged by European colonialism and invasions of the Portuguese, the Dutch, and the British. Efforts to convert the natives to Christianity were exerted, but Buddhist practice persisted. At one point *bhikkus* were imported from India to retain and fortify the presence of Buddhism. Buddhism prevailed, and today Sri Lanka is considered one of the few predominantly Buddhist countries.

Myanmar (Burma)

From Sri Lanka and India, Buddhism continued its march across the Asian continent. Monks from Sri Lanka left their home to spread the teachings abroad, having a powerful impact on other countries such as Burma, Thailand, Laos, and Cambodia. These southeastern transmissions were in the Theravada tradition. Buddhism originally came to Burma via trade with the people of India and via monks from Sri Lanka. With the aid of Sri Lankan monks and supporters, Buddhism was able to establish a firm foothold.

Originally, the predominant form of Buddhism in Burma was Vajrayana Buddhism, but by the year 1044 C.E., the powerful Burmese king Anawrahta sponsored Theravada monasteries and changed the country to a largely Theravada-supported nation. Anawrahta built monasteries, *stupas*, and shrines all over the capital city of Pagan, and the city soon became a center for Buddhist study and practice.

Buddhism flourished in Burma for many years, but ran up against a large threat with the British invasion of the nineteenth century. Today, Theravada Buddhism continues to flourish. There are more than 50,000 monasteries to be found and fully 88 percent of the population considers themselves Buddhist.

Thailand

Buddhism is said to have first appeared in Thailand among the Mon people in the third century B.C.E. The Mons left China about 2,000 years ago and settled in both Thailand and Burma. They are believed to be the first settlers in Thailand. Once established, they soon encountered other peoples arriving from the north. Many small kingdoms were subsequently established across the land, each vying for power over another. It is likely, considering the first settlers were from China, that some Chinese Buddhist influence was possible. However, Buddhism is generally considered to have appeared in Thailand from India and not from China.

By the thirteenth century, missionaries from Sri Lanka were able to convince the king of Thailand, Ramkhamhaeng, to convert to Buddhism. Pali was established as the religious language of Thailand and Theravada Buddhism firmly took root, where it thrives to this day.

There was a revival of the Theravadan traditions in the nineteenth and twentieth centuries across Southeast Asia. In Burma and Sri Lanka these reforms were part of the independence movement against colonial rule. In Thailand, which retained its independence, reform was initiated by King Rama IV (reign 1851–1868), who was a monk himself for twenty-seven years.

Cambodia, Laos, and Indonesia

From India, Buddhism spread to the East and South.

Cambodia

Cambodia was influenced by India early in its history, and Mahayana Buddhism took a foothold with its people. Early Cambodian history is not well documented, so it is not until the ninth century that we know Buddhism was being practiced there. Kings of the Khmer, who were dominate in Cambodia, started to build large temples and monasteries.

Then at the turn of the twelfth century, King Jayavarman VII came into power. He was a devout Buddhist, and Mahayana Buddhism became the dominant religion of the kingdom under his influence. Neighboring Thailand was soon to have a strong effect, however, and by the end of the thirteenth century Theravada was predominant.

FACT

Buddhism has exerted influence on Southeast Asia since the first century C.E. and has taken a predominately Theravada form (except in Vietnam). Great material and political resources were devoted to building what are now some of the world's most magnificent ruins: Angkor in Cambodia, Pagan in Burma, and Borobudur in Java.

When Pol Pot and the Khmer Rouge communists took control of Cambodia in the 1970s, they tried to eradicate Buddhism and nearly succeeded. There were 65,000 monks in the *Sangha* before 1970, and after Pol Pot, that number was reduced to 3,000. Approximately two-thirds of the Buddhist temples were destroyed. Today Buddhism is attempting to re-establish itself but political unrest continues. There has been resurgence in the *sangha*, and 95 percent of the population is Theravada Buddhist.

Laos

As in Cambodia, Laotian Buddhism was probably introduced by the Khmer. Later, it was heavily influenced by Thailand and thusly became Buddhist in the Theravada school. Communists also tried to rid Laos of Buddhism in 1975, and a large percentage of the *sangha* fled the country. The remaining religious communities were under strict state control. Recent reforms and dialogues are moving to declare Theravada Buddhism the state religion. Fully 60 percent of the population is considered to be practicing Buddhists.

Indonesia

The first Buddhists arrived in Indonesia sometime in the first century C.E. from India. It is believed that Buddhism spread here through Ashoka's missionaries as well. Both Theravada and Mahayana Buddhism were prevalent, though Mahayana eventually took hold in the eighth century C.E. In the nineteenth century, the largest Buddhist shrine in the world was built on the island of Java. It is known as Borobudur, and this monumental *stupa* was most likely built at the end of the ninth century by Hindu kings as a central sanctuary of the Buddhist religion. Until recent history, Borobudur was mostly covered and just a small portion was visible above the surrounding earth and forests. It was restored just 200 years ago. This enormous temple is said to be a *mandala*, a representation of the cosmos, constructed by practicing *tantric* Buddhists.

Northward Bound

Mahayana Buddhism was spreading northward from India as Theravada was spreading throughout the south and southeast. Vajrayana Buddhism headed north to Tibet and took a fast hold of that isolated mountainous country. Mahayana Buddhism proliferated in China, Japan, and Korea.

The Silk Road

Silk was a hot commodity in the ancient world, and in the second century B.C.E., a path developed across Asia that allowed the passage of silk from one country to another. This road, which came to be known as the Silk Road, was just north of India and west of Tibet. The 6,000-mile road traversed what would be Afghanistan, Pakistan, and northwestern China today. The Silk Road was a ferment of international trade that connected India to China. Silk went one way and gold and silver went the other. Early Chinese tradesmen started to hear of the wonderful teachings coming out of India, and curiosity in Buddhism was aroused in China. The first missionaries to China arrived in the first century C.E. They headed northward from India to spread the teachings of the Buddha. Literate Chinese started translating the *sutras* into Chinese and continued to do so for eight centuries.

China: Chan

As Chinese interest in Buddhism grew, a need for texts was established. Buddhism slowly flourished in China as new texts were brought into the country and translated, becoming available to practitioners. By the seventh century, different schools of Buddhism arose in China. The two most prominent schools were the Chan and the Pure Land schools. Chan Buddhism would come to be known in the West and Japan as Zen Buddhism. Both Chan and Zen mean "meditation."

Bodhidharma Enters China

Early in the sixth century C.E., Emperor Wu of China was a devout student of Buddhism. He had built many temples, translated many *sutras*, and considered himself well versed in the teachings of the Buddha. When he heard that Bodhidharma, a renowned Buddhist monk, had arrived in China, he requested a meeting with the Indian monastic. In reference to the great works he had done in the service of Buddhism through the construction of monasteries and translation of core texts, Emperor Wu asked Bodhidharma, "What merit have I accumulated for all my good to Buddhism?"

"None," Bodhidharma replied.

Emperor Wu was shocked; this contradicted everything that Emperor Wu thought he knew about Buddhism. It was a common belief that good deeds developed merit points. Giving food to a mendicant monk was considered good *karma* and insurance for a good rebirth, especially if the monk you gave to was a good student. Wu considered himself knowledgeable about Buddhism and wanted to engage Bodhidharma in conversation. He became defensive and decided to test the newcomer. "What is the meaning of enlightenment?" he asked.

"Vast emptiness, nothing sacred," Bodhidharma said.

This, too, must have confused the great emperor. This was not in line with his beliefs and he did not understand what it meant. Emperor Wu then asked in frustration, "*Who* are you?"

And Bodhidharma replied, "I don't know."

While Bodhidharma was at Shaolin Temple, he found the monks there to be in terrible physical condition. He helped them with their meditation practice and also helped them get back into top physical condition. It was here at Shaolin Temple that Shaolin Kung Fu was born.

Emperor Wu did not understand what Bodhidharma was telling him. Bodhidharma symbolizes a serious commitment to meditation practice and the concept of emptiness. He was the founder of Chan in China. The Chan school of Buddhism endeavored to keep Buddhism simple. It included none of the bells and whistles of the Vajrayana, but at its heart was the desire to get down to basics. Chan Buddhism promotes the belief that meditation is the direct route to enlightenment—and with meditation, *buddha-nature* is revealed.

Bodhidharma left the frustrated emperor and made his way up the mountains to Shaolin. It was here in a small cave that he meditated for nine years straight, facing a blank wall. Legend has it that he became frustrated with himself for falling asleep, so he cut off his eyelids to ensure he didn't fall asleep again. Artworks depicting Bodhidharma often show him with eyes wide open.

Bodhidharma became the first Chinese patriarch, starting a transmission of Chan from one person to another, from mind to mind, until the present day, just as the Buddha passed the teachings so many years before.

China: Pure Land

The other main school of Buddhism to start in China around the same time was called Pure Land. This school of Buddhism, unlike Bodhidharma's Chan, did believe in a system of merits and also promoted the idea that there is more than one Buddha.

They also believe that this realm has many different fields, the best being that of paradise, or Pure Land.

A purified field surrounds *buddhas* and *bodhisattvas*. The belief contends that out of their great compassion they create a space around them that is uncontaminated. This space is available for those who wish to join them. It is attributed to Amitabha Buddha (the buddha of Infinite Light). Amitabha is known as Amituo Fo in China and Amida Butsu in Japan. The Pure Land is also known as *Sukhavati* ("Abode of Bliss").

Pure Land Buddhists believe in a paradise after death. Amitabha, the Buddha of Infinite Light, is host there. If you invoke the name of Amitabha (*Namo Amituo Fo*), you will be reborn into the Pure Land. Pure Land in your mind is the place where enlightenment takes place; it is not enlightenment itself.

Therefore, in Pure Land Buddhism, if you invoke the name of the Buddha, you invoke the reality of Pure Land. This practice was less rigorous than the Chan practice and found widespread acceptability. One could be reborn into a paradise here at any time. All you had to do was recite the Buddha's name over and over, and paradise is yours. There were no impediments to enlightenment once you attained Pure Land, so much of the work of practice was alleviated.

The Jingtu Lun is an important Pure Land text that outlines five forms of devotion:

- Expressing reverence for Amitabha Buddha
- Praising Amitabha's virtue by reciting his name
- Spoken aspirations to be born in the Pure Land

- Contemplation on the physical form of Amitabha, *bodhisattvas* who live in the Pure Land, and the Pure Land itself
- Transferring one's own merit to assist others in reaching the Pure Land

According to Buddhist scholar Michael Willis, "The Pure Land is described as a kind of paradise devoid of diversion, such as women and conflict, and superior to any heaven because Amituo resides there, prepared to preach the *dharma* to all those who ask for assistance."

The Pure Land practice is comparable to the *bodhisattva* path, and its advocate Daochuo (562–645 C.E.) argued that it would be more expedient in this degenerate age because Amitabha was there to help. The Pure Land path was easier too, and therefore more accessible to common people. Pure Land Buddhism is popular in the West today.

Japan

Toward the end of the twelfth century, Chan arrived in Japan and became "Zen." The samurai warrior spirit was thriving in Japan, and the rigors of Zen practice were welcomed by the Japanese. There are two classes of Zen that arose in Japan. The first was called Rinzai and was brought back from China by the Japanese monk Eisai. Eisai's student Dogen brought the second class of Zen to Japanese shores from China. This school of Zen was called the Soto School. The two schools of Zen are covered in much greater detail in a later chapter.

Both schools of Zen emphasized the importance of seated meditation. Over many years, the Soto School became larger than the Rinzai School in Japan (today, it might be as much as three times as large), though both schools are still very prominent. The strictness of practice in the monasteries historically inhibited many people from practicing Zen. But as Zen headed west in the twentieth century, this would no longer be the case.

Nicheren Buddhism

There was another Buddhist tradition to arise in Japan in the early thirteenth century. A Buddhist monk named Nichiren was the founder of this school, which came to bear his name. Nichiren studied the Lotus *Sutra* and came to believe it was the embodiment of Truth. He believed that by reciting *Namu-myoho-renge-kyo* (Glory to the Lotus *Sutra*) one could evoke all of the wisdom contained in its verses. The Nicheren School has proliferated into many subschools and remains popular today in Japan and the West, including an evangelical branch that seeks converts. Much like the Hare Krishnas, someone encouraging you to chant the *mantra Namu-myoho-renge-kyo* may approach you at an airport or on the street.

Japanese Pure Land

The Pure Land practice went from China to Japan and was practiced from the aristocracy to peasants. One important text, written by Ojoyo-shu, "Birth in the Land of Purity," helped to promote the popularity of these practices that emerged from the ninth to eleventh centuries C.E. Honen (1133–1122) is considered the founder of the first Jodo (Pure Land) school in Japan. Honen's student gave up on getting to the Pure Land by personal effort. He forsook his monastic vows, took a wife, and substituted *tariki* (other power) for *jiriki* (self-power), feeling that this was more consistent with the Buddha's original teaching. He was discouraged that no *buddhas* had appeared since the time of Siddhartha, and the Pure Land was seen as an alternative path. Amida Butsu is the key to everything. His followers founded Jodoshin ("True Pure Land School"), which permitted its clergy to marry. The Jodoshin has persisted to contemporary times and remains the largest religious organization in Japan.

Honen's teachings created a paradigm shift for Buddhist practice, replacing the personal path of salvation with Amida, a universal savior who helped the faithful to reach his Pure Land. It was only in the Pure Land that one could achieve enlightenment. While initially suppressed, the Jodo School founded by Honen achieved great popularity and was the religion of the ruling class by the seventeenth century.

The Pure Land practices provided a "short-cut" through countless lifetimes to become a *bodhisattva*. It employs not only chanting but complex visualization of *buddhas*, *bodhisattvas*, and the Pure Land, especially Amitabha. In the text *Visualizing the Buddha of Limitless Life Sutra*, the story of Queen Vaidehi is presented. The Buddha gave her a vision visible in a golden ray of light emanating from his forehead. In this vision she saw all the celestial worlds and chose her wish to be reborn with Amitabha.

Buddhist scholar Michael Willis shares a segment of this text: "You should think of the *buddha* of Limitless Life. Why? Because the Body of the *buddha* is the Body of the Universe and it is within the mind of all beings. Therefore when you think of that *buddha* your mind becomes the One who has the thirty-two Magnificent Figures and the eighty Virtues. It is the mind that is to become a *buddha* and it is the mind that is the *buddha*. The Ocean of Omniscient Wisdom of all *buddhas* grows up from the mind."

What percentage of the world's population is Buddhist?
Today, it is estimated that approximately 6 percent of the world's population is Buddhist. Christianity weighs in with the largest percentage of adherents at 33 percent, and Islam comes in second at 18 percent. It is estimated there are 100 million followers of Theravada Buddhism worldwide; 500 million to 1 billion followers of Mahayana; and 10 to 20 million Tibetan Buddhists.

It is not clear whether belief in the Pure Land is taken literally or metaphorically as purified states of mind. For indigenous Chinese and Japanese, their relationship to Amitabha as savior is likely regarded as quite literal. In America, if you adopt these practices you have a choice. The Pure Land schools seem to move Buddhism from more of a rational psychology to a theistic, transcendent religion. The ease of these practices compared to arduous sitting meditation in Chan and Zen, and the promise (likely realized in bliss states as one chants the Amitabha mantras) of going to heaven increased its popularity in China and Japan. These practices resemble some of the Vedic practices that Siddhartha would have been familiar with in his search for the Way when he left the palace. Chanting the names of Shiva or Krishna, for example, was a common practice in pre-Buddhist India as it is today.

Tibet

Monks headed over the footpaths of the Himalayan Mountains into remote and isolated Tibet, taking their Buddhist practices with them. They reached

Tibet and began to spread the teachings, as so many others were doing all over Southeast Asia. But it wasn't until the seventh century, when the king of Tibet, Songtsen Gambo, married two Buddhist women—one a princess from Nepal and the other a princess from China—that Buddhism flourished in Tibet. It wasn't long before the king became very interested in Buddhism, sending representatives from Tibet over to China and India to learn more about it.

He became convinced of the benefits of the Buddhist lifestyle and his faith strengthened. He built many temples and encouraged the growth of Buddhism among his people. Eventually, Mahayana scriptures were translated into Tibetan. Buddhism remained a prominent part of life in Tibet until 1959, when the Dalai Lama took exile in India after ten years of Red Chinese occupation.

Korea

Buddhism arrived in Korea in 372 C.E. At that time, shamanism—a religion based on nature worship and the belief in a world of gods, demons, and ancestral spirits—was the native religion. Buddhism would eventually blend in with this shamanism to create Korean Buddhism. Shamanism promoted a belief in three gods: the god of the mountains, the hermit god, and the god of the seven stars. Korean Buddhism blended the belief in these gods into the teachings of the Buddha, and Korean Buddhism blossomed.

Pure Land and Son (Korean Zen or Chan) also found their way to Korea and took root there. Son emphasized meditation practice over text study, and eventually nine different Son schools emerged in Korea, which were called the Nine Schools of Son.

Today about half the population of Korea is Buddhist, though Buddhism has deep roots in the community and many others incorporate Buddhist practices into their lives, regardless of religious affiliation.

The East Today

Millennia ago Buddhism spread quickly over Asia and was soon well on its way to becoming a major world religion. Theravada Buddhism flourished in

Sri Lanka, Cambodia, Laos, Thailand, Myanmar, and Bangladesh. Mahayana Buddhism had deep roots in Tibet, Japan, China, Korea, Vietnam, Indonesia, and Nepal. The twentieth century saw Buddhism emerge in the West, and now vital centers of Theravada, Zen, and Tibetan Buddhism are here in the United States.

Today, the top ten countries with the highest number of Buddhist practitioners are:

1. Thailand
2. Cambodia
3. Myanmar
4. Bhutan
5. Sri Lanka
6. Tibet
7. Laos
8. Vietnam
9. Japan
10. Macau

Although the countries with the greatest number of Buddhists are all in the Eastern hemisphere, Buddhism has made great inroads in the West. In the past fifty years, Americans and other Westerners have been increasingly interested in changing their lives through the practice of the *dharma*. Writers, philosophers, artists, and teachers have spread the word of Buddhism all over North America and Europe.

Refugees from Tibet have brought Buddhism into the public eye, and the Dalai Lama tirelessly works with the hope of returning to his native Tibet. Emigrants from Asia have brought their practices westward and introduced new ideas and a new way of life into the hearts and minds of Americans and Europeans. Buddhism might be new to the West, but the seeds of *dharma* have been firmly planted in Western soil.

CHAPTER 11

Tibetan Buddhism

The plight of Tibet and the Dalai Lama's charismatic presence in the media has made Tibetan Buddhism a household name. The maroon and ochre pageantry of Tibetan Buddhism and the ongoing difficulty of its people has had a magnetizing effect on the West. Celebrities such as Richard Gere have been attracted to the practice, and Tibetan Buddhism in all of its variations flourishes in the United States.

Exile and Diaspora

Tibet is one of the few countries where secular and religious affairs of state were merged. His Holiness the Dalai Lama was both the spiritual as well as political leader of the Tibetan people. The Himalayan country of Tibet was invaded and occupied by the Chinese Red Army in 1949. Over the next ten years the Dalai Lama attempted to work with Mao Zedong, but in 1959 fled Tibet for fear of his life. With welcome, support, and blessings from India, the Dalia Lama set up the Tibetan government-in-exile in Dharamsala, an Indian hill station in the foothills of the Himalayas.

The Chinese were not the first to suppress Tibetan Buddhism; it was suppressed in 840 C.E. during a civil war. 200 years later, *siddhas* ("tantric yogis") and scholars were brought over from India to reintroduce it. Four schools emerged from this re-introduction. First, the Sakyapa sect headed the country, and then later the Gelugpa ("Yellow Hat") ruled the country. This was the first time in Buddhist history that the *sangha* assumed secular control of its country. Given this confluence of secular and religious forces, a large percentage of Tibetan men became monks—25 percent by the early twentieth century.

There are about 120,000 Tibetans living in exile, most of them in India. The Dalai Lama received the Nobel Peace Prize in 1989 for his efforts towards a peaceful resolution of the Tibetan occupation.

The Tibetan crisis has brought international attention to this isolated, mountainous country. Awareness and interest in Tibetan Buddhism and Buddhism in general has subsequently increased greatly in recent years.

Buddhist Origins

Tibetan Buddhism is unique in the Buddhist practices in that Tibetans believe that there are multiple *buddhas* living everywhere among them. They believe that Shakyamuni Buddha is the premiere *buddha* of this era, but he is by no means alone. They believe that the Buddha lives among humanity in many different forms, and any person at all can attain *buddhahood*.

Songtsen Gambo, an emperor of Tibet in the mid-seventh century, was one of the first to show an interest in Buddhism. He tried to convert Tibet from a militaristic society into a peaceful, more monastic society. He developed an interest in Buddhism and wed his two Buddhist wives, who brought Buddhist texts and teachings into Tibet. His court began to translate Sanskrit texts into Tibetan. But Buddhism wasn't to remain strong for long, and its popularity waned before returning to strength in the eighth century, principally due to Padmasambhava.

Padmasambhava

Padmasambhava, a Buddhist monk, originally brought Buddhism to Tibet from India. Padmasambhava is the patron saint of Tibetan Buddhism, credited with the founding of Buddhism in Tibet when he established the Samye monastery in the eighth century C.E. He was considered by Tibetans to be an example of a living *buddha*—a fully realized human being who lives among the people. The native religion at the time Padmasambhava arrived was Bön. Bön was a shamanistic religion, and practice included prophecies, rites, sorcery, sacrifice, and a belief in the interdependence of humans and nature. Bön rituals and ceremonies revolved around priests and priestesses, who were believed to possess supernatural powers. Tibetans deified elements of the natural world, such as mountains, and believed in a world of gods who inhabited all types of space from the underworld to the heavens above.

Tibetans live at great altitudes, many inhabiting land at an average of 14,000 feet above sea level. The climate and the isolating location bred a population of resilient citizens, and their history—both recent and ancient—speaks of their strength and their deep attachment to their cultural and spiritual beliefs.

Tibet was a militaristic nation with many different kingdoms spread across the Tibetan plateau. It was believed that the seven ruling kings were divine, having descended from heaven on a ladder. They practiced shamanism and believed the shamans could serve as intermediaries between the divine origins of the kings and the people of the Earth. Their belief system was based on magic, multiple deities, and ritual. In order for someone to influence this populace, that person would have to be a great charismatic teacher capable of teachings that would impress upon them his power over nature, life, and death. This was Padmasambhava.

Padmasambhava, with the help of his twenty-five disciples, helped to build the first monastery in Tibet, at Samye. He helped to translate many of the Buddhist scriptures into Tibetan, and educated the populace in Buddhist teachings. He traveled around the country, transforming it from militarism into a peaceful, spiritual nation. Padmasambhava strived to change the Tibetan people internally and spiritually, so that their warring external life would fall away. He was largely successful at making significant changes.

This peaceful spirit would continue in Tibet until the ninth century when Tibet entered a dark age and Buddhism was suppressed. Many of the teachings were kept alive during this dark time by twenty-five disciples who passed down the teachings. Eventually, the seeds of knowledge that were planted by Padmasambhava were to sprout again, and Buddhism would establish itself as a major force in Tibetan culture.

A Unique Form of Buddhism

As an example of the elaborate symbolism in Tibetan Buddhist practice, consider the Five Celestial Buddhas. Each *buddha* has a color, one of the five *skhandas* (mental aggregates), and a personality trait that the practitioner will need to overcome. Here, Professor Todd Lewis describes the elaborate symbolic system (note that these are also the colors of Tibetan prayer flags).

▼ **FIVE CELESTIAL BUDDHAS**

Celestial Buddha	Color	Skandha	Personality
Ratnasambhava (Born from a Jewel)	Yellow	Feeling	Ill-will
Vairochana (Resplendent)	White	Form	Delusion
Akshobhya (Imperturbable)	Blue	Perception	Anger
Amitabha (Infinite Light)	Red	Consciousness	Greed
Amoghasiddha (Infallible Power)	Green	Mental Dispositions	Envy

From *Buddhism: The Illustrated Guide*

Thunderbolt Wisdom

Vajrayana is the esoteric school of Mahayana. "Vajrayana" translates to "diamond" or "thunderbolt"; hence, Vajrayana is the Diamond-Thunderbolt vehicle. Diamond, being the hardest substance known, has the power to cut through ignorance or delusion, leading the practitioner to enlightenment. Vajrayana is based on secret *tantric* texts and powerful practices that can lead to enlightenment in this lifetime. Vajrayana is most closely associated with Tibet, since coming from India in the eighth or ninth century C.E.

Tantric practitioners known as *siddhas* broke away from the orthodoxy of Buddhist monastic life in sixth-century India; the *Mahasiddhas* were the great among them. They sought to replace intellectual knowledge with new meditative practices. Nagarjuna also contributed to the rise of Vajrayana by equating *samsara* and *nirvana*. Visualization of deities from the Mahayana pantheon is a common *tantric* practice. These practices provided a radical departure from the orthodoxy. And now, this radical practice is the orthodoxy in Tibet. The teachings were written down in *tantric* texts that were kept secret and whose meaning was kept obscure by using coded or esoteric language. These were not meant for the unitiated, and even today, one learns the *tantras* through a close relationship with one's teacher or *guru* (*lama* in Tibetan). These practices can be found in Tibet and other culturally Tibetan regions such as Bhutan, Ladakh, and parts of Nepal. *Tantra* also moved to the East and survives today as Shingon in Japan. Tibetan texts identify eighty-four *mahasiddhas* from 700–1100 C.E.

As Professor Lewis describes, these were a colorful group and came from every social status, from kings to prostitutes: "Luipa ate fish entrails, Virupa frequented taverns, Shaniripa was a hunter, Arydeva gave an offering of one of his eyes, Vinapa played the lute." Mahasiddhas you will have encountered (if you have had contact with Tibetan Buddhism) include Naropa, his disciple Marpa, and his disciple Milarepa. *Mahasiddhas* are in possession of *siddhis* (spiritual powers) that are believed to include clairvoyance, telepathy, superhuman strength, and the ability to fly. They are superstar *bodhisattvas*!

Triple Jewel Redux

The Triple Jewel takes on added meaning within Tibetan Buddhism. *Buddha* also refers to one's personal teacher, the *guru*. *Dharma* refers to all male *tantric* deities who are the subject of visualization in meditation and *sangha* refers to all the female *tantric* deities. Some of these deities have a wrathful form to ward off demons or other evil spirits. Again, these demons can be interpreted literally or symbolically as aspects of your own mind: greed, hatred, and delusion. All deities have a seed *mantra* that starts the process and a heart *mantra* to invoke compassion. The process of visualization is felt to bypass the intellect providing a more straightforward path to enlightenment.

One of these deities is Mahakala, known as the "Great Black" or the "Great Time." His job is to protect and his image may be seen outside temples. He can also be the focus of meditation (*yidam*), where he takes a wrathful aspect of Avalokiteshvara to destroy any obstacles to happiness. In his "Great Time" aspect he wields a sword to cut through intellectual concepts and a skullcap to represent wisdom. He may also wear a garland of fifty skulls to scare off evil spirits, and as a representation of the fifty vowels and consonants that comprise the Sanskrit alphabet. Wrath leads to transformation in the subjects who meditate upon him.

Another popular wrathful deity is Yamantaka, who is a manifestation of Manjushri ("Pleasing Splendor"), who represents wisdom. He wields a sword and carries a book. The sword is used to cut through ignorance or delusion. The myth has Manjushri descending to hell to scare Yama, the lord of death, to death. The myth provides a metaphor for meditation practice. As Michael Willis explains, "the individual who opens his or her body, speech, and mind to transformation by the visualization of these deities and through other *tantric* practices can effectively overcome the 'inner demons' that obstruct the path to liberation."

Tantra

Tantric yogis do not try to avoid desire but embrace it as a way to demystify it. In this way, they "use a thorn to remove a thorn." This path of embracing desire can be dangerous, especially if not properly supervised or if used for nonspiritual ends. It is, again, for these reasons that *tantras* are carefully guarded secrets and only passed from *guru* to disciple when the disciple is ready to receive them. While the path may be dangerous, it promises to be quick. A dedicated practitioner may attain enlightenment within seven years. *Tantric* practices overlap with Hindu yogic practices and make use of the *chakra* system (subtle energy centers) to move energy throughout the body. Some of these *tantras* take on an explicit sexual form. The goal in *tantric* sex is not pleasure or orgasm but rather generation of energy and modulation of that energy for spiritual purposes: to help the practitioner attain *nirvana*.

ESSENTIAL

Tantra seeks to merge the feminine and masculine and is portrayed in art, for example, as Lord Kalachakra in sexual union with his consort. Women enjoy a higher status in tantric practices because they are rich in spiritual power.

Sometimes *tantras* are enacted privately between *guru* and disciple and at other times *tantras*, such as the Kalachakra *tantra*, can be conducted for large audiences. Whatever the context, these practices can unleash powerful emotional and spiritual forces and are conducted in highly ritualized ways to provide a structure for that energy. The use of *mandalas* and ritual objects such as the *vajra* and the bell assist in this process of transformatiom. *Mantras* and *mudras* (hand gestures) are also used.

The Six Traditions of Tibetan Spirituality

Historically, there are six traditions, or schools, of Tibetan spirituality. Four of these schools are considered the principal schools. The six traditions are:

1. The Bön tradition
2. The Nyingma Tradition (the Old Ones)
3. The Bound by Command School (Kadam)
4. The Sakya Tradition
5. The Kagyu Tradition (The Transmitted Command School)
6. The Gelug Tradition (The Virtuous School)

The four principal schools are: Nyingma, Sakya, Kagyu, and Gelug.

The Bön Tradition

The Bön tradition is alive today and getting stronger after a long period of virtual invisibility in Tibet during the eighth to the eleventh centuries. The Bön community has been successful in establishing monasteries in India and Nepal. It is an integral part of Tibetan culture and history, and the Tibetans strive to preserve Bön customs.

The five other traditions of Tibetan spirituality are all Buddhist and combine elements of all three vehicles of Buddhism—Theravada, Mahayana, and Vajrayana—leaning heavily on *tantra* practices. They trace back to the different *gurus*, or *lamas*, who started the lineages.

The Nyingma Tradition (The Old Ones)

The Nyingma tradition of Tibetan Buddhism traces its roots back to Padmasambhava, and is the oldest school of Tibetan Buddhism. Padmasambhava mixed native Bön practices and beliefs with Tantric Buddhism to develop a very unique and mystical form of Tibetan Buddhism.

FACT

Atisha wrote *Lamp for the Path of Enlightenment* for the Tibetan people to answer the questions they had about practice and show them all of the Buddha's teachings—distilled from *sutras* and *tantras*—in a short guide that simplified direction for practice. These teachings on the stages of the Path were known as *lam-rim*. *Lamp for the Path of Enlightenment* is still used in practice today.

It is believed that Padmasambhava found his disciples unready to experience the full disclosure of his knowledge, so he hid hundreds of teachings from them, to be revealed in the future to teachers more prepared for the knowledge he had to impart. Subsequently, teachers through the years have revealed these hidden treasures, known as *terma*, to their students to aid in their enlightenment.

There are nine paths to enlightenment in Nyingma, six based on the *sutras*, and three based on the *tantras*. Nyingma is based on the practice of Dzogchen—a practice of meditation that presupposes the existence of *buddha-nature* and strives to allow it to manifest.

Dzogchen has recently become very popular in the United States as a meditation practice.

The Bound by Command School (The Kadam)

The Bound by Command school traces its roots back to Atisha, a monk who taught in Tibet starting in 1040 B.C.E. Atisha was born Chandragarbha to a royal family in Bengal. He was renamed Atisha, which means "peace," by a Tibetan king.

Atisha brought to Tibet a synthesis of the three major vehicles of Buddhism. His coming initiated the era of the Second Transmission of Buddhism to Tibet, seminal for the Bound by Command School of Tibetan Buddhism, but also for the Virtuous School and Transmitted by Command School.

Atisha was also known as one of the living *buddhas* among the Tibetan people. He promoted the premise that the teachings of the *guru*, the *lama*, should be held above all else as the *lama* can demonstrate the living nature of the teachings and directly shows the student how to practice. The teacher could choose the specific practices that would benefit the specific student.

The Bound by Command School of Tibetan Buddhism did not last long. It was considered too strict for the Tibetan people, prohibiting intoxicants, money handling, sexual relations, and travel.

The Sakya Tradition

Founded in 1073 by Khön Könchok Gyelpo, the Sakya School took its name from the monastery of the same name in central Tibet. Sakya means "Gray Earth." The Sakya tradition, which developed out of the earlier Nyingma teachings, has been preserved to the present day through the unbroken succession of the heads of the Khön School. The Khön lineage is hereditary, but does not pass directly from father to son, but rather indirectly from uncle to nephew. The lineage holders of the tradition pass down the transmission of the Path and Fruit (*Lam-dre*) teachings. The Path and Fruit teachings synthesize the teaching of the *sutras* and the *tantras*, and are designed to bring the student to enlightenment in a single lifetime.

The Sakya tradition continues to this day. The current head of the Sakya School is the forty-first in the lineage and practices in exile from Tibet.

The Kagyu Tradition (The Transmitted Command School)

The Transmitted Command School of Tibetan Buddhism can trace its roots back to two Indian masters: Naropa and Tilopa. These masters were skilled in advanced yogic practices. The emphasis in the Transmitted Command School has been and still is on practice and mysticism rather than academics. Kagyu tradition has some of the more familiar names in the history of Tibetan Buddhism. Naropa taught Marpa, and Marpa took the teachings back to Tibet with him where he continued to practice as a layperson.

Marpa in turn passed the teachings on to his most famous student, Milarepa (1052–1135 C.E.), one of the most popular figures of all time in Tibetan Buddhism. Milarepa started out as a dark figure in history—he was a black magician bent on revenging his widowed mother and sister who were being mistreated by relatives—but became a poet and a supremely powerful yogi who mastered self-knowledge and achieved liberation. He was legendary for his mystical powers.

Among Milarepa's disciples was Gampopa, who wrote *The Jewel Ornament of Liberation.* Gampopa received the Six Yogas of Naropa from Milarepa as well as the practice of Mahamudra ("Great Seal" and one of the most important practices in Vajrayana focused on realization of emptiness), and then combined them into one lineage—Dakpo Kagyu. The Dakpo Kagyu School then gave rise to four additional schools. One of the most successful of these schools, the Karma Kagyu School, is still going strong today and is passed down through the reincarnations of the Karma Kagyu teachers.

The Six Yogas of Naropa is one of the *tantric* practices unique to the Transmission by Command School. It is a system of advanced *tantric* meditation passed down by Naropa that represents the completion stage teachings. Mahamudra practice is explained according to interpretations of *sutra* and *tantra*—with the goal being direct understanding of *buddha-nature.* Mahamudra was an effort to get back to the basics of meditation practice much like Chan did in China. Each of the schools within Kagyu tradition approach Mahamudra differently.

The Gelug Tradition (The Virtuous School)

The Virtuous School could be called the reform movement of Tibetan Buddhism. Started by Tsongkhapa in the fifteenth century, Gelug can be traced back to the Bound by Command School and was greatly influenced by the teachings of Atisha. Tsongkhapa reiterated the emphasis that Atisha had made on the monastic traditions and the importance of the *guru*. Tsongkhapa was extremely well educated in various schools of Buddhism and engaged in extensive meditation practices as well. Tsongkhapa was a renaissance man undertaking prostrations, meditation, incantations, scriptures, monastic study, ethics, and more. He founded the Ganden Monastery in 1409, which was later divided into two colleges. He died at the age of sixty and left behind a legacy that has lasted to this day. The emphasis in the Gelug tradition is on monastic and academic study. Few masters, if any, are laypeople. Monks who train in the Gelug tradition receive advanced degrees in Buddhist philosophy and thought. These monks are known as *geshes*.

A *geshe* has the equivalent of a PhD in Tibetan philosophy. They become experts in a spirited form of discourse called ritualized dialectical debate. The curriculum includes topics such as the Abidharma, Madhyamaka, and the Prajna Paramita, and can last between twelve and twenty years.

The Dalai Lamas come from the Virtuous School of Tibetan Buddhism and have been the spiritual and secular leaders of Tibet ever since. However, the Dalai Lamas are not the heads of the Virtuous school itself. The Dalai Lamas receive training in many if not all the Tibetan schools of Buddhism, and the leader of the Virtuous school is the abbot of the Ganden monastery.

Common Threads

All of the principal Tibetan traditions of Buddhism have more in common than not. The energy behind Tibetan Buddhism is the spirit of Avalokiteshvara ("Lord who looks down in compassion"), the *bodhisattva* of compassion. The Tibetans believe that anyone can attain enlightenment. The bedrock of Tibetan spiritual culture is the commitment that each individual makes to help all sentient beings towards enlightenment. These Vajrayana schools come from the Mahayana tradition and mix native and *tantric* elements into their practices.

FACT

According to Buddhist scholar Michael Willis, Avalokiteshvara was invoked as a protector against the "Eight Great Perils" of the first millennium: shipwrecks, wrongful imprisonment, thieves, conflagrations, lions, poisonous snakes, wild elephants, and disease. Avalokiteshvara became the feminine Guanyin in China and Kannon in Japan. Avalokiteshvara is also known as Chenrezi in Tibet and remains male with his feminine aspects as Tara.

The role of the *guru* (or *lama*) in Tibetan spirituality is key, especially when it comes to the more sophisticated *tantric* practices, for which a student needs attentive guidance. The *mantra Om mani padme hum* ("Hail to the jewel in the lotus") is woven into the very fabric of their society. This *mantra* is ubiquitous. It is on the lips of all Tibetans, on the walls of buildings, on prayer flags, in art, in jewelry, in stonework, on prayer wheels. The *mantra* captures the spirit of Tibetan Buddhism.

Tara

Tara is one of the important *bodhisattvas* in Tibetan Buddhism. She is the female embodiment of compassion (*karuna*) and lovingkindness (*maitri* in Sanskrit, *metta* in Pali). Atisha introduced the cult of Tara to Tibet in the eleventh century. According to myth, Tara was born from a lotus growing in a pool formed by tears of compassion shed by Avalokiteshvara when he saw the enormity of suffering that humanity experiences. Tara is also the mother of all *buddhas*. She also comes in different colors: green for divine energy and white for transcendent wisdom. In another myth, Amitabha Buddha radiated his thoughts into a lake where a lotus grew and later revealed Avalokiteshvara. He then changed himself into a monkey and mated with Tara to produce the ancestors of the Tibetan people.

The Quest for the Dalai Lama

The current Dalai Lama is regarded as the fourteenth incarnation of the *bodhisattva* of compassion, Avalokiteshvara. The original Dalai Lama came out of the Gelug or Virtuous school of Tibetan Buddhism. This third teacher in the Gelug lineage appeared as the incarnation of the compassionate *bodhisattva* and was subsequently named the Dalai Lama, or Ocean of Wisdom.

The current Dalai Lama was born on July 6, 1935, to a family of poor farmers in the province of Amdo in Tibet. His eldest brother, Thubten Jigme Norbu, had already been recognized as a reincarnation of a high *lama (tulku)*, Taktser Rinpoche, so it was a surprise that another Rinpoche would be found within the family.

Tulku is a special *lama*, one who is reincarnated from a previous teacher. Since the Dalai Lama is the fourteenth in his lineage, he is a *tulku*. Thousands of *tulkus* have been recognized over the centuries and most of these have been men. The Dalai Lama has considered the idea that he will return as the fifteenth Dalai Lama in female form. The identification of a *tulku* was portrayed in the film *Kundun*, where monks disguised as peasants arrived at the future Dalai Lama's home when he was a child of three years old. The monks were following clues provided by the thirteenth Dalai Lama—dreams, or information provided by oracles to find candidate children. Once children are identified they are examined for special marks or signs and their parents interviewed in regards to their moral character. Finally, a test is provided where the young child must identify items that belonged to his predecessor, picking them out from similar items. If he can do this correctly, he will be designated a *tulku*.

Stories abide about *tulkus* being able to remember details from their previous lives, including His Holiness the Dalai Lama. *Tulkus* are also known by the title, *Rinpoche* ("Precious One"). The Dalai Lama is not only the reincarnated *tulku* of the Gelugpa clan and secular and religious leader of Tibet, he is also believed to be the reincarnation of Avalokiteshvara.

The Fourteenth Dali Lama

The thirteenth Dalai Lama had died in 1933, and while his body was in its period of sitting in state, his head had been found to have mysteriously turned toward the area near Amdo—this was just one of the clues that sent the search party on its way.

Once the search party had narrowed down their focus, they found Tenzin Gyatso. The small boy is said to have immediately recognized one of the monks and when handed some items as a test, he was able to pick out the ones belonging to the thirteenth Dalai Lama; he is said to have cried out, "It is mine!"

The three-year-old child was taken away from his family to be trained and prepared for his role as the fourteenth in the long succession of Dalai Lamas. He was eventually reunited with his family and continued his intensive education and training. At the age of fifteen, with the Chinese invasion threatening on the horizon, the Dalai Lama was formally made the leader of Tibet. The young leader tried to secure the assistance of Great Britain and America but was turned down. Tibet was going to have to face the might of the huge Chinese government alone.

His Escape

On March 17, 1958, the Dalai Lama consulted with the Nechung Oracle and was instructed to leave Tibet. For nine years the Tibetan people had tried to hold back a full-scale invasion of the Chinese government, but in the winter of 1959, the Dalai Lama knew it was time to go. On a winter's day, General Chiang Chin-wu of Communist China invited the Dalai Lama to see a Chinese dance troupe—the invitation stipulated that no Tibetan soldiers were to go with the Dalai Lama and his bodyguards should remain unarmed. The people of Lhasa became upset as the news spread, and soon a mob of tens of thousands of citizens surrounded the palace where the young leader resided. The Dalai Lama, disguised as a soldier, slipped through the crowds and fled his homeland.

The Succession of Dali Lamas

The first thirteen Dalai Lamas were:

1. Gedun Drub (1391–1474)
2. Gedun Gyatso (1475–1542)
3. Sonam Gyatso (1543–1588)
4. Yonten Gyatso (1589–1616)
5. Ngawang Lobsang Gyatso (1617–1682)
6. Tsang-yang Gyatso (1683–1706)

7. Kezang Gyatso (1708–1757)
8. Jampel Gyatso (1758–1804)
9. Luntok Gyatso (1806–1815)
10. Tshultrim Gyatso (1816–1837)
11. Khedrup Gyatso (1838–1856)
12. Trinley Gyatso (1856–1875)
13. Thubten Gyatso (1876–1933)

The current Dalai Lama, the fourteenth, is named Tenzin Gyatso.

Contemporary Tibet

The status of Tibet remains a contentious international issue. The Chinese government insists that Tibet is now and has been for 700 years an integral part of China, and that the matter is an internal affair. Tibet considered itself a sovereign nation and wishes to resume this sovereignty, even if seen as an autonomous part of China. Thus far, China has resisted, and the international community has not challenged China's position.

When the People's Republic of China defeated the small Tibetan army in 1949 when it first crossed into Tibet, it subsequently imposed the Seventeen-Point Agreement for the Peaceful Liberation of Tibet on the Tibetan government, in May 1951. The agreement was signed at gunpoint and Tibetans do not recognize its validity.

FACT

According to the exiled Tibetan Prime Minister Samdhong Rinpoche, approximately 7.5 million Chinese have been transferred to Tibet from China since 1949. The total population of Tibetans living in their country stands at 6 million. The Chinese influx has more than doubled the population of Tibet.

By the end of the Tibetan uprising in 1959, more than 80,000 Tibetans were dead and the government-in-exile was established in Dharamsala, India. Native Tibet has been devastated by the loss of its people and the environmental impact of the invasion. Deforestation, overpopulation, mining, and pollution have adversely impacted the ecosystem of this Himalayan country. March 10 is now a national Tibetan holiday called Uprising Day.

Tibetan Buddhism and the United States

The Buddhist history of Tibet is colorful and diverse. Tibetans forged their own kind of Buddhism that is unique and intense. Tibetan Buddhism in different forms has found great popularity in the United States. There are monasteries and study centers for the various forms of Tibetan Buddhist all over the country. One of the most well known teachers of Tibetan Buddhism to emigrate to the United States was Chögyam Trungpa.

He fled Tibet at the age of twenty in 1959. In 1970, he moved to the United States and established his first American meditation center. He started Naropa University—the first Buddhist-inspired university in North America. There are more than 100 Shambhala Meditation Centers throughout the world that were founded by Chögyam Trungpa. He was a prolific author, including the classic *Cutting Through Spiritual Materialism,* and was responsible for bringing many teachers to the United States from Tibet. Although he died in 1987 at the age of forty-seven, he left a legacy of study and education that continues strongly to this day. The *Shambhala Sun,* a bimonthly periodical, recently celebrated its thirtieth anniversary.

CHAPTER 12

Zen Practice

The origins of Zen are found in China when Bodhidharma went there in the sixth century. In China it is called Chan, in Korea it is called Son, in Japan it is called Zen, all meaning "meditation." This chapter will explore Zen history, philosophy, and practice. Zen has captured the popular imagination in the West, and the center of gravity of Zen practice worldwide has shifted to the West. Zen offers a fresh interpretation of the Buddha's teachings and forms of practice that are straightforward and profound.

Zen History

Meditation is the core practice of Zen and teachers are notorious for irreverent, unpredictable, and unorthodox methods of teaching. For example, in one temple, the bell would ring after meditation and all the practitioners who had been in seated meditation for a long period of time would have to get up, legs still asleep, and run down the hall to the Zen master's chamber. Only those who showed up first would get an interview for that day. The novices stumbled over each other in this mad procession to get to the teacher.

Zen is the transliteration of the Chinese Chan, which itself is an abbreviation of *chan-na*, the transliteration of the Sanskrit *dhyanas* (meditation). Zen has had a large influence on Taiwan, Korea, Vietnam, Japan, and now the West, especially the United States, which is now the most vital center of Zen practice in the world. Zen emphasizes enlightened masters over scriptures, and is the least academic of all the Buddhist schools.

According to Professor Mark Blum, Zen is comprised of four principles:

1. Transmission outside the orthodox Buddhist teachers through its lineages
2. A belief that truth is not dependent upon established doctrine and a belief in the value of experience over the value of scripture
3. A direct pointing to the mind
4. An emphasis on examining one's original nature and the attainment of enlightenment

The Buddha's disciple Kashayapa (or Mahakashyapa) was the forebear of Zen. It was he alone who understood the Buddha's teaching when he held up a flower and smiled. Seeing that flower occasioned Kashyapa's enlightenment and reflects the emphasis in Zen that transmission does not require language. Kashyapa was the first of twenty-eight Indian patriarchs, culminating in Bodhidharma, who went to China around 520 C.E. where he became the first Chinese Patriarch of Chan. Sudden enlightenment, like that of a peasant who heard the Diamond *Sutra*, led to the Southern school, versus the gradual enlightenment through long practice that led to the Northern school. These historical schools correspond to Rinzai and Soto Zen, respectively. From China, Chan went to Vietnam in 580 C.E. and to Japan and Korea around the twelfth century. In Japan, the monk Eisai founded the Rinzai School and Dogen founded the Soto School. Eisai's monastery, Kenninji, is still active today.

Rinzai

Rinzai emphasizes sudden enlightenment that is predicated on the fact that everyone already has *buddha-nature*. The right context will bring this sudden realization of what is already there. This sudden burst of insight is called *kensho*. *Koan* practice is integral to the pursuit of sudden awakening (and so, too, might be the rationale for having the monks race to get an interview with the Master). The Rinzai schools bristles against slow and silent illumination found in *shikintaza* ("just sitting"). While the schools disagree, both value meditation. In Rinzai, you meditate not to attain wisdom but as an expression of wisdom. Wisdom is not confined to the cushion, and awakening can be found in the most mundane experiences of everyday life. Historically, Rinzai was practiced in urban centers by the elite shoguns and samurais, while Soto was more of a rural practice. As military culture declined in the nineteenth century, so did Rinzai.

QUOTE

"Body and mind of themselves will drop away and your original face will be manifested. If you want to attain suchness, you should practice suchness without delay."—Dogen, on *zazen* practice

Rinzai *zazen* practice employs the waking stick. If you slump during meditation or fall asleep, an attendant will strike you across your trapezius muscles with a wooden stick. The blow is designed not to harm but to wake you up to the task at hand: meditation. You can also request a blow if you feel your energy is flagging. Performed correctly, the blow will not injure.

Koans

Koans are designed to short circuit the rational mind and provide the basis for a sudden spiritual awakening. The most famous of these inscrutable puzzles is, "What is the sound of one hand clapping." As one Zen master said, "It is the place where truth is." *Koans* are an important part of Rinzai practice. Rinzai also emphasizes meetings with the Master (*dokusan*) more so than Soto schools, as these meetings (whether one runs or not) can also facilitate *kensho*. Students are normally assigned a *koan* in *dokusan*. As a Zen student you would try to answer the *koan* when you meet with the teacher. Answers are usually not verbal, but can be. They are not "yes/no," "this/that" answers. When you know the answer, you will know how to convey the answer to the teacher, and the teacher will recognize that the *koan* has been passed by the way you are in the interview. During your meditation practice you will reach a stage known as *samadhi*. *Samadhi* is a deep and focused meditation wherein concentration is effortless and complete absorption has been attained. *Koan* practice is done in the *samadhi* state.

Are You Worthy?

The life of a Zen monk in Japan is arduous with rigorous periods of meditation, work practice, and exposure to the elements. It's not for the faint of heart, for those not serious about the practice, or not prepared for the rigors that await you. If you show up at the gates of a Zen temple in Japan you may have to wait two days to get into the temple. This is the first test. If you pass this test, you may then sit alone in small room for three to five days. Having passed this test you will then be admitted into the Zendo with the rest of the monks, and after a few days more of practice you will then meet the Zen master. Better pack a lunch before you go!

The Eight Gates of Zen

If you study at Zen Mountain Monastery and the Zen Center of New York City (part of the Mountains and Rivers Order of Zen), you will be exposed to the Eight Gates of Zen.

1. *Zazen: Zazen* is the formal seated practice of seated meditation and the "cornerstone of Zen training."
2. Zen Study: Zen is an ancestral lineage, and the Zen teacher is "indispensable in helping to navigate the difficulties along the way, directly pointing to your inherent perfection."

3. Liturgy: An outward manifestation of what is known intuitively, and involves bowing and chanting as expressions of the truths that are cultivated in practice.
4. Art Practice: "Creativity and spirituality share a common source." Art, both traditional and contemporary, can help the practitioner, as with liturgy, to express the truths experienced in Zen practice.
5. Body Practice: Exploring the physical body as a "vehicle for self-realization." These practices range from Tai Chi to eating meals.
6. Buddhist Studies: "Academic study of Buddhist texts and commentaries is an essential part of establishing sound religious practice."
7. Work Practice: Every dimension of life can be "transformed into a sacred activity." Work practice becomes an opportunity to broaden spiritual practice.
8. Right Action: The study and practice of the Buddhist Precepts, "the moral and ethical teachings of the Buddha. Engaging the precepts teaches you to embody compassion as the selfless activity of the awakened mind."

Zazen

The heart of Zen practice is *zazen*. *Zazen* is seated meditation, and the total concentration of mind and body. *Zazen* can be described to you with words, but the words are not *zazen* and you will not have experienced *zazen*. You can study, discuss, and read about *zazen*, but that is not *zazen*.

Instructions for Zen Meditation

In Zen there tends to be a paucity of instruction for meditation technique. Rather, the emphasis is on the posture. The practice is to sit and just sit! But of course, something else is always being added. Shunryu Suzuki encourages a very precise way of sitting that is dignified and stable. You would sit in the lotus or half-lotus posture with your back straight and your hands in your lap, left palm resting on your right palm with your thumbs touching and forming a bridge. This posture is dynamic and full of energy. In some Zen practices, you may be instructed to count your breaths, counting on each exhalation up to ten, and then back from ten to one.

Breathing

In beginning *zazen*, you will pay careful attention to the breath. Breathe in through your nose and out through your nose. Breathe from your diaphragm and feel it rise and fall with your breath. Let your breathing fall naturally, in and out, in and out. Now start to count your out breaths. Breathe in, breathe out, count "one." Breathe in, breathe out, count "two." Continue doing this until you get to ten and begin again. When you notice that you are no longer concentrating on the counting but instead your mind has started to wander to the future or the past, start counting at one again.

Dogen was the founder of the Soto lineage of Buddhism in Japan. Dogen taught a way of sitting called *shikantaza*, which means "just sitting," nothing else—no breath counting, no *koan* practice at all. *Shikantaza* means that sitting *is* enlightened mind. You don't sit to become enlightened; you sit to enjoy your enlightened mind.

Acknowledge the thought and go back to the breath. In and out, one. In and out, two. Continue to do this until the bell rings. You will notice how hard it is to bring the mind back to the breath. The mind can be full of unruly monkeys jumping from tree to tree. Sitting practice helps you to train the monkeys, and eventually make them still.

Being Present

The practice of Zen is the practice of sitting. Just sitting with *nothing* else added. When nothing else is added, you experience your enlightened nature. But, most of the time the mind will be active with thoughts and images. It may get swept away by emotions and stories. Your job is not to get rid of thoughts but to come back. You are learning to be present in the moment.

Try to sit still. Do not move. This may seem impossible at first, but the more you move the more you will want to move. This will require working through discomfort and even pain. Zen is a hard path in this way because it has such a strong emphasis on form. You will learn a lot about yourself by doing so. Sometimes the physical pain can be quite powerful. Not all teachers are strict with posture and suggest moving rather than fighting through pain. But sometimes you'll be moving just out of habit. You will see how you wiggle around to get away from the moment. If you can, sit still as a mountain. *Be* a mountain.

Beginner's Mind

As with all forms of Buddhism, the aim of Zen practice is enlightenment. Zen assumes that you are already enlightened; enlightenment is not something you do or a destination you get to; it's already here. Zen is the here and now. *This* moment. This moment, just as it occurs; just as it is without adding anything to it. Zen is something you experience intuitively. It is not about your rational, intellectual thoughts. In fact, your rational, intellectual thoughts will only get in the way when it comes to Zen practice.

Shunryu Suzuki, in *Zen Mind, Beginner's Mind*, says, "The beginner's mind knows many possibilities, the expert mind few." Having no preconceived notions and a willingness to be open to new experiences is the key to transformation. Having a taste of enlightened mind, you will recognize something you have always had, and somehow lost your connection to. Tasting enlightened mind is like going home.

You have, throughout your life, constructed an idea of who you are. Zen is being in the moment without the "I" construct, the "me" you have created for yourself. Zen exists in the moment with no thought, no ego, bringing nothing to the table. You achieve this realization of emptiness through *zazen*.

Group Practice

The *sangha* is key to Zen practice. The *sangha* usually meets in the zendo, a large hall or room where *zazen* is practiced. When a group gets together to practice, certain rules must apply to ensure that order and the quality of practice is maintained. Each practice group might have its own rules of practice, and there might be some variation. Some of the practices used by a *sangha* might include: walking meditation, a *dharma* talk given by the teacher, tea service, *sutra* recitation, and bowing. Lighting of candles and incense might be part of the *sesshin*, or Zen meditation retreat.

When the teacher gives a talk to the group it is called *teisho*. *Teisho* is not a lecture or a sermon. It is more of a presentation of insight to the students. Often the subject of a *teisho* will be a *koan*. A private encounter with the teacher is called *dokusan*. In *dokusan* the teacher will gauge the student's progress and do what is necessary to encourage the student's practice.

When the Student Is Ready

It is said that when the student is ready, the teacher appears. Although at the heart of Zen is the realization that you are already enlightened, the student/teacher relationship in Zen is a very important element of practice. A teacher will guide the student through the various stages of practice, helping the student toward enlightenment.

Zen is transmitted from person to person. A teacher will have become a teacher through direct transmission from his or her teacher. The teacher in Zen is called the *roshi*.

Sesshin

A *sesshin* is a Zen meditation retreat. *Sesshins* vary greatly in length, from a weekend to several weeks or more. *Zazen* is usually practiced for ten or more hours a day, broken with *kinhin* (walking meditation), work practice, rest periods, *teisho*, and ritualized eating known as *oryoki*. The *sesshin* members rise before dawn and do *zazen* before breakfast and end the day with *zazen*. *Dokusan* is held anywhere from one to three times during the day.

Sesshins are periodic intensive practice sessions to augment daily practice. *Sesshins* are the optimum time to work on *koan* practice (Rinzai) or *shikintaza* (Soto) and the *dokusan* is most helpful and provides encouragement to a flagging spirit. *Sesshins* are extremely difficult and rewarding. They are wonderful opportunities for practice in a safe environment with no distraction except for your own monkey mind.

Mu

Joshu Jushin was a renowned Zen master of the T'ang period in Chinese history. He is best known for his *Mu koan*, but appears in many of the *koans* still in use today. One of the *koans* most frequently assigned to newcomers to Zen practice is *Mu*. *Mu* gained fame from the story of Joshu.

A Zen master said to Joshu, "Does a dog have *buddha-nature*?"

Joshu replied, "Mu!"

Mu is a negative symbol in Chinese meaning, "no-thing."

Opening the Gate

Chanting is an integral component to Zen practice, especially the Heart *Sutra*. It is woven into the ritual fabric of Zen practice. For instance, a formal Zen practice period (in the Soto Zen tradition) will begin with a series of bows followed by the recitation of the Heart *Sutra*. The Heart *Sutra* begins (in transliteration), "MA KA HAN NYA HAR RA MIT TA SHIN GYO" that translates to Great *prajna* (wisdom) *paramita* (transcendental) *sutra*. An excerpt from the text can be translated:

> *Avalokitesvara Bodhisattva practice deep Prajna paramita when perceive five skandas all empty, relieve every suffering. Sariputra, form not different from emptiness. Emptiness not different from form. Form is the emptiness. Emptiness is the form. Sensation, thought, active substance, consciousness, also like this. Sariptura, this is everything original character; not born, no annihilated not tainted, not pure, does not increase does not decrease. Therefore in emptiness no form, no sensation, thought, active substance, consciousness. No eye, ear, nose, tongue body, mind; no color, sound smell, taste, touch, object.*

Once the chant is complete, another series of bows are made. These prostrations, while done in front of an image of the Buddha, are not meant as idol worship. The Buddha sits as a symbol of human potential and your nature as an awakened being, and serves as a reminder of that possibility. The ritual of bowing and chanting creates a gate that the participants go through to mark the beginning of the formal practice period. Silence is maintained. While the participants do not talk with one another, the practice of Zen is communal.

ESSENTIAL

Walking meditation in Zen is called *kinhin*. *Zazen* is often broken up with a period or periods of *kinhin* to stretch the legs and give them some relief. The walking meditation is very slow and the steps are usually synchronized with the breath so that you step with the in-breath and step with the out-breath.

At the beginning of each sitting (that may last approximately forty-five minutes), each participant bows to the wall, turns 180 degrees clockwise, and waits until everyone in the room has done likewise. When everyone is standing ready to bow (hand in *gassho*—prayer position), then everyone bows together, turns 180 degrees clockwise again, and sits down on their cushion. At the end of the sitting meditation period, the bell rings and everyone arises from meditation, first arranging their sitting space neatly, bows to the wall (Zen is practiced facing the wall), and turns 180 degrees as before and waits for everyone to be ready to bow, and then the group bows together as one. A typical meditation period may last two and a half to three hours with alternating periods of sitting and walking (*kinhin*) and is followed by a group meal known as *oryoki*.

Oryoki

At a *vipassana* meditation retreat participants eat in slow, isolated silence. Like eating at a *vipassana* retreat, the Zen meal continues silent practice but in communal form, and with speed variations. Everyone assembles around the table. For example, at the Shao Shan Spiritual Practice Center (a Soto Zen Temple) in East Calais, Vermont, the group may be approximately ten people. Once everyone has arrived in the kitchen, the group, standing, places their hands in *gassho* and bows. Once seated, Japanese-style on the floor, the Zen master claps wooden sticks together to mark the start of the meal practice, and there is another *gassho*. Now the food is served. A simple meal is offered for lunch of homemade squash soup, hummus, some greens, and steamed bread.

The Food Service

The food service is an exercise in remaining attentive. Participants are required to pay keen attention to maintain the group harmony. The Zen master serves the soup from a large pot. The person furthest from her sits with hands in *gassho* watching. When enough has been served, the hand is lifted towards the sky to signal "enough." That bowl is then passed back along the participants until it reaches that person, who sets it down. This process is repeated until everyone has soup. Then the hummus is passed around in a bowl. The people on one side of the table become the servers. You serve the person sitting across from you, who sits in *gassho* and raises one hand when enough has been served. You then serve yourself and pass the bowl to the person next to you. The bread is served in the same way. Once all the food has been served, the meal chant is recited in Japanese:

Hitatsu ni wa, ko no tasho o hakori, kano raisho o hakaru

Futatsu ni wa onore ga taku gyo no zen ketto nakatte k ni ozu

Mitsu ni wa, shin o fusegi toga o wanaruru koto wa tonto o Shu to sa

Yatsu niw a, masa I ryo yaku o Kot to suru wa gyoko o ryozen ga

Itatsu ni wa, jodo no tame no yue ni, ima Kono jiki o uku.

These five stanzas roughly translate to:

This meal is the labor of countless beings; let us remember their toil

Defilements are many, exertions few; do we deserve this offering?

Gluttony stems from greed; let us be moderate.

Our life is sustained by this offering; let us be grateful.

We take this food to attain the Buddhaway.

To recite the meal chant is to become intentional about eating. The goal is to be awake while food is consumed and to come out of the trance where eating is taken for granted. The first stanza reminds you that countless events took place in order to get this food to the table that you are about to eat. It had to be prepared, bought, delivered to the store, planted in the ground, nurtured by rain, sun, and bacteria, and so forth. It is a reminder of the interconnected web of life and also a reminder that events do not occur out of this interconnected context. This helps to foster appreciation for the unique gift this food represents.

The second stanza asks you to reflect upon your efforts to date and to see where your effort may be strong or where it needs improvement. The third stanza is self-explanatory and at a deeper level resonates the Buddha's message of the Middle Way. Remember, in his own path he experienced both extremes of indulgence and starvation. Moderation with food is a reminder of moderation in all things, avoiding extremes whenever possible. The fourth stanza reminds you that this food is vital to your survival, to nourish the body with nutrients. And the fifth stanza builds on the fact of the fourth stanza to put that nourishment to good use—to use it to work towards awakening.

And you thought you were just having lunch! Once the meal chant is recited and the reflections on its meaning made, there is one more step: the food offering. Everyone takes a small bit of bread and places it into a bowl. Later, the group will go for a walk and offer this bread to the fish living in the pond near the Zendo. Then eating begins!

The Eating Process

Unlike *vipassana* meditation retreats where eating made be a very slow process, the group eats at relatively normal rate. One must be efficient and mindful of others while eating. Once the Master has finished her portion, an offering of seconds is made. Everyone stops eating and the process of serving begins anew. Once everyone who wants seconds is served, another *gassho* is performed and then everyone resumes eating. As with bowing before and after meditation, this is a group process and the meal does not end until everyone has finished eating. This communality is a natural deterrent to gluttony, because no one wants to be the last one eating when everyone else is finished!

The meal ends with tea served as the hummus and bread were served; you serve the person across from you and then serve yourself. Then a serving tray is passed for the dishes and each of the participants wipes their portion of the table. Then *gassho.* Then standing. Then *gassho.* Lunch is now over and the entire process has been conducted in noble silence—when it goes smoothly, no words or eye contact is exchanged.

Eating the meal in this ritualized way provides continuity to the practice and functions as a living reminder that all moments can be lived with intention. The entire Zen practice is an invitation to awaken. After lunch, a volunteer is solicited or someone is appointed the opportunity to do work practice by washing the dishes. Then a communal walk to make the food offering takes place. Then *zazen* practice resumes. This is a taste of the way of Zen.

CHAPTER 13

Buddhist Practice

Meditation is an elemental part of Buddhism. The various schools of Buddhism approach meditation differently; however, mindfulness is a common core. For Westerners, meditation is one of the key attractive features of Buddhism, providing a methodology for personal transformation. Meditation provides an antidote to problems of self that Westerners find so vexing. Buddhism also provides a philosophical system that speaks to many people who want to live a life less ruled by greed, hatred, and delusion.

Why Meditate?

Meditation can transform your life. It can change your brain and it can reduce stress and anxiety, help you to sleep better, energize you, make you more patient, get you in touch with how you feel both emotionally and physically, provide a quiet space in your day, and much more. Meditation is the method the Buddha used to reach his own awakening, to cut through the veils of illusion to find unconditioned existence.

John Daido Loori Roshi, the late Abbott of Zen Mountain Monastery in Mt. Tremper, New York, told a story about visitors coming to the monastery. People frequently came in to see the building, which was a national and state historic landmark. The monastery is nestled among acres of fields and forest in the Catskill Mountains. The visitors often ask if they can watch a *zazen* session, if they can stand quietly and witness the meditation. Abbott Daido always said no. *Zazen* may look peaceful on the outside, but inside it can be anything but peaceful for the one who is sitting. Picture a calm lake, the water completely still, like glass—serenity. But underneath those still waters can be a tumult of activity. Getting to the stillness on the inside takes some work.

According to the meditation teacher Shinzen Young, mindfulness meditation provides three benefits:

- Sensory clarity
- Concentration
- Equanimity

Twenty minutes a day can change your life. If meditation improves sensory clarity and your experiences are twenty percent richer than they were before meditation, then the twenty minutes per day you spend meditating actually increases how much life you experience. What if meditation made things twice as rich? You can do the math! Improved concentration is another benefit of meditation. Can you use more concentration in your life? Would your work performance improve? Your relationships? Your golf game? Equanimity is the ability to handle any situation with a matter-of-fact and engaged attention. It is the ability to be calm in the midst of a storm. Meditation helps to cultivate equanimity along with sensory clarity and concentration.

Meditation Gear

Of course you don't actually need any supplies to meditate, but traditionally many Buddhists have things that accompany their meditation routines, from altars and incense to cushions and bells. Here are some supplies you might want to consider:

- A meditation cushion (*zafu*)
- A cushion to put your meditation cushion upon (*zabuton*)
- Incense
- Timer, bell, or Tibetan singing bowl
- Altar
- Altar cloth
- Candles
- Flowers
- Devotional objects such as a statue of the Buddha
- Prayer beads

Buddhists call their meditation cushions *zafus*. Zen practitioners traditionally have round *zafus* and Tibetan practitioners usually have square *zafus*. The *zafu* can be placed on a *zabuton,* which is a large, flat, square cushion that protects the knees from the floor.

Traditionally, incense is burned for the duration of the meditation. Incense can be used as a timer for meditation sessions. Once the incense is burned, the time is up. This could be one of the original uses for incense. Incense also covered unpleasant body odors that may have arisen during meditation sessions, and helped keep flies out of the *zendo.* An altar is used for several reasons. First, repetition, habit, and ceremony play a large part in meditation practice. The altar is a visual reminder of the importance of practice. It is an indicator of your commitment to practice. And an altar sets the stage for energizing the senses: gazing at the Buddha, smelling the incense, bowing or doing prostrations all combine to form a context for the practice itself.

If possible, it is a good idea to have the altar in a room or part of a room you will not use for any other purpose. If this is not possible, the altar can be in a corner of a room that can be accessed for practice. If you choose to have an altar, make it your own. You might find altars configured in the following way. A Buddha statue is placed in the center of the altar to focus attention on the two Jewels of the Buddha and the *dharma*. Implements (such as bells or a *vajra*) are placed to the side of the Buddha. The incense and incense holder are placed in the center of the altar. You can put incense in an incense holder or fill a small bowl with rice to hold the incense stick. Flowers can be placed on the altar to symbolize the nature of impermanence. A candle can also be placed to one side. The candle symbolizes the light of truth brightening the darkness of delusion.

A timer or Tibetan singing bowl would stay by your *zafu* and *zabuton* and would be struck to begin and end the meditation sessions. You can follow the sound of the bell with your mind and start your meditation.

FACT

Tibetan singing bowls traditionally come with a striker and a silk-covered cushion to rest the bowl on. They come in a variety of sizes from quite small to large. You can use a Tibetan singing bowl to mark time, as an alarm, a timer, or to hold your incense sticks.

Prayer beads and devotional objects can be placed on the altar, and prayer beads would be held during Tibetan-style meditation. Prayer beads traditionally came from the wood of the Bodhi Tree. A typical strand of prayer beads would have 108 beads on a strand. Similar to a rosary, these prayer beads are used in the practice of *japa*, repeating a *mantra* such as *Om mani padme hum*, using the beads to keep track of the number of repetitions. Different schools of Buddhism use different meditation items.

Posture

In virtually all Buddhist meditations, you are required to take a specific posture. Put on some comfortable clothing and take off your shoes. Sit with your legs crossed, in lotus (legs crossed with each foot on the opposite thigh), or half lotus (one foot on the opposite thigh and the other foot folded on the floor) position if you can. Put the *zafu* underneath you and sit forward on it so that your knees are touching the ground, if possible. You can also put the cushion between your legs or sit on a special small bench and kneel with the majority of your weight resting on the cushion so your legs don't fall asleep. This is called sitting *seiza*. If you are flexible enough, you can also sit Burmese-style (both legs folded and flat on the floor with either the right or left foot forward), or seated in a chair with back straight and feet firmly on the floor. If your knees do not reach the floor you may want to place a towel or another cushion underneath to support them. Make sure you are in a quiet space with no distractions such as television, radio, or other people who are not practicing.

ESSENTIAL

For thousands of years, yogis have perfected postures for supporting meditation. The ultimate of these is the lotus position. The lotus position is not readily attained, but if you are interested, sit on the floor with your legs stretched out in front, slightly apart. Place your right foot on your left thigh with the sole facing up. Your right knee should now rest on the floor. Take your left foot and place it high on your right thigh with the sole facing up. Your left knee should now rest on the floor. This will be difficult at first and you should be careful not to strain yourself.

Keep your spine as straight as possible and the top of your head pointed toward the ceiling. Rest your hands in your lap, palms up, with one hand cradling the other. Touch your thumbs gently together. You can also rest your hands palms up or palms down on your thighs. Your lips touch lightly and your tongue can gently touch the roof of your mouth. Make sure you are not holding tension in your shoulders or anywhere else. Your eyes can be open or closed. If open, try to relax them and loosen their focus.

Set a time limit for your meditation and use a bell, timer, or incense to indicate when time is up. You can start with very short periods, such as ten minutes, building up to longer periods of sitting as you continue practicing.

When your timer goes off or your sitting time is over, be careful that you do not jump to stand up. Often your legs can go to sleep and if you stand up quickly you might fall over. Take your time, shake out your legs, and then stand slowly. You may want to bow to honor the practice you just completed.

It may help to do light stretching before getting into your meditation position. If you go to a practice center you will get further instructions.

The Breath

Awareness of breathing is fundamental to Buddhist-style meditation. The breath is your constant companion and if you're not breathing, becoming enlightened is not going to be your top priority! Breathing is also happening now and will help to bring you into the present moment and into your body as it is now. You will taste the sense of being a living, breathing human being (rather than a human "doing," which you may be most of the time). Every breath you take is colored by your emotional experience and so familiarizing yourself with the process of breathing helps you to monitor your emotional state and to intervene early if anxiety or other distressing emotions arise. When you breathe, allow the process to be natural. Don't try to breathe a "meditative" breath, whatever that might be for you. You will probably find that your breathing will slow naturally and that is fine. If it doesn't that is also fine. Just notice the breathing that is happening now.

Shamatha Meditation

There are different techniques for meditation. *Zazen*, or Zen meditation, was covered in the previous chapter. Two other types of meditation are *shamatha* meditation and *vipassana* meditation. *Shamatha* means "calm abiding" or "dwelling in tranquility," and *vipassana* means "insight." *Vipassana* is therefore also called "insight meditation." Most Buddhist traditions employ these as central practices (that is, Theravada) or as component practices (for example, Tibetan).

The *Sathipathana Suta* provides very detailed instructions on breathing mediation with sixteen different ways to attend to breathing. These myriad ways of attending to breathing are outlined in Larry Rosenberg's classic book, *Breath by Breath: The Liberating Practice of Insight Meditation.*

Shamatha meditation techniques involve concentration on one thing in particular, whether it is your breath or the sound of rain. "Calm abiding" means sitting with one's breath, or other point of concentration, gently coming back to this point whenever attention wanders. Concentration is the foundation for later insight practices and is not the final goal. Remember that Siddhartha was able to reach very high states of concentration and these did not lead to his final awakening. But concentration is valuable as the foundation for awakening.

The benefits of one-pointed concentration are many. You can make great progress in any undertaking you choose if you have the ability to focus diligently on the task at hand. *Shamatha* meditation has you focus on one point calmly and quietly without undue exertion. The quality of this concentration is firm but not forced. Think of holding a bird in your hand. If you hold it too loosely, it will fly away. If you hold it too tight, you will crush it. Pursue concentration along the Middle Way, with effort, zeal, and interest.

Vipassana Meditation

As compared to one-pointed concentration, *vipassana* meditation—insight meditation—is a more open awareness. Attention is directed to whatever arises in the field of experience. In the Burmese tradition, the field of awareness is limited to the body, and in the Thai tradition, for example, the field of awareness is open to any mental content including thoughts, images, feelings, sights, and sounds, in addition to bodily sensations. Attention to the arising and fading away of bodily sensations or other experiences will show you impermanence in action. It will show you how these experiences are "empty" of any underlying substantial reality. You will experience yourself in a dramatic new way.

The *Visudhimagga* (Path of Purity), written in the fifth century by Buddhagosa, outlines hundreds of pages on various kinds of mindfulness meditation practice. The two most basic categories are *shamatha* (calming) and *vipassana* (insight).

Shamatha is the foundation for *vipassana* meditation. Once your mind is still and calm, you will have the ability to watch whatever arises in your mind. Once the mind is quiet, you can notice when your mind wanders off. If your mind is perfectly still, you can abide with your breath. If your mind wanders off, just observe where it goes. When you catch your mind wandering away, you can do one of two things, and the instructions will vary according to your teacher's tradition.

One approach is simply to come back to whatever is happening in the body and to move away from the story of the thoughts to the recognition that thoughts are happening. Another approach is to give the mental content a label. This practice is called mental noting. So if thoughts arise, note "thoughts" or "thinking." You just stick a label on it and move on to the next moment. Mental noting helps you to be objective with your experience and avoid self-judgment. If you notice judgment is active, such as when you are criticizing yourself for attention wandering, note this "judgment" and move your attention from the judgment to the next breath.

Other Forms of Meditation

Shamatha and *vipassana* are the basic Buddhist meditation practices. *Vipassana* can also be taken "on the road" in the form of walking meditation. There are also other practices based on the Four Immeasurables, such as lovingkindness and compassion. There are also other meditative techniques such as visualization, *mantras*, and chanting.

Lovingkindness (*Metta*) Meditation

The Buddha said, "You can search through the entire universe for someone who is more deserving of your love and affection than you are yourself, and that person is not to be found anywhere. You yourself, as much as anybody in the entire universe deserve your love and affection."

Compassion, generosity, open-heartedness, and lovingkindness are all wonderful qualities to acquire, and are what the Buddha called the Four Immeasurables or Heavenly abodes. What is lovingkindness, or as it is sometimes translated, lovingfriendliness? *Metta* (lovingkindness) practice is a curious hybrid of Buddhist and yoga practices. Instead of just working with whatever arises as you would in *vipassana*, you intentionally direct your attention to the generation of loving feelings. To do this, you may bring to mind someone who is very dear to you, someone whom you can readily access loving feelings for. You can feel how this suffuses your heart with love and a sense of openness. Depending on the specific teacher, you will direct that loving feeling in various ways. There are some commonalities. With that loving feeling, you would direct it to others and with four specific intentions:

- May you be free from danger; May you be safe
- May you have happiness; May you have peace
- May you have physical well-being and health; May you be free from illness
- May you have ease of well-being; May you be free from unnecessary struggle and pain

You direct these feelings towards yourself as well. You might start with a loved one where making these wishes is easy. You could then go to a stranger and offer the stranger the same intentions. Then you could move on to a more difficult person. Perhaps someone you are angry at or someone who has harmed you in the past. And, again, the practice is to direct these loving feelings toward them.

Tara Brach teaches a form of *metta* meditation that has spoken to the "trance of unworthiness" that afflicts so many in the West. This lack of self-acceptance is humorously and compassionately explored in her bestselling book, *Radical Acceptance: Embracing Your Life with the Heart of a Buddha*. She is the founder and senior teacher of the Insight Meditation Community of Washington.

You might be thinking this is an incredibly difficult task. But this is the real challenge of *metta*, being open and loving towards everyone, even your enemies. The Dalai Lama practices lovingkindness towards the Chinese, so you could try to be open to the difficult people in your life. The secret is that this is really good for you. Staying in a state of unforgiveness towards people and situations leads to elevated stress levels and can damage your health. You can expand the circle of *metta* further to your *sangha*, your community, your country, the world, and all sentient beings.

Another meditation that focuses on compassion is called *tonglen*—sending and receiving. Pema Chödrön writes about *tonglen* in *When Things Fall Apart*. *Tonglen*, she says, is "designed to awaken *bodhicitta*, to put us in touch with genuine noble heart. It is the practice of taking in pain and sending out pleasure and therefore completely turns around our well-established habit of doing just the opposite." The way to practice *tonglen* is to breathe in suffering—your own suffering, the suffering of others, those with disease, with heartache, with pain—and breathe out wellness and kindness and direct it toward others, toward yourself. Breathe in pain, breathe out healing. Breathe in hatred, breathe out love. In this manner, you cultivate *bodhicitta* and awaken a compassionate spirit inside yourself.

Mantra Meditation

Mantras are often used as meditation devices by Buddhists. A *mantra* is basically a sound vibration. A constant repetition of a *mantra* (whether silent or aloud) can help to clear the mind of debris. Distractions fall away as the mind focuses on the repetitive sound. You can use a specific *mantra* for a specific spiritual purpose or you can use the *mantra* in a general way for focusing the attention and clearing the mind.

Different vehicles of Buddhism tend toward using different *mantras*:

▼ MANTRAS

Tradition	Mantra	Translation
Pure Land	Namo Amito	Glory to Amitabha
Tibetan	Om mani padme hum	Jewel in the Lotus
Nichiren	Namu myoho renge kyo	Glory to the Lotus Sutra

For example, according to Gen Rinpoche, *Om mani padme hum* is associated with Avalokiteshvara, the *bodhisattva* of compassion. This *mantra* has six syllables. Each of the six syllables is said to aid you in the perfection of the six *paramitas* of the *bodhisattvas*. The six *paramitas* are: generosity, ethics, patience, perseverance, concentration, and wisdom. Chanting the *mantra Om mani padme hum* will help you master these six perfections. Mastering these six perfections will help you to become a more compassionate person.

Chanting

The Buddha discouraged attachment to rites and rituals. Nevertheless, all of the Buddhist traditions engage chanting of liturgical texts. To chant the texts is to concentrate the mind and to send a powerful vibration into the atmosphere surrounding you. Chanting in a group can be a very powerful experience. In Tibetan Vajrayana practices, chanting rituals can last for hours. Traditional Buddhists will chant *mantras* and *sutras* for the accumulation of merit.

The Triple Refuge Chant is popular in many traditions. You recite the phrase, "I take refuge in the *Buddha*, I take refuge in the *dharma*, I take refuge in the *sangha*" three times.

Buddham saranam gacchami

Dhammam saranam gacchami

Sangham saranam gacchami

Dutiyampi Buddham saranam gacchami

Dutiyampi Dhammam saranam gacchami

Dutiyampi Sangham saranam gacchami

Tatiyampi Buddham saranam gacchami

Tatiyampi Dhammam saranam gacchami

Tatiyampi Sangham saranam gacchami

Chanting sacred texts can help to secure a favorable rebirth, and families with this belief will enjoin a Buddhist monk to recite *sutras* at the time of death. These texts will be heard by the deceased in the bardo state. The monk will chant from the classic text the *Bardo Thodol* (The *Liberation Through Hearing in the Intermediate State* and popularly known as the *Tibetan Book of the Dead*). The *bardo* is an intermediate state, a way station of sorts that will determine the place of the dead person's rebirth. What happens during this forty-nine day period is believed to be crucial for the rebirth. So, too, the moment of death is crucial for what comes next, so the Tibetans undergo a great deal of preparation for this moment. The *Bardho Thodol* and practices such as *Powa* are detailed field manuals preparing for this moment.

Visualization

Visualization is a key practice in Vajrayana (Tibetan Buddhism). In visualization practice you would select an object to visualize such as the Buddha, *bodhisattvas*, *mandalas* (cosmic diagrams of the spiritual realm) or other sacred objects and concentrate on that image in the image space of your mind (that is the mental screen that appears to be around where your forehead is). In these practices, rather than letting the imagination run wild into future and past scenarios, it is recruited to aid practice. Visualization can help you to achieve mindfulness and spiritual empowerment by taking on the qualities of the imagined deities, changing habit patterns of mind, and so forth.

According to Buddhist scholar Michael Willis, *mandala* literally means "circle" or "enclosure," but they represent more than this—a sort of cosmic diagram that provides a structure to guide meditation practice. A typical *mandala* would have outer rings of concentric circles representing the oceans and mountains. Inside these circles would be a square form with four gates, one on each side representing the cardinal directions. Each has its own characteristic color: white for the east, red for the west, green for the north, and yellow for the south. In the middle of the form resides a special meditation deity.

Willis explains, "Elaborate *mandalas* painted on cloth scrolls or on temple walls were once common in many parts of the Himalayas, the best preserved examples being found in Buhtan, Nepal, and those parts of India which are culturally Tibetan, such as Ladakh."

The most spectacular *mandalas* are also the most ephemeral. Tibetan Buddhists monks will labor for weeks creating an elaborate *mandala* made of colored sand. These *mandalas* can be six, eight, or ten feet in diameter. Once completed, the sand is swept away in a closing ritual and then deposited in a nearby body of water.

Visualization was practiced in China in the late fourth and early fifth centuries from texts that were newly authored at that time. Here, practitioners would meditate on images such as the "Medicine King." Visual contemplation of Amitabha Buddha became a central component of Pure Land Buddhism in sixth century Chinese Buddhism. These practices had many forms. To visualize the Buddha in your mind is to make your mind Buddha.

Walking Meditation

Zen walking meditation, *kinhin*, was covered in the last chapter, and walking meditation is not particular to Zen practice. Walking meditation is a wonderful complement to seated meditation, mindfulness, or *mantra* practice. Walking meditation is a way to practice mindfulness while moving around the world you inhabit. If you leave your meditation on the floor with your *zafu*, you won't make as much progress as you will if you take it with you into your day.

Because walking meditation proved so beneficial, the Buddha and his disciples used it in their practice. In Thailand, walking meditation is such a fundamental part of practice that a walk is built into each meditation center for the monks' use. There are obvious physical benefits to walking meditation as well. Even slow walking provides stretching and a respite to the strenuousness of prolonged seated practice. Walking meditation can rejuvenate the mind and the body. Walking aids concentration, digestion, promotes physical fitness, and rejuvenates the body—all the while still practicing mindfulness.

CHAPTER 14

Ceremony and Celebration

For some, Buddhism is principally a meditation practice and a way of living life that strives to maximize wakefulness and minimize suffering. For others, Buddhism is religion and central to their cultural heritage. In the West, you have a choice. You can approach Buddhism as a secular practice of meditation and ethics, or you can elaborate this into a cultural affiliation with a sectarian form of Buddhism such as Tibetan Buddhism or Zen. This chapter looks at some of the ceremonies and celebrations you can find in the Buddhist world.

Pilgrimage

On his deathbed, the Buddha instructed his followers to visit the important sites from his life, the places of his birth, enlightenment, first sermon, and death, because these would inspire powerful emotions and propel their practice. These places were imbued with a magical sense and the Buddha suggested that dying in one of these places with a serenely joyful heart would guarantee a good rebirth.

This "sacred geography" was expanded by the dissemination of the Buddha's remains and other relics. Subsequently, mountains became sacred pilgrimage sites, including Mt. Kailsh in Tibet, Mt. Fuji in Japan, Mt. Wutai in China, and "Adam's Peak" in Sri Lanka. Tibetan pilgrims may circumambulate long distances making full-body prostrations. Some of these journeys may be hundreds of miles and take years to complete, one prostration at a time. To protect themselves, the pilgrims wear leather aprons and hand and knee protectors. Pilgrimage is a special form of practice, away from daily routines; the pilgrim brings the intention of devotion to the journey.

"These, Ananda, are the places that a devout person should visit and look upon with feelings of reverence. And truly there will come to these places, Ananda, devoted monks and nuns, laymen and laywomen, reflecting: 'Here the Tathagata was born! Here the Tathagata became fully enlightened in unsurpassed, supreme Enlightenment!'"
—The Buddha

The Sennichi Kaihogyo

A May 2010 NPR news story, "Monk's Enlightenment Begins with a Marathon Walk," presents an intriguing account of walking Japanese Zen monks. These monks aren't going for a stroll. One monk completes the "Sennichi Kaihogyo, 1,000 days of walking meditation and prayer over a seven-year period around Mount Hiei. He walked twenty-six miles a day for periods of either 100 or 200 consecutive days." That's the equivalent of a trip around the earth. Japanese Zen is notorious for such feats, but the Sennichi Kaihogyo is a walk in the park compared with the "test" that occurs 700 days into the process.

Here, he "prays nonstop for nine days, without eating, drinking, sleeping or even lying down. It's a near-death experience, the monk says." Such a test burns away all traces of self-related story and resistance and provides the practitioner with an unencumbered look at existence. This is an existential experience of purity and one must be willing to relinquish everything to have it. "Finally, his old self dies, at least figuratively, and he is reborn to help and lead all beings to enlightenment."

This extreme experience cuts away at the illusion of separation, helping the monk to pursue his *bodhisattva* path—working for the betterment of all sentient beings. Such experiences are the equivalent of Buddhist Olympics and not the sort of thing that you might contemplate or practice on a daily basis. They are certainly not necessary for you to have a taste of that interconnectedness with everything and everyone around you. Certainly, the Buddha spent a lot of time walking around northern India with his retinue of followers, and walking meditation is an important practice for mindfulness. So, you can embody this spirit each time we walk in a deliberate manner. As a lay practitioner, you may not have the time to spend 1,000 days walking the equivalent of a marathon each day, but as Tich Nhat Hanh said, "peace can be in every step."

A pilgrimage is much more than a holiday with a spiritual destination. A pilgrimage is a journey to a shrine or sacred place that can change the traveler in an irrevocable way. The Buddha made pilgrimages all over India, traveling from place to place, spreading his teachings. Today, you can walk in the Buddha's footsteps and follow his path. If you are interested in experiencing some of the sacred places in the history of Buddhism, you will have many to choose from.

The Holy Sites of Buddhism

The four holy sites of Buddhism are: Lumbini, the Buddha's birthplace; Bodhgaya, the site of his enlightenment; Sarnath, the site of the First Sermon; and Kushinagara, where the Buddha died. This list is not comprehensive. You can also visit Sri Lanka, Myanmar, Bhutan, China, Taiwan, Tibet, Thailand, Vietnam, Japan, Korea, and more. The Buddha himself may not have left footsteps in these countries, but Buddhist culture and history is rich and there are many wonderful places to experience.

Nepal

The Buddha was born in Lumbini in what is now Nepal. Places of interest to visit in Lumbini include Lumbini Garden, which contains the Ashokan Pillar and the image of Queen Maya (Maya Devi); Puskarni, the sacred pool; Sanctum-Sanctorum of the Birthplace; and the Buddhist Temple. The Ashokan Pillar was erected by King Ashoka in homage to the Buddha and contains an inscription dedicating the site to the Shakyamuni.

The image of Maya Devi is inscribed into a pagoda-like structure. The image itself is in bas-relief and pictures Maya holding onto the baby Buddha who is standing on a lotus petal. Puskarni is the sacred pool in which it is said that Maya bathed the baby Siddhartha soon after he was born. Sanctum-Sanctorum is the holiest of places in the garden—within the Sanctum-Sanctorum is a stone slab that marks the exact spot the Buddha was born. Also of interest is the nearby Buddhist Temple. And not too far from Lumbini is Kapilavastu, where Siddhartha's father, Suddhodhana, had his palace.

India

Bodh Gaya is, perhaps, the most important of the pilgrimage sites, the place where Siddhartha attained awakening under the pipal tree. This Bodhi Tree (tree of awakening) is believed to be the ancestor of the tree that currently grows in Bodh Gaya next to the great *stupa* at the Mahabodhi temple. Cuttings from the original tree have been planted around the Buddhist world and temples erected next to them.

Ashoka set up the first building in Bodh Gaya in the third century B.C.E. The current Mahabodhi temple was built in the sixth century C.E. on the orders of the Sri Lankan monk, Mahanama. Today, the temple has been restored and is a great icon of Buddhist devotion. For example, in 1985, His Holiness the Dalai Lama came to Bodh Gaya to give the Kalachakra Tantra ceremony. 250,000 (or two and a half *lakh* in Hindi) Tibetans descended upon this tiny village to participate in this ritual, many of them in exile and others receiving special permission from the Chinese government to attend.

Among them were 10,000 Tibetan Buddhist monks and approximately 1,000 Westerners. This was the Kalachakra Tantra's largest audience to date. The Dalai Lama chose this spot as the most auspicious to offer these teachings, including teachings from Shantideva's *Guide to the Bodhisattva's Way of Life.* Everyone in attendance took the *bodhisattva* vows from His Holiness. The place of Siddhartha's enlightenment is known as the *vajrasana* ("diamond throne").

One of the more well-known Buddhist pilgrims was Hsüan-tsang, a monk from eighth-century China who traveled vastly throughout central and southern Asia and spent many years in India and Sri Lanka studying Buddhism. Hsüan-tsang spent sixteen years in India on a pilgrimage. He studied at Nalanda University and visited all the important Buddhist pilgrimage sites.

You can also see a cave where Siddhartha practiced asceticism and the village of Uruvela, where the young Siddhartha broke his fast after attaining enlightenment.

Sarnath, several miles from Varanasi, is another major pilgrimage site where the Buddha gave his First Sermon in the Deer Park and started the wheel of *dharma* turning. Sites of interest in Sarnath include Ashoka's Pillar (which used to have the Lion Capital on top of it that now resides in the Sarnath Museum), the ruins of the Mulagandhakuti, and the enormous Dharmek Stupa—a tower that dates back to the fifth or sixth century.

To the east is the modern Mulagandhakuti Vihara, which is said to house the original relics of the Buddha in a silver casket. The casket was recovered from the ruins of the first-century temple. The temple has beautifully painted walls that depict the Buddha's life story. The Sarnath Museum contains some of the greatest treasures of Indian Buddhist art. There is also an archaeological museum and the remains of a monastery from the third century B.C.E.

Also of interest in India is Rajgir, the home of Vulture Peak, the site of many of the Buddha's teachings.

Kushinagara is the site of the Buddha's death. It is here in the Sala Grove that he reached *paranirvana* and passed into death. Places of interest in Kushinagara include the Nirvana Stupa, built over the spot where the Buddha died; the Makutabandhana Stupa, which marks the place of the Buddha's cremation; and a large stone reclining Buddha, housed in the Nirvana Temple.

Tea Ceremonies

Most Westerners think of tea as a breakfast drink or something to enjoy with crumpets at four o'clock in the afternoon. Most drink tea in a cup with a bag or an infuser and maybe a garnish of lemon and honey or a little bit of milk and sugar. In Zen Buddhism, tea is a ritual. Once you experience tea the Zen way, you will never look at a cup of tea quite the same way. Tea is ceremony itself.

Tea was originally used as a medicine, not a beverage. It was not only taken internally, but externally as well. Rubbing some tea in paste form on joints was thought to alleviate joint pain.

The tea ceremony is called *chanoyu.* It translates into "hot water for tea." *Chanoyu* is based on the principles of respect, harmony, purity, and tranquility. If you could bring these qualities into your everyday life, your life would be filled with utter peace. Everyone in the tearoom is equal, and great respect is paid to each person present. Everything in the tearoom matters, from the air you breathe to the flower arrangement to the actual space it is served in—everything contributes to the enjoyment of each moment of the tea ceremony.

The rules for the tea ceremony are to be followed exactly. Each moment matters, and the sequence of events is laid out rigidly. The ceremony flows, and there is meaning in every gesture; each moment is to be savored. The tea ceremony is the way of life itself. It captures the essence of Zen—life in the moment with great attention.

In this regard, the tea ceremony is a mindfulness meditation. It is a moving meditation, practiced to cultivate *samadhi*. The repetition and rigidity of action allows you to enter a deep meditative state, as you know each movement. As you perform each part of the ceremony, you do so with mindfulness, paying careful attention to each and every movement. When you whisk, you whisk. When you pour, you pour. When you drink, you drink.

"In the liquid amber within the ivory-porcelain, the initiated may touch the sweet reticence of Confucius, the piquancy of Lao-Tzu, and the ethereal aroma of Shakyamuni himself."—Okakura Kakuzo

In *The Book of Tea* by Okakura Kakuzo, the author says there are actually schools of tea. These schools can be classified as Boiled Tea, Whipped Tea, and Steeped Tea. Practioners in the West would fall into the latter category. Caked tea is boiled, powdered tea is whipped, and leaf tea is steeped.

Vocabulary

First is an introduction to the vocabulary of the tea ceremony. The tea ceremony takes place in the *chashitsu*—a room designed for the tea ceremony. This room is usually in the teahouse itself, which is usually within the gardens. Here are some other words you will want to familiarize yourself with:

- *Sayu*—hot water with which to make tea
- *Furo*—brazier (a pan for holding hot or burning coals)
- *Chabana*—tea flower arrangement
- *Fukusa*—a cleansing cloth, usually a square of silk, folded into a triangle, which hangs from the host's sash
- *Kama*—a container for boiling water (kettle)
- *Kashi*—sweet candy snack
- *Mizusashi*—container for cold water
- *Chawan*—tea bowl

- *Chakin*—napkin
- *Chashaku*—scoop for tea
- *Chaki*—tea container
- *Kensui*—water waste container with futaoki (lid rest)
- *Hishaku*—water ladle

In order to have a tea ceremony, you will also need the tea and charcoal for the fire.

Procedure

The guests are greeted by the host and ushered into the tearoom. The guests take their seats and the *kashi* is served and eaten. The *kama* has been set on the *furo* so that the water can boil. Then the host brings items necessary to start preparation of the tea. First he brings over the tea bowl containing the wiping napkin, the whisk, the tea scoop, and the container holding the tea. He then brings over the wastewater container, which holds the lid rest and the water ladle. The lid rest should be placed near the kettle with the water ladle on top of it. The lid rest is used to hold the lid of the kettle and is usually made of green bamboo. Now the host is ready to start preparations.

The host takes the *fukusa* and wipes the tea scoop and the tea container. This is done with intense concentration as the host's focus on meditation increases. This cleansing gesture signifies to the guests that everything is clean and the host cares about the purity of the service. Taking the ladle in hand, he scoops hot water out of the kettle and pours it into the tea bowl, and the whisk is then rinsed in the water. The water is then poured into the wastewater container, the bowl is cleaned with the wiping cloth, and the cloth is put back in its place. Now the tea can be made.

The tea used in the tea ceremony is powdered tea, so it has to be whipped. The host picks up the tea container in his left hand and the scoop in his right, and puts three scoops of tea into the tea bowl from the tea container. The water ladle is filled nearly to the brim with hot water, and enough water is added to the tea to make a paste. More water is added as necessary to get the correct consistency for the tea. The tea is briskly whisked, and then the host picks up the tea bowl and places it on top of his left palm. He holds the right side of the bowl with his right hand, then turns it twice away from himself, a full turn of the wrist each time, so that the front of the bowl is facing away from the host. Then the tea bowl is placed in front of the guests, and the first guest picks up the bowl and holds it the same way.

The tea ceremony traces its origins to the fifteenth century and conversations between Zen monks and the nobility. The goal is to combine aesthetics with meditative calm. The monk Shuko formulated the four principles. Sen no Rikyu changed the *chanoyu* from opulence to elegant simplicity in the sixteenth century. The door to the newly designed *chashitsu* was so low that participants had to bow on their way in. Samurai were asked to leave their swords outside. The interior was blank with the exception of a single piece of art.

The first guest to pick up the bowl will turn to the next guest, *gassho,* and offer the tea bowl. The guest will bow back and decline. Then she will *gassho* to the host, pick up the bowl and hold it in the same way. She raises it a little bit while bowing again to show gratitude, then turns the bowl toward herself. She then drinks from the side of the bowl.

She wipes off the bowl with her thumb and finger and then turns the bowl back to the front. She admires the craftsmanship of the bowl—tea bowls are a work of art and the choosing of the tea bowl is part of the beauty of the ceremony—and returns the bowl to the host, turning it so the front of the bowl faces the host. Before she returns the bowl, she can ask questions about the bowl, such as "Where was this bowl made?" and "Does this bowl have a name?" The host pours water into the tea bowl, swirling it around to cleanse the bowl, then pours the water into the wastewater container.

The process is repeated for the next guest. When the last guest has had tea, the host cleans the tea bowl with the cold water and reverses the process. In the winter and spring months, a *ro* (a sunken hearth) is used instead of the *furo,* which is used the rest of the year so that the tearoom does not get uncomfortably hot.

This is a basic explanation of the tea ceremony. If you are interested in learning more, you can often take classes on tea ceremonies at a university in your area, or perhaps visit a monastery for instruction. Also see the bibliography for resources on the tea ceremony.

Holidays

A Buddhist likes to celebrate as much as anyone else, and while there might not be a Buddha Claus, there are many traditions and celebrations worth noting. However, dates of holidays vary from country to country, and the different vehicles and traditions of Buddhism celebrate different festivals and holidays. For example, the Mahayana Buddhists honor different *bodhisattvas* throughout the year. However, because the holiday dates change depending on which country you are in and which calendar is being used (for instance, the Japanese do not use the lunar calendar, but use the Gregorian calendar), a listing of holidays is provided, but frequently not the time of year they might be celebrated.

The Buddhist Festival

A typical Buddhist festival day starts off with a visit to a local monastery. Food is very often brought as an offering for the monks, who in return might give a *dharma* talk. While at the monastery, visitors might affirm the Five Precepts, pray, and meditate.

The monasteries and various local Buddhist organizations will perform acts of generosity *(dana)* within the community, such as visiting and providing for those in need, adopting caged animals, donating blood, providing transportation, medical care, and so on. Laypeople will commit acts to accumulate merit, such as feeding the poor or helping the needy. In the evening a visit to a *stupa* often takes place, where practitioners make three walking circles around the *stupa* to signify respect for the Triple Gem: *buddha, dharma,* and *sangha.*

Sampling of Celebrated Days

This listing is by no means exhaustive. There are many days of celebration and festivities in a Buddhist calendar year, but here are some of the more important ones. The most important holiday of the year in Buddhism is Buddha Day. On Buddha Day, which usually falls on the first full moon in May (but as mentioned above changes from country to country), the birth, death, and enlightenment of Shakyamuni Buddha are celebrated. Buddha Day is also called *Vesak*, which is the Indian month Buddha Day falls on.

Buddhists have a Buddhist New Year celebration. However, it is not usually celebrated on the first day of January. Different traditions have a different time of year to celebrate the New Year, again depending on their calendar. For example, Theravada Buddhists will celebrate the New Year in April. People in Cambodia, Laos, Myanmar, Sri Lanka, Thailand, and parts of Indonesia will be having festivals and sometimes water fights (if you're in Thailand and you are a tourist, watch out!—you might be a special target for good, but wet, fun). Mahayana Buddhist countries tend to celebrate the New Year in January, and in Tibet in February.

Here are some other Buddhist celebrations:

- Birthday of Maitreya, the coming Buddha
- Magha Puja Day (*Sangha* Day)
- Birthday of Avalokiteshvara
- Asalha Puja Day (*Dharma* Day): marks the turning of the *Dharma* Wheel (or First Sermon)
- Ploughing Day: celebrating the day of Buddha's first moment of awakening—when he was a child sitting in the fields watching the plowing
- Ullambana Day (Ancestor Day): celebrating the time period where the gates of hell open and ghosts visit for fifteen days

There are, of course, many other celebrations and ceremonies in a Buddhist's life. Birth and marriage will be considered in the next chapter, as well as rites of passage, and how Buddhists handle death.

CHAPTER 15

Life and Death and Other Practical Matters

What does Buddhism have to say about children, education, marriage, aging, and death? Family values were not the cornerstone of the Buddha's teachings. This can be seen in the example of his own life: finding the way beyond suffering was more important than his wife, newborn son, or duty to his father's expectations. The Buddhist *sangha* has a strong monastic component. Yet at the same time, the Buddha and the Buddhisms that have developed over the past two millennia are not anti-family at all, as this chapter will explore.

Children and Practice

Babies are not born Buddhist. Parents train their children in the *dharma*, teaching them the skills of meditation and mindfulness, the ethical precepts, moral codes, and rituals. The children will take refuge in the Three Jewels if and when they decide to do so. There is no passing of the religion through the parents to the children, as in some of the other great religions of the world.

There is no baptism or naming ceremony, no monastic intervention in the birth of the baby whatsoever. Family is very important in Buddhist life, but as there is no central Buddhist office, church, or higher authority, Buddhism does not have much to do with family ritual. Families are largely a secular matter and not a matter of monastic relevance. Everything falls to the individual and each person's enlightenment is his own responsibility. But Buddhism nonetheless infiltrates the daily life and spirit of the Buddhist family as the family practices together.

How old should a child be when starting a meditation practice?
Young children have trouble sitting still. Forcing them to sit still for long periods of time is probably an exercise in futility or unnecessary punishment. However, innovative practitioners are finding ways to engage children of all ages in mindfulness practice through music, games, and altering the instructions, such as focusing on the souls of your feet when you walk. Teens and young adults can do seated practice, and many retreats are available for these kids, as well as family retreats at the Insight Meditation Society and other retreat centers.

As Buddhism moved to the West, the problem of how to simultaneously maintain a meditation practice and raise a family became a pressing issue. Where could parents find the time to dedicate to their practice if they had young children to care for? As James William Coleman tells us in *The New Buddhism*, Western Buddhist centers have not done a satisfactory job of providing for children so their parents can practice. Some have offered limited childcare to encourage parents to practice, but even those are few and far between.

Parents come up with creative solutions, such as sharing childcare time with other families who practice. But as Buddhism moves away from monastic focus and laypeople get more involved with Buddhist monasteries and centers, a solution will have to emerge that frees up parents to practice while their children are well cared for.

Rites of Passage

All spiritual traditions have their rites of passages, such as bar mitzvahs and confirmations. Buddhism is no exception, but traditions vary from school to school and country to country.

In Thailand and Myanmar, young men become monks in a rite of passage and live a monastic life for at least three months, while Tibetan children are given a herd of yaks to take care of. In the West, programs are being developed for children as Buddhism comes of age in this part of the world and children become an active part of the Buddhist community.

Education

Although you don't meet American children who are going to "Buddhist" schools as you do children who are going to Catholic schools, Buddhism has always had a strong foundation and history in encouraging education.

When Buddhism reached China it became apparent to the Chinese government officials that Buddhism had much in common with the prevalent tradition of Confucianism. A ministry was created to be in charge of Buddhist education in China. There was a Confucian educational system as well as a Buddhist educational system. The Buddhist educational system took off and spread across the country quickly. Within the Buddhist learning centers—the temples—one could find books on all different traditions, and not just on Buddhism. The monks encouraged learning that went beyond Buddhism and the Buddhist educational system began to take over the traditional educational system.

Buddhist educational facilities provided educational opportunities across Asia. That tradition continues in the West to this day. Today, Naropa University in Boulder, Colorado, is based on Nalanda University, the ancient

Indian university. The mission statement of Naropa University affirms its intention to promote awareness of the moment through intellectual, artistic, and meditative disciplines; create and foster a learning community that reveals wisdom; cultivate communication; stay true to the origins of the original Nalanda University; encourage integration of modern culture with ancient wisdom; and remain nonsectarian and "open to all." The Buddhist educational system seems to be as alive today as it was millennia ago.

Visiting Monasteries and Retreat Centers

When laypeople visit monasteries they often wonder how they can be respectful and what behavior is expected of them. Although many people are curious as to what goes on in a Buddhist monastery and would like to speak with the monks or watch a meditation session, they are afraid they will be pestered for donations or pressured to convert.

However, you could say that Buddhism is a program of attraction rather than evangelism. Traditionally, Buddhism was a missionary religion, although in the West, Buddhists do not try to convert others to Buddhism. They might speak enthusiastically of their personal practices if asked, but it is highly unlikely that you would be solicited for money or anything else at a monastery or through mail, e-mail, or other means. A donation *(dana)* might be suggested at certain monasteries, much like a museum will have a suggested donation box in the admission area.

FACT

> If you visit a monastery it is customary to take a small offering, such as a bouquet of flowers or an offering of food. You may also donate money. All of these are part of generosity practice (*dana*) aimed to overcome the poison of greed.

Most monasteries welcome visitors and most visits are free of charge. Classes, retreats, and lectures might charge something to cover meals, lodging, and depending on the institution, instruction may be part of the fee or be addressed separately through *dana*. Having said this, some retreats have become very expensive and out of reach to the person of average means.

Fancy retreats at spa locations are more and more common. In typical American style, the *dharma* has become a status symbol in some, but not all, circles. Some monasteries have stores where they sell art, meditation supplies, and clothing to help generate money to support the monastery. Most sitting sessions will be free of charge. Check the Internet for a monastery near you if you would like to visit, and you can probably find information on the site that will put you at ease before you visit. Call ahead or e-mail with any questions you might have. Most centers will have a scholarship program.

Marriage

Buddhism has long been silent on the subject of marriage. There are no great romantic figures in Buddhist history as there are in other great religions. There are no Samsons and Delilahs, no Muhammads and Khadijahs. In Buddhist countries marriage is considered a secular affair, and therefore there is no turning to your monk or religious figure for a marriage ceremony. Perhaps this is due to Buddhism's strong monastic tradition. However, it is common for couples to turn to a monk for a blessing after their civil ceremony has been performed.

In the United States, a Buddhist monk, *lama*, or other Buddhist officiate can perform a marriage ceremony, depending on the laws of your state. Check your local marriage laws to verify that a Buddhist monk or nun can officiate. However, as there are not Buddhist marriage ceremonies within the Buddhist tradition, you might make up your own ceremony with the input of a Buddhist monk, Zen priest, teacher, or similar *dharma* teacher or friend. A Buddhist blessing on a civil ceremony is still a lovely alternative if a Buddhist cannot officiate.

FACT

The Buddha had a son named Rahula (which interestingly enough means "fetter" in Sanskrit). Although Siddhartha left his family when his son was newly born to search for spiritual truth, he did return after his enlightenment and welcomed Rahula into the *sangha*. Rahula followed in his father's footsteps and eventually became a fully ordained monk.

In a Buddhist wedding ceremony the couple might affirm their commitment to the Three Jewels of *buddha*, *dharma*, and *sangha*. They might vow to support each other on the path toward awakening. A Buddhist union may differ from the standard Western-style union. Each partner commits to working on his or her own salvation through dedication to Four Noble Truths and other teachings. As the poet Rilke elegantly said, "each appoints the other the guardian of his solitude, and shows him this confidence, the greatest in his power to bestow." There is no ideal of two halves becoming a whole. Buddhism does not encourage marriage or discourage marriage, but it will lend advice on how to live a good married life.

The Buddha wasn't exactly the best role model for marriage. He left his wife and newborn son on his quest to find a Way beyond suffering. Buddhists could be said to view romantic love as suffering, just as all desire leads to suffering. But Buddhist marriages can be filled with compassion and friendship, and the challenges of being in a relationship can help each partner towards awakening. A relationship can be a path in itself. Living the precepts will promote a household of ethical strength, honesty, and faithfulness. However, if one were to wonder if the Buddha was against marriage you would only need to turn to the Maha Mangala *Sutra* (the Blessings *sutra*), which tells us: "To support one's father and mother; to cherish one's wife and children, and to be engaged in peaceful occupations—this is the highest blessing."

Buddhism and Sex

It's not difficult to figure out that sex wasn't high on the Buddha's list of things to do with his spare time. According to the Four Noble truths, desire is suffering, and the way to end suffering is to end desire. Naturally, sexual desire would fall into this category. However, the message here is not to avoid pleasurable things but to examine your potential attachments to them. Buddhism is not anti-hedonistic, just anti-attachment. The Buddha cautioned against harmful sexuality but did not discourage healthy sexuality. Every experience can be your teacher, including and especially, sexuality. Most Buddhist monastic traditions preserve celibacy, although not all do, and especially not in the West. Some Zen priests, like Protestant clergy, can marry.

FACT

Zen Master Ikkyu, who lived from 1394–1481, was an eccentric and mischievous Zen monk. He frequented brothels and wine houses, saying (according to John Stevens in *Lust for Enlightenment*), "Follow the rule of celibacy blindly and you are not more than an ass. Break it and you are only human."

The ideal of the *arhat* was based on a life of celibacy and devotion to practice. For many years the tradition in Buddhism was for monks and nuns to remain celibate for life. However, as Buddhism spread and laypeople became more involved in practice, the emphasis on celibacy shifted in some traditions and practice. While remaining celibate can certainly free a person's energy—energy that could then be devoted to practice—it wasn't always convenient or practical for people to forgo a sexual life. As mentioned earlier, the tradition of celibacy may have been advocated to control the numbers of the *sangha*. A thousand monks is a lot of mouths to feed; a thousand monks with families would increase the demands on the community of lay supports manifold.

The Asian ideal of a celibate monastic didn't weather the journey west very well. When Buddhist teachings took hold in the late 1960s, it was happening in conjunction with the sexual revolution. Love-ins were not celibate affairs! Getting people to restrict themselves in a time of newfound liberation was neither feasible nor likely necessary.

There is no standard set of sexual behaviors that all Buddhists would agree upon. For instance, Zen teachers in the United States are often married with families. And some Tibetan monks are celibate while others practice *tantric* sex. *Tantric* sex takes sexual activity and transforms it into a spiritual practice where the partners practice meditation while engaging in sexual behavior. *Tantric* sex is a ritual thought to bring about strong states of awareness and to heighten practice. However, it is supposedly reserved for those who are extremely advanced in their practice. The sexual activities themselves are shrouded in secrecy and are different from the many books on the shelves of your local bookstore that purport to teach you the secrets of *tantric* sex (these would be based on Hindu mysticism rather than Buddhism).

Women in Buddhism

Like most of recorded history, the early years of Buddhism report few stories of women. The Buddha's mother is mentioned, but she died soon after Siddhartha was born. He was then raised by his aunt, his mother's sister, Prajapati. In fact, it was Prajapati who, after the Buddha's enlightenment, went to Shakyamuni and asked him if women could also join the *sangha*. She was refused by Shakyamuni but persisted, asking a second time, and then a third. But the Buddha was unmovable and denied his good aunt's request.

Prajapati cut off her hair and donned the yellow robes of the mendicant monks. She followed the Buddha and pleaded with him to allow women to become members of the *sangha*. It wasn't until Ananda interfered on Prajapati's behalf that the Buddha finally relented. The Buddha believed women were equal to men as regards the ability to attain enlightenment, but practical matters, such as not offending the *sangha*'s wealthy patrons, kept him from agreeing that it was a good idea to allow them into the community. However, he did finally say yes and women were subsequently permitted to give up their worldly lives and enter as members of the *sangha*. Five hundred women joined Prajapati, including Yasodhara, the Buddha's abandoned wife. However, the women were given eight rules they had to follow that separated them from the monks and made them subordinate to their male counterparts. Monks and nuns are segregated in Asia and are discouraged from having physical contact.

There is the traditional story of two monks who are walking down the road. They come to a small stream and there is a frail woman waiting at the water's edge. One monk offers to carry the woman across the water and does so and puts her down on the other side of the stream. The monks walk on for miles and the other monk says, "I can't believe you touched that woman; it is forbidden." The monk laughed and said, "I put her down miles ago, why are you still carrying her?"

The Mahayana texts support the Buddha's statement that men and women were equally equipped for enlightenment, and most traditions in Buddhism have included nuns *(bhikkunis)*. But Buddhist literature portrays the difficulties that men had accepting the women as part of monastic life. Women were portrayed as seductresses and unclean creatures—most likely due to men's unfulfilled sexual drives and inability to stave off lust and desire.

But women struggled in Buddhism as they have struggled in most other religions. For many years and in many traditions in Buddhist history, women were proclaimed to be equal in theory but were in fact subordinate in practice. As late as 1979, Irish-American Maureen "Soshin" O'Halloran wrote home to America to tell her family that she was the first woman ever admitted to Toshoji Temple in Japan.

In the West today a great percentage of the teachers of Buddhism are women. Teachers such as Pema Chödrön, Tara Brach, Charlotte Joko Beck, Sharon Salzberg, Silvia Boorstein, Joanna Macy, Narayan Liebenson, Grace Schireson, and many others have strengthened the *dharma* with their wise teaching.

In *Zen Women: Beyond Tea Ladies, Iron Maidens and Macho Masters,* Grace Schireson tells the untold story of women in Zen. The unfortunate truth is that the history of Buddhism is not one of gender equality. While the Buddha did finally relent after persistent pressure from his aunt Prajapati to admit women into the *sangha* against the norms of the time, admittance has not translated to equivalence of opportunity. She tells the story of a male Zen master who responds to a female student's question, "How many women teachers were at the conference?" (a North American Zen conference). The Zen master replied, "We were all women." Huh? His answer speaks to the unity beyond the gender duality of male and female and the apparent lack of need to worry about gender discrepancies. *We are all women; we are all men.*

But this begs the question of why the male version of Oneness (since the conference was predominately male). Empowered by writing about the forgotten histories of women in Zen, Grace would now reply to this Zen master, "How many of you women used the ladies room at the Zen conference?"

Grace Schireson is a *dharma* teacher in the lineage of Suzuki Roshi and received her empowerment from Sojun Mel Weitsman Roshi, abbot of Berkeley Zen Center. She has also been empowered to teach *koans* by Keido Fukushima Roshi, chief abbot of Tofukuji Monastery in Kyoto Japan. Grace is the head teacher of Central Valley Zen Foundation and has founded and leads three Zen Groups, including Empty Nest Zendo.

In *Zen Women*, Schireson has "moved beyond the question of why and how female Zen ancestors had been erased from Zen history. I have sought to identify these erased women and put them back in the Zen practice I loved."

Death

Death is a subject fraught with anxiety and denial in the West. "Everything must die, perhaps even me." Our death rituals are somber and morose and it is unclear whether they provide adequate meaning and solace for the bereaved. Death is a shrouded mystery, and for most children and most adults, death is an uncomfortable topic of conversation, one often populated by platitudes.

Buddhism asks you to consider your mortality daily. Meditations on impermanence can be meditations on death. The Buddha used to encourage his disciples to sit with the dead, with the rotting and decomposing corpses, so that the nature of impermanence would be understood and experienced. In Zen you might be told to "Die on the cushion."

Buddhism encourages you to face death as a part of life. Tibetan Buddhism has the *Tibetan Book of the Dead*, which is a study of death and the stages one goes through immediately after death.

The Tibetans believe there are forty-nine days between lives, forty-nine days in which the living read from the *Tibetan Book of the Dead* to help the dead gain insight and move away from the attachments of the body. Buddhists see death as just another transformation. Impermanence is the nature of the world. Some Buddhists believe that if they are aware in the moment when death comes they can direct their rebirth in a beneficial way.

Remember in the traditional story of the Buddha that he started his search for the truth after having an encounter with death. As he saw the sick and dying outside his palace gates, and a corpse being carried through the streets, he realized that all that was alive comes to an end. Death is inevitable. This realization was the catalyst that set him on his quest to end suffering.

The *Bardö Thodol* (*the Tibetan Book of the Dead*) was passed down orally for centuries. It was first put into written form by Padmasambhava in the eighth century C.E.

If you stay close to the awareness that any moment could be the last moment of your life (after all, you never know what might happen: aneurysm, accident, atom bomb), then you realize that each moment is precious. Each moment is a gift and a blessing. So many people when given the news of terminal illness say they realize the joy of life as soon as the reality of death becomes clear to them. Hospice work can also bring this truth into focus. Death meditation practice can be a powerful way to keep you aligned with the present and alive in the moment, aware that everything changes.

And so the practices in Buddhism remain steady from birth through death. Buddhists, Muslims, Christians, Jews, and every person, whether atheist or religious, shares the commonality of birth and death. Buddhism stresses how everyone and everything is interconnected.

CHAPTER 16

Buddhist Art

Religions have inspired much of the world's great art, such as Michelangelo's Sistine Chapel and the Taj Mahal. Buddhism has also inspired beautiful and ambitious artwork, from the ephemeral to the enduring. These arts forms include painting- and sculpture-filled caves, architecture, *thangkas*, *mandalas*, statuary, calligraphy, and contemporary art. Buddhist art is some of the most distinctive and recognizable art in the world.

Architecture

The beginning of Buddhist architecture can be traced to King Ashoka in the third century B.C.E. Ashoka built great *stupas* and pillars in tribute to the Buddha. Two of the most famous pillars are the one at Sarnath that used to house the Lion Capital (the Buddha was known as "Lion of the Shakyas") and the one in the Lumbini Gardens. There are more incredible works of Buddhist architecture than can be listed here, but some of the more outstanding ones deserve special mention.

Stupas

The Buddha died somewhere between 483 and 400 B.C.E. and his remains were quickly taken for custodial protection by King Ajatasattu of Magadha, India. According to legend, the king divided the remains into eight portions and gave each piece to one of eight different kings to protect and cherish. Each king was directed to build a *stupa* to house the remains, and these *stupas* were erected all over India and present-day Nepal.

FACT

When the Buddha was cremated, rulers from various kingdoms came quickly to reclaim the relics of his body. Arguments ensued, but a Brahmin named Dona was quick to quell the disagreement. His clever speech convinced the kings to divide the relics between them and build *stupas* to honor the holy Buddha.

King Ashoka was thought to have opened up seven of the eight *stupas* and relocated the relics of the Buddha to structures that he subsequently had built. The Hill of Sanchi, one of the most well known Buddhist *stupas*, is one of Ashoka's most famous creations.

The Hill of Sanchi is a group of Buddhist monuments. The foundation was laid by Ashoka but was later damaged, rebuilt, and added to over the centuries. When two of the *stupas* on the Hill of Sanchi were excavated in the nineteenth century several of the relic caskets were recovered. Today, relics of the Buddha are scattered and appear in China, Burma, Sri Lanka,

India, and elsewhere—fingers, teeth, hair, and bone have all been preserved. Three *stupas* at Sanchi have been recovered.

Another of the greatest works of architecture in Buddhist history is the Borobudur Temple, a stonework of wonder standing in Java, Indonesia. The size of the temple is awe-inspiring, with nearly 200,000 square feet of lava rock. The temple is composed of six rectangular terraces. The top of the structure contains three more circular terraces and a spire *stupa* forms the top. The temple is thought to have been the Buddhist cultural center in the seventh and eighth centuries.

It is a massive structure overlooking the misty mountains and green valleys of Java. The whole structure is in a *mandala* version of a lotus, a symbol of Buddhism.

It also represents the Buddhist cosmos, with realms of desire, form, and formlessness depicted from bottom to top. The lowest level of the structure has 160 carved panels illustrating the joys and horrors of life in the realm of desire. There are more than 1,400 scenes in all from top to bottom, with ninety-two Buddha statues for each direction. The structure is a marvel of devotion and endurance. Borobudur has been used for devotional practice for centuries—you can walk around the terraces while meditating, walking clockwise until you reach the top.

The Cave Temples of Ajanta

In Western India you can find the cave temples of Ajanta. These "caves" are actually man-made structures carved out of living rock. Hsüan-tsang, the famous Chinese Buddhist pilgrim who traveled in India for sixteen years, first wrote about the Ajanta caves in the eighth century C.E. The caves were originally used as dwelling and meeting houses for Buddhists. Frescoes decorate the cave walls. There are approximately thirty such temple caves, some created as early as 200 B.C.E., and some as late as the seventh century. It is not known who painted the brilliantly depicted scenes from the Buddha's life and from the Jataka tales, but they are colorful and larger than life. The caves were rediscovered by the British in 1817.

The Magao Caves of Dunhuang

One of the greatest repositories of Buddhist art is found in China amidst the Magao caves. There are 800 caves, built between the fourth and fourteenth centuries C.E., of which 492 are decorated with murals and statuary. The start of the caves is attributed to a Buddhist monk named Yuezun who, in 366 C.E., responded to a vision of a thousand Buddhas by carving a small meditation cell in the rock. Others followed, and the practice became more and more ambitious. Emperors would outdo their predecessors with magnificent projects.

It is estimated that these murals cover a half-million feet of wall space, forty times larger than the Sistine Chapel. And as for sculptures, there are over 2,000 of them (and this has been reduced from tens of thousands due to plundering).

FACT

The oldest printed book was found in cave seventeen at Magao. It is a copy of the Diamond *Sutra* and was printed with woodblock on a sixteen-foot scroll in 868 C.E., nearly 600 years before the Guttenberg Bible. You may visit the scroll at the British Library.

These magnificent caves on the Silk Road reflect the great influence that Buddhism had on China, more so than any of the other religions that have appeared in China.

The June 2010 issue of *National Geographic* featured an article on the caves: "Within the caves, the monochrome and lifelessness of the desert gave way to an exuberance of color and movement. Thousands of Buddhas in every hue radiated across the grotto wall, their robes glinting with imported gold."

The caves employ a staff of 500 and receive a half million visitors each year. The caves have survived centuries of sandstorms, plundering archeologists, and the Cultural Revolution. Its biggest threat today is the moist breath of its multitude of tourists.

Buddhist Statuary and Images

The image of the Buddha is familiar worldwide. The first images of the Buddha appeared during the reign of King Kanishka during the first century, greatly influenced by the Hellenic art coming out of Central Asia. The Buddha image conveys serenity and calm. The proportions of the Buddha are always ideal. Though there is some variation in measurement and scale from school to school and country to country, most Buddha images have the following characteristics:

- The top of the Buddha's head has a raised area that symbolizes enlightened mind
- The hands and the feet are equal in length and scale
- The nose is long, straight, and noble
- There is a mark in the center of the forehead—the Eye of Wisdom
- The ears are elongated

Buddha images portray grace and great beauty. One of the most famous Buddha images is Wat Pho: The Temple of the Reclining Buddha, in Thailand. The gold-plated reclining Buddha is more than 150 feet long and 49 feet high and represents the Buddha's *paranirvana*. The temple grounds contain more than 1,000 Buddha images scattered around.

Mandalas and Sand Paintings

A sand painting is exactly what it sounds like—a painting made of sand. Sand paintings represent the impermanence of all things. *Mandalas* are maps of the spiritual world. They are usually represented in artwork as a graphic symbolic pattern. The pattern is usually in the form of a circle with intricate designs within. The patterns are representative of the sacred place where the Buddha or deity abides. They are used for contemplation and meditation and are designed to awaken spiritual potential.

Native Americans are also known for their sand painting *mandalas*. Many similarities can be found between the Navajo sand paintings and the Tibetan sand paintings. Both contain images of the cosmos in a circular form.

Sand paintings are often *mandalas*. Tibetan *lamas* create them to promote healing. Sand paintings are made with vegetable-dyed sand, flowers, herbs, grains, stone, and sometimes jewels. A platform is laid out and the sand and other materials are placed on the platform over a period of time that serves as a meditation. Once the platform is in place the *lama* will start a healing ceremony that blesses the area. When the sand painting is finished, it is dismantled, demonstrating the impermanence in action. After a ceremony, the sand is swept into a large vessel and deposited in a river or a lake, again with ceremony.

Thangkas

Thangkas are paintings. They are often done on canvas and turned into scrolls, framed in silk, and hung from a dowel. The dowel can be made of wood with decorative metal knobs on the ends. *Thangkas* are also often *mandalas*. They depict images of different deities, such as the *bodhisattva* Avalokiteshvara or any of the numerous Tibetan deities. As compared to sand painting *mandalas*, *thangkas* are a more permanent art form. They are often used as meditative devices and are hung by the altar.

Gardens

The earth itself is a work of art—the colors, the textures, the sensory depth.

Japanese gardens are some of the most exquisite gardens to be found. Their simplicity, stark beauty, and serenity are moving and inspire peace. For centuries, Japanese Zen masters created gardens out of rocks and sand, raking the sand into patterns that could be destroyed quickly, like the sand paintings, emphasizing the impermanence of all things. These gardens are designed for contemplation and meditation. In a dry element garden, movement can be depicted using sand, and rocks can be used to represent mountains or islands in the sand streams. Bridges are a common element in many Japanese gardens as well.

Garden design under the Japanese became a spiritual activity. Gardens in Zen monasteries became objects for meditation and an appreciation for natural beauty. While constructed, these gardens represent more than human creation. The best-known designer of Zen gardens was Muso, who lived in the thirteenth and fourteenth centuries. Ponds were created to represent mind, and in one walking garden sharp rocks were juxtaposed with soft moss to represent the confluence of beauty and monastic austerity. Raked rock gardens are also striking examples of Zen symbolism, with rocks representing thoughts in the sea of the mind.

Haiku

Haiku is Japanese poetry form that traditionally follows a pattern of five-seven-five syllables. This is generally a good way for haiku beginners to start but it is not a rigid rule. Instead, it is important that the haiku uses no spare words—no unnecessary words and syllables.

Haikus are written in a moment of inspiration where the self-conscious mind drops and the poet is in touch with the unity of all things. Haiku is a mindfulness meditation. Haikus are about everyday life and usually have a nature theme. One of the lines usually contains a word that indicates to the reader to which season the haiku refers, thereby giving it a sense of time and place. Wild plums, for instance, would indicate summer.

Basho is known as a great haiku poet. He was born Matsuo Munefusa in seventeenth-century Japan. In his youth, Basho was a samurai but exchanged his sword for poetry. He lived in a hut made of banana leaves, which is how he came by his pseudonym. *Basho* means "banana leaves."

Haikus do not usually refer to a participant: in other words—no self. This usually extends to mean no adjectives are included, as adjectives imply there is a person judging (a beautiful tree implies an opinion, therefore someone who holds the opinion).

Here is an example of haiku from Basho:

Winter rain
falls on the cow-shed;
a cock crows.

Notice that the haiku does not follow the five-seven-five rule but a similar beat is found: three-five-three. Haikus are not intended to be brilliant and pithy. They are strokes of inspiration and honesty coming from the heart. Most of all, haikus are reverent towards the sanctity of the small things, and of everything. Children love to create haiku poetry, which says a lot about the simplicity and honesty to be found in the haiku.

Art Practice

Buddhist art is approached the same way everything in Buddhism is approached—with concentration and mindfulness. Ideally, there is no separation between artist and art—the artist is the work of art and the work of art is the artist. The artist strives to use the creative process as an expression of awakening. When the artist does a sand painting, the artist *is* the sand painting and the sand painting *is* the artist. No division exists.

Chogyam Trungpa Rinpoche founded Shambhala Art and said, "Genuine art tells the truth." For example, *miksang* is the Tibetan word for "good eye" and is a form of contemplative photography. His son and successor, Sakyong Mipham Rinpoche, said, "Without seeing things as they are, it is hard to create art. Our perceptions are obscured and our mind is not fresh, so making art becomes a troubled, futile process by which we're trying to create something based on concept."

Zen Art

Many of the Zen arts trace their origins to China but receive their fullest expression in Japan. These art forms include painting, calligraphy, poetry, photography, archery, swordsmanship, tea ceremony, flower arranging, and garden design. Typically, Zen art eschews narrative for an aesthetic sensibility that simultaneously conveys openness and compactness. The aim of the art is to inspire insight rather than devotion. In this way Zen art is similar to a *koan*.

Zen painting takes as its subject landscapes, depictions of famous Zen stories, *koans*, and Zen masters. For example, landscape paintings seek to depict the enormity of the universe and the smallness of humanity in the context of nature.

There is a tradition of art practice within Zen. Art arises spontaneously and manifests the *buddha-nature* within you. Art practice is mindfulness training. The art relies on a foundation of technical training that is then expressed in spontaneous practice. Zen art tends to be simple, sometimes stark, and always lovely.

FACT

The ten ox-herding pictures are attributed to Kakuan Shion, twelfth-century Zen master from China. Early ox-herding pictures have existed, but Kakuan Shion is known to have created the entire sequence of ten that has survived to this day.

Calligraphy (*Zenga*)

Japanese calligraphy is an art form spiritually expressed through Zen. The artist must be in touch with *buddha-nature* in order to create an expression of enlightenment. The brush stroke must come from a union with the world; no separation must exist—no *I* and *pen*, just the act itself.

Japanese calligraphy dates back to the seventh century, where it was part of art practice and meditation in monasteries. Often, the subject of a Japanese calligraphy and painting would be a *koan*. One of the most common examples of *zenga* is the open circle, called *enso*. The simplicity of the *enso* was particularly popular during the Edo period of Japan in the eighteenth century. *Enso* symbolized enlightenment, emptiness, and life itself. In the series of ox-herding pictures previously mentioned, the eighth step in the sequence (both ox and self vanish) is represented by *enso*.

During the execution of the calligraphy, the slightest hesitation on the part of the artist will cause the ink to blot on the thin rice paper, and the calligraphy will be ruined. Technique is learned and perfected over many years before such spontaneity is possible. Once the boundary between art supplies, art, and self are gone, the art can be executed.

Flower Arranging

Japanese flower arranging is called *ikebana. Ikebana* evolved in Japan over the course of many centuries. The written history of *ikebana* can be traced back to the fifteenth century, to the first *ikebana* school. Many years of training are required before someone achieves the technique necessary to perform *ikebana* well. Many different ways of fastening the flowers into an arrangement are possible, using various techniques. The essence of *ikebana* is simplicity, and in contrast to Western flower arrangement, very few flowers, leaves, and stems are used to achieve the desired effect. *Ikebana* uses the flowers, the container, and the space around the flower arrangement as part of the artistic impression.

There are different styles of *ikebana.* Some styles use low containers and the flowers are piled on top. Other styles use tall, narrow vases and the flowers have a tossed-about look to them. *Ikebana* strives to use seasonal flowers and foliage in a naturalistic presentation. Traditional forms of *ikebana* used three points to represent the realms of heaven, human, and earth.

The essence of Buddhist art is the Buddhist practice of the artist. The art itself is an expression of enlightenment and the creation of the art an act of enlightenment. Years of technical study can go into a single moment of expression. From the centuries' old *stupas* to the Zen gardens of today, Buddhist art is integral for awakening. Art can depict the cosmos in a painting or a single moment in a photo. Art can last for centuries, such as the Borobudur Temple of Java, or it can last hours, like a Tibetan sand painting. No matter the outcome of the durability of the art, the essence is in the creation itself.

The ability to become one with the act of creation is at the heart of Buddhist art forms. Art in Buddhism is an act of the deepest love and connection with the world.

CHAPTER 17

Buddhism and the West

There have been many expressions of the Buddha's teachings across the past 2,500 years. As the *dharma* moved from India it was adopted by each host nation, combining indigenous religious and cultural elements to make new forms of Buddhism. Each culture has "owned" Buddhism in its unique way, whether in Japan, Tibet, and now the West. What elements should be retained from Japanese Zen and Tibetan Buddhism? Is the *dharma* in danger of dilution if it is changed on Western soil?

Westward Bound

In 1893, the first formal gathering of representatives from the world's religions —both Eastern and Western spiritual traditions—was held in Chicago. It was called the Parliament of the World's Religions and is seen today to be the foundation of the continuing formal dialogue between the world's religions.

That year in Chicago, Zen master Soyen Shaku spoke for the first time on Western shores. It wasn't until after World War II, however, that Zen attracted a readership in the West. More than any other figure in history, D. T. Suzuki, Soyen Shakyu's student, is credited with opening the West to Buddhism with his writings on Zen. Suzuki communicated to Westerners the experiential aspect of Zen and explained Zen in a way that left Westerners hungry for more.

In the 1950s the Beat Generation brought a new crowd of Zen enthusiasts, with an experimental nature and generous outlook. Soon, Zen centers spread all over the country, and Zen took root. Buddhism, in all its forms, has gained popularity in Europe, Russia, Australia, Canada, and South America. Westerners fighting wars in Asia in World War II, Korea, and Vietnam brought back interests in things Asian, including Buddhism. After the Holocaust, Jews were disillusioned and many could not find comfort or the answers they were seeking in the synagogue. Buddhism provided an attractive alternative and many of American *dharma* teachers are Jewish, while Jews only comprise a small percentage of the population.

FACT

Many of the poets and writers of the Beat Generation were Buddhists, such as Allen Ginsberg, Jack Kerouac, Kenneth Rexroth, Gary Snyder, and Anne Waldman. Jack Kerouac wrote a book entitled *Wake Up: A Life of the Buddha*.

Political unrest in Asia has become a boon for Western Buddhism. His Holiness the Dalai Lama left isolated Tibet and entered the world stage, exposing countless millions to the colorful pageantry and deep wisdom of Tibetan Buddhism. S. N. Goenka left Burma and found a worldwide audience for his teaching of *vipassana*. Tich Nhat Hanh, one of the most popular and revered Buddhist authors and teachers, came into the public eye during his protests of the war in his native Vietnam. Asian immigrants also contributed to the rise in Buddhism, such as the Chinese establishing Buddhist temples in San Francisco during the gold rush.

Zig Zag Zen

The beautifully illustrated book *Zig Zag Zen* chronicles the interrelationship between Buddhism and psychedelic drugs. While at first this may seem an unlikely pairing (given that one of the precepts prohibits intoxication), there is a fascinating concordance. First, the brain state the Buddha was likely in sitting under the Bodhi tree may have been neuro-physiologically similar to the brain states found by people ingesting LSD or sacred plants such as peyote cactus, psilocybin mushrooms, and ayahuasca root. Many future Zen leaders experimented with these consciousness-altering drugs and later turned to Zen as a way to stabilize the experience that opened to them with the drugs. However, these same teachers do not advocate the use of psychedelic compounds as a path to liberation. Stephen Batchelor confirms that "It is undeniable that a significant proportion of those drawn to Buddhism and other Eastern traditions in the 1960s (including the present writer) were influenced in their choice of religious orientation by experiences induced by psychoactive substances such as marijuana and LSD."

Thich Nhat Hanh and Jesus

Perhaps one of the most beloved Buddhist teachers in the West is Thich Nhat Hanh, whose teachings on mindfulness, peace, and religious tolerance have touched the hearts of millions of Westerners. Thich Nhat Hanh was chairman of the Vietnamese Peace Brigade during the Vietnam War and was subsequently nominated for a Nobel Peace Prize by Martin Luther King Jr. His tireless efforts to promote peace and interreligious tolerance have won him a steadfast and loyal following the world over.

In his book *Living Buddha, Living Christ,* Thich Nhat Hanh, known as Thầy to his followers and friends (*Thầy* means "Teacher"), writes about the similarities between Jesus and Buddha, trying to erase the lines of religious intolerance. The spirit of Jesus and Buddha cannot be found in their names, he tells us. The spirit of Jesus and Buddha can be found in practicing the actions they took in their own lives: by becoming a *living* Jesus and a *living* Buddha ourselves. Both men showed us how to live by the actions each took in his life. Jesus said, "I am the way." Thich Nhat Hanh points out that Jesus meant that his *life* was the way—not his name. The same applies to the Buddha.

Thich Nhat Hanh runs a Buddhist monastery in France called Plum Village, which he founded in 1982. When he is not traveling around the world teaching mindful living, he teaches, writes, and gardens in Plum Village.

Thich Nhat Hanh works tirelessly to promote tolerance, peace, compassion, and true understanding. He writes, "Buddhism and Christian practice is the same—to make the truth available—the truth about ourselves, the truth about our brothers and sisters, the truth about our situation. This is the work of writers, preachers, the media, and also practitioners. Each day, we practice looking deeply into ourselves and into the situation of our brothers and sisters. It is the most serious work we can do." Thich Nhat Hanh teaches the essence of Zen and also the essence of all religions. At the center of each religion is the desire for love and true connection.

Thomas Merton

Thomas Merton was an American Christian monk, poet, social critic, and mystic. He was born in France, moved to the United States, and became a Roman Catholic at age twenty-three. He eventually became a Trappist monk, which is one of the strictest orders in Catholicism. But something about Buddhism drew Thomas Merton, and in 1968 he found himself on a plane to Asia for a monastic conference. He welcomed the opportunity to learn more about the Eastern religion he felt compelled to study. Merton remained a devoted Christian monk his entire life, but he actively worked for interreligious tolerance as his appreciation for the Eastern religion grew.

D. T. Suzuki was an influential presence in Merton's life. Their correspondences formed an essay collection called *Zen and the Birds of Appetite*, which was a dialogue about the similarities and differences between Christianity and Zen Buddhism. Merton came to believe that Buddhism and Christianity were completely compatible with each other and that the emptiness found in Zen could be related to the true self and the idea of unknowing found at the heart of Christian practice.

QUOTE

"Thich Nhat Hanh is my brother. We are both monks, and we have lived the monastic life about the same number of years. We are both poets, both existentialists. I have far more in common with Nhat Hanh than I have with many Americans."—Thomas Merton

While he was in Asia, Merton met three times with the Dalai Lama and each was very impressed with the sincerity, humanity, and compassion of the other. They were able to give each other an understanding that their vision was perhaps not the only vision of truth, and each had come to the same realizations, had similar experiences from different approaches. Merton had a powerful awakening experience while in Sri Lanka, and believed that Buddhism had given him an ability to practice Catholicism in a very powerful way.

The Western Face of Buddhism

It would appear that Buddhism is one of the fastest-growing religions in the West. But who are all of these new Buddhists? Not everyone is a "card-carrying" Buddhist; many in the West integrate Buddhist principles into their own value systems, religious orientations, and daily behavior. For example, you can partake of the value of Buddhist meditation without identifying yourself as a Buddhist. Many Americans are taking some of the practices of Buddhism and incorporating them into their own religious traditions. You might find Jews and Catholics in a zendo one night during the week, but come their own holidays, you also might find them celebrating at temple or church as well.

His Holiness the Dalai Lama has done more than anyone else to bring Buddhism into public awareness. His great compassion in the face of adversity, his peaceful demeanor regarding exile, his lack of dogmatism, and his projection of kindness draw people to him with curiosity. In a time when so many Americans are unsure how to cope with their own suffering, the smiling presence of His Holiness coping with his loss with equanimity and serenity is a great comfort and source of inspiration. Americans, like everyone, want to be happy, especially in the face of so much uncertainty.

More and more people are opening to new spiritual experiences. In the United States, many people make a distinction between spirituality and religion. Some people do *zazen* to bring them closer to god, regardless of their religious background. *The New Buddhism* tells us the interesting fact that most of the best-selling books that are sold today on Buddhism offer direct advice on how to practice.

Actress Sharon Stone is a Buddhist. After achieving a high degree of fame too fast, Stone took some time off from acting to regain her footing. "My practice is Buddhism, but I believe in God." Stone says. She doesn't see any conflict between her belief in God and her practice of Buddhism. However, she does say, "I don't believe in Buddha as my God…I believe in the practical ways of Buddhism as a way to live."

American Buddhists come from all religions, they are equally represented by male and female, they are both young and old, are white, Hispanic, black, and Asian. Some are devout and some are merely curious. Some devote their entire lives to practice and some balance it with their other religious beliefs. The new face of Buddhism is the face of America: diverse, curious, and hopeful.

Contemporary Buddhist Literature

Buddhism has had a great effect on contemporary American literature. Go to a bookstore anywhere and you will be hard pressed not to find a book on

Buddhism. The Eastern religion sections of bookstores are overflowing with books on Zen, Buddhism, mindfulness, meditation, and more.

One of the most popular books in the United States on Buddhism is *Zen Mind, Beginner's Mind* by Suzuki Roshi, with nearly a million copies in print.

You'd think Buddhism would be hard to talk about with emptiness being a major theme. But nevertheless people make great effort to put down on paper that which has transformed their lives. The Dalai Lama's *Art of Happiness* was an international bestseller. *The Miracle of Mindfulness* by Thich Naht Hanh is another popular book, which appears on bookshelves all over the country.

You can find daily meditation books, calendars, diaries, and quote books with Buddhist themes. Some of the wonderful writings available in your local bookstore include books by Stephen Batchelor, Tara Brach, Pema Chödrön, Bernard Glassman, Joseph Goldstein, Bhante Gunaratana, Thich Nhat Hanh, Jon Kabat-Zinn, Philip Kapleau, Ayya Khema, Jamyeng Khyentse Rinpoche, Jack Kornfield, Noah Levine, David Loy, Melvin Mcleod, Sakyong Mipham, the Dalai Lama, John Daido Loori, Andrew Olendzki, Larry Rosenberg, Sharon Salzberg, Grace Schireson, D. T. Suzuki, Shunryu Suzuki, Mu Soeng, Robert Thurman, Chogym Trungpa Rinpoche, Brad Warner, Alan Watts, Shinzen Young, Polly Young-Eisendrath, and many more.

A sampling of poets who use Buddhist themes include Kenneth Rexroth, Albert Saijo, Anne Waldman, Lew Welch, Allen Ginsberg, Jack Kerouac, Michael McClure, Peter Levitt, Al Robles, Gary Snyder, and Philip Whalen.

From haiku to novel, nature writing to illuminating nonfiction, Buddhism has permeated our literature and our lives.

The Zen of Everything

One indication that Buddhism is here to stay is that it is showing up in pop culture as well as in art and bookstores. From movies to golf, Zen is everywhere. A trip to a bookstore may illuminatie how far Zen has infiltrated popular culture. There may be tiny Zen gardening sets, Zen calendars, Zen mugs, et cetera. Titles that had nothing to do with Zen claimed Zen roots. This is the Zenning of America and it goes beyond Zen to represent all of the Buddhist traditions.

Buddhism and Zen have even made it to the movies. Movies like *The Matrix* have Zen themes running through them. Martial arts films have taken off in popularity, from the Jackie Chan films to the Hong Kong imports. *Seven Years in Tibet* and *Kundun* are both popular movies whose plots concern the Dalai Lama. *Little Buddha,* by Italian director Bernardo Bertolucci, gained widespread release. Why is Zen and Buddhism showing up everywhere?

Buddhist stories inspire and make you pause, such as this Buddhist parable about living in the moment:

> *A man traveling across a field encountered a tiger. He fled, the tiger chasing after him. Coming to a precipice, he caught hold of the root of a wild vine and swung himself down over the edge. The tiger sniffed at him from above. Trembling, the man looked down to where, far below, another tiger was waiting to eat him. Only the vine sustained him.*
>
> *Two mice, one white and one black, little by little, started to gnaw away the vine. The man saw a luscious strawberry near him. Grasping the vine with one hand, he plucked the strawberry with the other. How sweet it tasted!*

The world is such where it is possible to wake up on a Tuesday morning and watch the World Trade Center buildings fall down. You may feel the imperative to find meaning in your life now more than ever. Americans are *longing* for meaning in their lives and are turning to spirituality. Everything today goes at such a fast pace and life feels as if it is flying by.

Buddhism teaches you to live in the moment, or more accurately, it reminds you how to live in the moment since you already have this natural talent. It shows you that everything matters: that work matters, that dinner matters, that walking the dog matters. The Buddha's teachings can bring sanity and comfort, and help you to reclaim your life. Living mindfully elevates the mundane into the sacred and can give you the meaning you may be desperately searching for. The Buddhist traditions that have taken root in Western soil share timeless messages that translate into other faiths: compassion, faith, truth, suffering. Buddha is everywhere because *buddha* is in everything. It's not silly to talk about the Zen of golf. It's amazing. When you swing, just swing.

Buddhism and Psychotherapy

A cartoon in *The New Yorker* magazine by Robert Mankoff portrays a psychoanalyst addressing his patient. The analyst, says, "Look, making you happy is out of the question, but I can give you a compelling narrative for your misery." At heart, both Buddhism and psychotherapy address the same fundamental issue: human suffering. Both promote methods of self-observation. The Buddha saw himself as a physician and might have seen himself as a psychotherapist had that concept been around 2,500 years ago. Buddha was both psychoanalyst and cognitive-behavioral in his approach, looking deeply at the conditionings that give rise to emotions and changing the behaviors that give rise to suffering.

Buddhist meditation practice and the process of psychotherapy are not instant fixes. Each practice takes time to mature. In other words, one therapy session or one seated meditation session will not change much—unless of course a curiosity and faith are born that bring you back to the couch or the cushion. A synergy can arise if both processes are engaged concurrently.

Both meditation and psychotherapy address the sense of lack that many people feel. Psychotherapy attempts to construct a better functioning self while Buddhist psychology aims to deconstruct that self into no-self (*anatta*). Psychotherapy can help to identify patterns that can become obstacles in your meditation practice, and meditation can show you where you are holding on to painful identifications with stories and attachments to things that are changing.

In the West, there is a lot of attachment to having a self (a "thinker") and difficulty grasping what means to have no-self. This idea strikes the Western mind as counterintuitive: "Of course, I have a self, who else is having this thought?" What the Buddha meant, though, is that there is no fixed self that is unchanging over time. The self, rather, is a set of processes that in the aggregate give the appearance of an enduring entity that you would call your self.

What is this collection of processes? They are called the *skandhas* (translated as "aggregates" or "components"). There is the physical body (*rupa*) and this body is comprised of the four elements (earth, water, fire, and air); feelings (*vedana*) that arise from sensory contact with the world (that is, sight, sound, smell, taste, touch, and thought); perceptions (*samjna*) that put sensory experiences into categories of pleasant, unpleasant, or neutral (telling you whether to approach, avoid, or ignore any experience); and habitual mental patterns (*sankharas*) that are conditionings that arise from experience. These are the results of local *karma*—things that happened in the past affect how you feel in the present; and the final aggregate is consciousness (*vijnana*) that arises when the elements of body and mind make contact with the world around you.

Learning to sit through the rise and fall of thoughts can bring about a profound realization: *I am okay.* Despite the tendency to believe that obsessively thinking about something will actually change it, the realization dawns that thinking isn't always necessary. Whether or not you obsess over the dent in your new car, the car will either be fixed or remain unfixed and rumination will not change that. With the increase in Buddhist practice in the West came a willingness on the part of psychotherapists to explore the possibilities of using Buddhist practices for therapy.

Thoughts Without a Thinker

Mark Epstein, author of *Thoughts Without a Thinker,* is a therapist who practices Buddhism himself. He tells a story about the great psychologist and philosopher William James (1842–1910), who thought that Buddhism would be a major influence on Western psychology. James was lecturing at Harvard when he noticed a Sri Lankan Buddhist monk in the lecture hall. "Take my chair," he said to the monk. "You are better equipped to lecture on psychology than I."

Epstein explains that meditation, often misunderstood to be a retreat from emotional and mental experiences, requires that you slow down to examine the day-to-day mind. And, he concludes, "This examination is, by definition, psychological."

There are also many different and new forms of Buddhist-inspired psychotherapies. These include Mindfulness-Based Stress Reduction (MBSR), Mindfulness-Based Cognitive Therapy (MBCT), Mindfulness-Based Relapse Prevention (MBRP), Dialectical Behavior Therapy (DBT), and Acceptance and Commitment Therapy (ACT).

Positive Psychology

Buddhism is also enjoying a dialogue with the emerging field of positive psychology. For much of its history, psychology focused on psychopathology rather than on optimal states. The Buddha had quite a head start in that his psychology is explicitly what would now be called positive psychology. Buddhist scholars Shauna Shapiro and B. Allan Wallace point out, "The goal of Buddhist practice is the realization of a state of well-being that is not contingent on the presence of pleasurable stimuli, either external or internal." Contemporary research studies are confirming this insight. Transient things like material wealth, praise, and pleasures cannot provide enduring happiness. It turns out the Buddha was right about clinging and aversion: they lead to misery. And this still holds true today. Happiness from internal mental training, that is, meditation, is more durable than stimulus-driven pleasures.

"In the first place a man never is happy but spends his whole life in striving after something which he thinks will make him so; he seldom attains his goals and, when he does it is only to be disappointed: he is mostly shipwrecked in the end, and comes into harbor with masts and riggings gone. And then it is all one whether he has been happy or miserable; for his life was never anything more than a present moment, always vanishing; and now it is over."—Arthur Schopenhauer

Buddhism and Technology

Modern technologies have created unprecedented opportunities for the spread of the *dharma*. You can find countless scriptures, teachers, and teachings online. There are online communities such as the one sponsored by *Tricycle* (*www.tricycle.com*). Some teachers, such as Shinzen Young, use telephone conference calls to conduct live online retreats (*www.basicmindfulness.org*). This gives participants the opportunity to attend from home without the travel and accommodation costs of going away on retreat. A company called eMindful (*www.emindful.com*) offers a variety of mindfulness-based courses online and also offers free daily meditations in a live video-conference room. These technologies have created a worldwide *sangha* that will continue to grow. You don't have to wait outside the gates of the Zen temple for days in the rain to find a teacher. You can get on the Internet right now and find the *dharma* in all of its varied glory.

CHAPTER 18

Brain of a Buddha

Buddhist meditation affects the brain in a positive way. Neuroscience studies of meditation have demonstrated enduring changes in both the function and structure of the brain that persist beyond the period of meditation. Recent research that takes advantage of advances in brain imaging technology is demonstrating very exciting findings on the benefits of meditation. These benefits lead to changes in how people feel, how they handle stress, and how they relate to each other.

Brain Basics

Your brain is a three-pound miracle. It is the most complex thing in the known universe. It is a powerhouse; despite being only three pounds, it utilizes 25 percent of your body's energy. It contains 100 billion nerve cells known as neurons. Each of these cells can make connections to other neurons, forming a vast array of interconnections. These connections can range from 100 to 100,000, averaging at about 10,000. And in any given moment, each of these connections can be in any one of ten electrical states. If you do the math, the numbers are staggering. At 100 billion neurons, there is one neuron for each star in the Milky Way galaxy. The brain is also closely wired to the body, with 3 million nerve connections going from the body to the brain and one million going from the brain to the body. These connections will turn out to be very useful when you are doing body-based *vipassana* (mindfulness) meditation.

"Simple calculations show that the number of humanly graspable sentences, sentence meanings, chess games, melodies, seeable objects, and so on can exceed the number of particles in the universe."
—Stephen Pinker

Plastic Fantastic

Not that long ago, say twenty years ago, neuroscientists believed that neurons did not regenerate. If you lost a neuron, whether due to a brain trauma or a night of heavy drinking, these neurons were lost forever. Now, with advances in brain imaging technology, scientists have realized that the brain is much more plastic (that is, its capacity to change in response to experience) than they thought. In fact, not only do neurons form new connections with each other promiscuously, after loss there can be neurogenesis.

This discovery of what is called "neuroplasticity" has invigorated the field of meditation research and provides a neurophysiological explanation for the benefits seen from meditation practice. The discovery of neuroplasticity highlights the amazing fact that experience changes the brain. It's not just Prozac in your brain that can make changes. Like all experiences, meditation can change the physical structure of your brain, and each time you sit down to meditate you are forming new neural connections and perhaps even developing new neurons. Of course, the Buddha didn't have this scientific knowledge, but his insights are now being confirmed by science. How cool is that?

A Million to One

Despite the brain being the most complex thing in the known universe with a prodigious processing capacity, consciousness is not what you think. Most of what the brain does is unconscious. Of all the information coming into your brain, only one millionth of that information gets to consciousness. Consciousness seems vast and everywhere, but this is an illusion.

The late psychologist Julian Jaynes likened consciousness to "asking a flashlight in a dark room to look around for something that does not have any light shining upon it." As far as the flashlight is concerned the room is completely bright.

At any given moment your brain is processing approximately 11 million bits of information per second from your sensory organs. By way of comparison, your television processes 4 million bits per second and your telephone about 4,000.

Of these 11 million, you can only be consciously aware of fifty at the maximum. Tor Norretranders estimates that the average is closer to sixteen bits. It makes you think of those t-shirts bemoaning the fact that all you got was a lousy t-shirt: "You mean my brain is the most complex entity in the known universe and all I got was a lousy sixteen bits of information?!"

"Many of our core mental processes such as awareness and attention and emotion regulation, including our very capacity for happiness and compassion, should best be conceptualized as trainable skills. The meditative traditions provide a compelling example of strategies and techniques that have evolved over time to enhance and optimize human potential and well-being."—Antoine Lutz

This bottleneck is where meditation is aimed. You would not want to be conscious of *everything* that came your way; that would be overwhelming. However, you do want to have more choice in how the precious resource of your present moment attention is directed and this is what mindfulness meditation will give you—choice.

Selective Inattention

Why is this important? Attention is one of humanity's most precious commodities. Being in the present is the currency of living. You either spend this currency living in the present moment or by squandering it, worrying about the future, or regretting the past.

If consciousness is a precious and fragile resource, it behooves you to be as attentive as possible to make the most of those sixteen bits of information. Who knows, with practice you can even expand that bandwidth to the maximum of fifty!

One of the consequences of this bandwidth problem is called *selective inattention*. Selective inattention is a fascinating phenomenon. Imagine that you are watching a video of six people, three in black shirts and three in white shirts, with each team passing a basketball back and forth to each other. Your job is to count how many times the basketball is passed between the players on the team. Meanwhile, a guy in a gorilla suit walks into the middle of the scene, beats his chest, and exits stage left. Of course you would notice the gorilla, right? Maybe. About half the people watching the video did *not* see the gorilla! If you are not seeing the "gorillas" in the course of your day, what else are you missing?

Chocolate Cake or Fruit Salad

An intriguing study shows just how fragile attention can be; how easily overwhelmed it can become. In this study, research subjects were given digits to remember. One group had to memorize a two-digit number and the other group a seven-digit number. After memorizing the number the subjects walked down the hall where they were presented with a snack choice: "decadent" chocolate cake or "healthy" fruit salad. Will power is a function of the prefrontal cortex (this part of the brain is examined in more detail below). What would you predict? The subjects who had to memorize the longer number chose the chocolate cake twice as much as the subjects memorizing the shorter number. Your poor consciousness gets so easily overwhelmed. Better beef it up with some meditation!

The Monk Who Loves Science

His Holiness the Dalai Lama has enjoyed a life-long fascination with science as recounted in his science memoir, *The Universe in a Single Atom: The Convergence of Science and Spirituality.* This interest in science has resulted in his reaching out to scientists over the past twenty-five years and his receptivity to their work. In 1987, the Mind and Life Institute was established to hold annual meetings with the Dalia Lama and Western scientists to discuss issues such as the mind, emotions, compassion, et cetera.

The precursor to the Mind and Life meetings was the Inner Science Conference. The first Inner Science Conference of 1984 was held at Amherst College and focused on Buddhist psychology as taught by the Dalai Lama. Western scientists and philosophers gave commentary on his talks and included: Robert Thurman, Richard Davidson, Frances Vaughan, Roger Walsh, David Bohm, Daniel Brown, Jack Engler, Seymour Boorstein, Kenneth Pelletier, Charles Tart, Bonnie Strickland, Renee Weber, Joseph Loizzo, Seymour Epstein, and G. Perry.

The Dalai Lama was the center of controversy in 2006 after he had been invited to give the keynote address at the annual "Neuroscience" meeting, a conference with 14,000 attendees. Some scientists protested that a religious figure should not be addressing this august scientific body. When interviewed and asked how he would feel if science made discoveries that contradicted his Buddhist beliefs, His Holiness promptly replied, "Change my beliefs." What other religious leader could make that claim?

The Dalai Lama has also sent some of his monks into the laboratory of Richard Davidson at the University of Wisconsin to be studied. These monks have shown exceptional differences in their brains and prodigious capacities to concentrate and generate compassion. These preliminary brain-imaging studies sparked a new wave of interest in the brain effects of meditation. While monks with thirty years of meditation experience had remarkable brains, you don't need to meditate for thirty years to get some of the benefits of meditation. In fact, as few as eight weeks of practicing mindfulness can result in significant changes in your brain.

Emotional Intelligence

Emotions are critical to functioning in the world. According to researchers Mayer, Salovey, and Caruso, there are four features of "emotional intelligence":

1. Perceiving emotions accurately in oneself and others
2. Using emotions to facilitate thinking
3. Understanding emotions, emotional language, and the signals conveyed by emotions
4. Managing emotions so as to attain specific goals

Emotional intelligence (EI) is the "ability to engage in sophisticated information processing about one's own and others' emotions and the ability to use this information as a guide to thinking and behavior. That is, individuals high in EI pay attention to, use, understand, and manage emotions, and these skills serve adaptive functions that potentially benefit themselves and others." Emotional intelligence was popularized by Daniel Goleman's book by that name, and you will see below how EI can be directly affected by meditation in areas such as empathy and emotional regulation.

Nine Benefits of Mindfulness Meditation

Mindfulness can bring your brain into an integrated state of harmony, balancing chaos on the one hand and rigidity on the other. This scientific wisdom is brought to you by neuroscientist Dan Siegel, author of several important books, including the *Developing Mind, The Mindful Brain, Mindsight*, and his latest, *The Mindful Therapist*. The middle prefrontal cortex, located behind your forehead and part of the newest part of the brain evolution-wise, (it's known as the "rational brain" in contrast to the "emotional brain" that is older evolutionarily) is critical to the following nine functions:

- Bodily regulation
- Attunement
- Emotional balance
- Response flexibility
- Downregulation of fear
- Insight
- Empathy
- Morality
- Intuition

Each of these functions is positively affected by meditation. When you meditate, your prefrontal cortex will actually change. It will become thicker in places, indicating new neural connections and perhaps even new neurons. It will be more efficient and more integrated.

Bodily Regulation

Bodily regulation is accomplished by regulating arousal and relaxation through the sympathetic and parasympathetic branches of the autonomic nervous system (think of the gas pedal and a brake in a car). If you are overly stressed or anxious, your sympathetic nervous system is overly active—think of a lead foot on the gas pedal—the car lurches forward and uses a lot of gas. Mindfulness helps to regulate the sympathetic nervous system, making it less reactive (no more lead foot), and helps you to drive the car more slowly. This cuts down on wear and tear on your body and reduces the risk for long-term health problems.

Attunement

Attunement is being connected to others, or being "in tune." By being mindful you can better connect to others because you are more present and less preoccupied with your own story. Attunement sows the seeds of compassion. Attunement provides the optimal environment for babies to develop in; healthy development happens when babies are attuned with their caregivers.

Emotional Balance

Emotional balance refers to how you engage with experiences. It balances apathy on the one hand and feeling overwhelmed on the other. Like bodily regulation, it's a Goldilocks phenomenon, not too much and not too little. This is the optimal place for neural integration. Like bodily regulation, this helps you to be more nuanced and less clumsy in your emotional responses. This will come in handy in your relationships and dealing with the day-to-day frustrations of life.

Response Flexibility

Response flexibility refers to the pause that can develop between a stimulus and response. It aims at the impulsive reactions that often occur in response to a stimulus. This pause comes from mindful awareness and can help you to be less impulsive and less destructive with what you say and do.

Downregulation of Fear

This important feature is your ability to adjust the signals from the emotional brain that can often overwhelm you. The emotional brain, which is responsible for emotions like fear and anger, has the job of keeping you safe. It does so by figuring out what you should be paying attention to. It is prone to making mistakes that err on the side of caution: "Is that a snake or a stick? Let's assume it's a snake and let's get the hell out of here."

That kind of mistake is less costly than guessing wrong. It takes longer to recover from a snakebite than to catch your breath for running away for no good reason. To be more accurate in detecting what should really get your precious attention resources, the prefrontal cortex (the rational brain) needs to have more nerve fibers going from the rational brain to the emotional brain to tell it, "Hey, it's a false alarm." This is accomplished through the development of inhibitory nerve fibers that go from the middle prefrontal cortex to structures like the amygdala in the emotional brain (limbic system). Mindfulness practice can help to develop these nerve fibers.

Insight

Insight refers to what Siegel calls mental time travel or what you might call imagination. Mindfulness can help you to refine this capacity in the service of living skillfully rather than being subjected to out-of-control worry, regret, and self-criticism. If you are not using your imagination for these destructive purposes it will be free to be creative, and that would be a much better thing to do with your attention.

Empathy

Empathy, or what Siegel calls "mindsight," refers to the ability to take the perspective of the other. Obviously, this is connected to compassion and once again hinges upon the ability to transcend your own self-preoccupied stories to meet the person you are with where they are. While some people are naturally more empathic than others, you are not stuck where you are. As with all of these features, empathy is a trainable skill. The more you meditate, the more empathic you can become.

Morality

Morality is also a function of the middle prefrontal cortex and includes not just your ability to be moral in public settings but also in private. As you already know, morality or ethics is a cornerstone of Buddhist teaching and practice, so it may not be a surprise to find morality showing up on this list too. Buddhist meditation practice helps you to discern skillful from unskillful actions in all domains. In the context of morality, this may require inhibiting an impulse, or inserting a pause before you say something.

Intuition

Intuition is the capacity to access the wisdom of the body by monitoring your bodily sensations. For example, a brain structure called the insula has a map of the interior body, and studies have found the insula gets thicker with meditation practice. The more you meditate, the more aware you will be of your body. This awareness can help you to cope with whatever the body is experiencing, whether that is pain, anxiety, or any discomfort whatsoever.

Before he took an interest in mindfulness, Siegel came up with the same list of brain function as mindfulness researchers had compiled independently. And it's not just brain researchers; this list has been striven for in many spiritual traditions since ancient times. When you recognize the plasticity of the brain, you can understand why you respond in certain situations the way that you do. Your previous conditioning will have you react in sometimes-harmful ways. But it is the fault of conditioning. However, at the same time, it is your responsibility (and potential) to change these conditionings through mindfulness and meditation. The middle prefrontal cortex develops optimally in an interpersonally attuned environment during infancy. Mindfulness provides the possibility of self-attunement to develop these same brain areas. So sit down and change your brain! (For more information visit: *http://drdansiegel.com.*)

Other Brain Benefits

One study found that people who had participated in an eight-week mindfulness meditation class had measurable shifts in the way their brains handled emotions, shifting their emotional set-point towards more positive feelings. This study also found a boost in their immune systems (chronic stress can reduce immune functioning).

Mindfulness meditation has also been shown to reduce the recurrence of major depression in patients who have had multiple episodes of depression. Mindfulness can also help with anxiety disorders including posttraumatic stress disorder. There is also some evidence suggesting that mindfulness meditation discourages self-destructive behavior in response to stress by encouraging acceptance rather than avoidance of negative emotions such as sorrow, guilt, or loneliness. This might seem backwards, but acceptance is the key and is at the core of the Buddha's teaching. When you accept something, you are in clear contact with reality. It doesn't mean that you like sorrow or want to be lonely, but you accept the fact that you are. Then a space opens up where you can experience these emotions as they are without having to change them into something else. This gives you freedom and can help to prevent covering these feelings over with potentially self-destructive behaviors such as smoking, eating, and drinking.

Two Modes of Being

A 2007 study by Farb and his colleagues, published in the journal *Social Cognitive and Affective Neuroscience*, confirms something that anyone who has done the Buddha's meditation has experienced first hand. In fact, it confirms what the Buddha experienced 2,500 years ago. It appears there are two basic modes of being that humans can be in at any given moment. The first mode can be called the "narrative mode," and is the default mode of being. This is where you are engaged in the running commentary of stories about the future and past and complaints about the present. It is the place where "I, me, mine" is confirmed through internal dialog. If you're like most people, it's where you spend most of your time. This kind of self-talk lights up certain parts of the brain. The other mode of being is called "experiencing," and is the mode that is active during mindfulness meditation, where you would be paying attention to the moment-to-moment activity in your body. This lights up a different part of the brain.

In their study, they trained half the subjects in mindfulness during an eight-week mindfulness-based stress-reduction class. They then compared them to the subjects who had not yet been trained in mindfulness. They had all subjects try to turn "off" their narrative mode; that is, focus attention on the present moment instead of future/past. The subjects who had mindfulness training were able to reduce the narrative mode significantly greater than the subjects who had not received mindfulness training. In addition, the mindfulness subjects were able to reduce activity in the amygdala, the fear-processing center of the brain, and increase activity in the areas of the prefrontal cortex that are responsible for monitoring the body. In other words, less narrative means fewer stories and less stress. Mindfulness training in as few as eight weeks produced noticeable and significant changes in the way the brain functioned, allowing the participants to enjoy being in the moment.

Social Brain

As you may have noticed in the section on the nine benefits of meditation, two of the benefits were explicitly social. The prefrontal cortex is very important for what is known as "social intelligence." Scientists have recently discovered a system in the brain called "mirror neurons." This system functions to help understand the intentions and behaviors of others by essentially trying to replicate what you see out there in your own brain. These mirror neurons were discovered in monkeys. They became active, whether the monkey grasped at a banana or simply watched another monkey grasp a banana. The brain of the watching monkey creates an estimate of that perceived experience in its own brain. In other words, empathy. As Professor Siegel explains in the *Mindful Brain*, "What we see we become ready to do, to mirror other's actions in our own behaviors." Not surprisingly, these mirror neurons become active during meditation.

Attachment

There has been a lot of discussion about attachment being something to avoid in order to follow the Buddha's teachings, but in biology, attachment has a different meaning. It refers to the process that infants undergo with their caretakers early in life. Attachment is necessary for survival and also for optimal brain development. Good attachment is attachment that is *attuned.* Attunement refers to the capacity for the caretaker, in most cases the mother, and the baby to be in a synchronized perceptual and emotional state. The attuned mother is very attentive to the baby's fleeting facial expressions (showing emotion) and behavior. This attunement provides an optimal environment for the prefrontal cortex of the infant to develop rich connections and lay the foundation for later social and emotional intelligence. Healthy or "secure" attachment via attunement helps the infant to develop a sense of safety and predictability in the world. Secure attachment helps infants grow into kids and adults who can be intimate, resilient, and enjoy well-being. In fact, as attachment researcher Phil Shaver points out, "security enhancing interactions with attachment figures increase a person's capacity for mindfulness."

Self-Attunement

There is an appealing parallel between infant attachment and mindfulness meditation, the meditation the Buddha did under the Bodhi Tree thousands of years ago. As mentioned above, a loving secure environment helps people to be naturally more mindful—that is, able to be in the present moment without regret and worry. The amazing finding is that the regions of the brain affected by mindfulness meditation are the very *same* areas of the brain that develop during infancy; the very same circuits that lead to social and emotional intelligence. Dan Siegel refers to mindfulness as a process of *self-attunement.* In a sense, when you meditate you are reparenting yourself, attuning to the moment-to-moment changes in your perceptual and emotional states. Siegel describes this process through the acronym COAL: curiosity, openness, acceptance, and love.

Mindfulness Benefits

To summarize the positive changes that mindfulness promotes in the brain, think of the following six steps:

1. When you are mindful, you are paying attention to the reality of the present moment with accuracy and clarity.
2. This clarity redirects your attention away from ruminative stories about the future and the past to pay attention to the richness of the moment (the experiencing mode rather than the narrative mode).
3. This, in turn, turns down the reactivity of the emotional brain and leads to relaxation without having to keep mounting a stress response to imagined threats.
4. Over time (and as few as eight weeks), this will lead to neural connections developing in the prefrontal cortex of your brain that will help you to be more mindful and have more social and emotional intelligence.
5. This leads to a state of self-attunement and either an enhancement of your ability to be intuitive or empathic or to helping to overcome deficits in these areas if you did not have optimal attachment growing up.
6. Finally, you experience a state of equanimity with an increased ability to cope with whatever life throws your way.

All this from sitting down on a cushion and being quiet!

CHAPTER 19

Can Buddhism Save the Planet?

There is wide recognition that the planet is in trouble. Climate change, overpopulation, and the depletion of natural resources threaten the future of humanity. Do Buddhists have something unique to offer toward the solution of these problems? Thich Nhat Hanh warns that the future of all life on earth hangs in the balance of whether humans can be mindful of Mother Earth. The quiet solitude of meditation and the mindfulness it cultivates is integral to Buddhism in action, so that humans can see clearly and cause no harm.

Individual Poisons, Collective Problems

If you recall the Three Poisons, greed, hatred, and delusion, these could explain much of the world's problems today. What you experience on an individual level is reflected in the collective. Individuals walking a Buddhist path are working to become awakened, that is, to overcome the pull of greed, hatred, and delusion. But cultural institutions, corporations, and governments are very much in the shadow of greed and delusion (or ignorance or denial, take your pick). The planet is out of balance. The 20 percent richest of the world's population consume 60 percent of its resources. Americans do more than their fair share of the damage, whether it is oil, food, or narcotics. After the economic downturn that followed the terrorist attacks of September 11, 2001, President Bush urged Americans to "go shopping."

The Lotus *Sutra* mentions Dharanimdhara. She is a special *bodhisattva* whose name means "Earth Holder" and whose job is to preserve and protect the earth.

Is there a better solution? Current rates of consumptions are not sustainable, and how awake is humanity to this reality on a moment-to-moment basis? Recall the antidotes to the Three Poisons: generosity, lovingkindness, and wisdom. Could these contribute to a solution of the looming disaster? If humanity cannot figure out how to live mindfully, there is not much hope for the future.

Fortunately, many Buddhists teachers are getting out in the world and doing the work that needs to be done to generate awakening on a global scale. This is part of what is called "Engaged Buddhism." Living a peaceful life and causing no harm is a foundation; after all, you don't want to be a "violent" peace advocate. However, it will probably take more than individuals sitting on cushions to produce needed social and environmental change. Thich Nhat Hanh claims Buddhism is the "Strongest form of humanism we have." Imagine if everyone followed the Buddha's ethical precepts of not harming and consuming mindfully. The world would be a different place.

Be a *Bodhisattva* Now: Engaged Buddhism

The *bodhisattva* vows to help others to wake up by working diligently towards enlightenment. This spirit of service to others is a large part of being a Buddhist—cultivating an open heart and practicing not only "random acts of kindness" but committing yourself to social and environmental good. In *Peace Is Every Step*, Thich Naht Hanh writes, "When I was in Vietnam, so many of our villages were being bombed. Along with my monastic brothers and sisters, I had to decide what to do. Should we continue to practice in our monasteries or should we leave the meditation halls in order to help the people who were suffering under the bombs? After careful reflection, we decided to do both—to go out and help people and to do so in mindfulness. We called it engaged Buddhism. Mindfulness must be engaged. Once there is seeing, there must be acting. Otherwise, what is the sense of seeing?"

So, engaged Buddhism is getting out there and making the world a better place; it's connecting with other people and forming relationships. Once a Buddhist, through diligent practice, sees clearly that everything is interdependent, it becomes difficult to sit back and do nothing. "If anyone is hurting, I too am hurting" becomes the philosophy of the engaged Buddhist.

What is socially engaged Buddhism?
Socially engaged Buddhism is a *dharma* practice that flows from the understanding of the complete yet complicated interdependence of all life. It is the practice of the *bodhisattva* vow to save all beings. It is to know that the liberation of ourselves and the liberation of others are inseparable. It is to transform ourselves as we transform all our relationships and our larger society. It is work at times from the inside out and at times from the outside in, depending on the needs and conditions. It is to see the world through the eye of the *dharma* and to respond emphatically and actively with compassion. Source: Donald Rothberg and Hozan Alan Senauke from the Buddhist Peace Fellowship (*www.bpf.org/socially-engaged*).

You can also practice engaged Buddhism by working toward promoting peace in the world. Buddhist Peace Fellowship (*www.bpf.org*) is the oldest socially engaged Buddhist nonprofit organization in the United States. There is an environmentally aware group called Earth Sangha (*www.earthsangha.org*) that encourages the practice of Buddhism as an answer to the global environmental crisis. There are as many ways to help as there are varieties of people in the world. Celebrate life by improving the quality of someone else's life. You might find a happiness you never imagined in the joy of serving others.

What Can One Person Do?

Isabel Losada, author of the *Beginner's Guide to Changing the World*, asks this question and wonders how Buddhists should be engaged in the cause of Tibet. She has noticed protests against China that are angry and very "un-Buddhist" and bereft of Buddhist practitioners. Where are the Buddhists, and what are they doing?

Buddhists, like anyone, can get engaged in the political process, lobbying their members of parliament or congress to inform them on the situation and to urge action. These meetings or letters should be suffused with lovingkindness and wisdom, not polemics or anger. This reflects the Dalai Lama's strategy of nonviolence in his efforts to reconcile with China.

Taking an approach of nonviolence does not equate with non-action. Sitting on the cushion and meditating is not enough. Losada urges you to ponder this question, "How can I engage in this with joy?" This reflects the wisdom that it is through generosity, lovingkindness, and wisdom that change occurs rather than greed, hatred, and delusion disguised as a righteous cause. Indeed, when you can set aside preoccupation with your stories of fear and trying to protect "I, me, and mine," a space opens up for action that helps others. As Losada points out, this action can be joyful.

Liza Smith speaks to the relationship between the practitioner and the rest of the world: "I don't think Buddhist practice would be relevant to me if it weren't engaged with the rest of the world. It just doesn't feel useful to me if it's always inwardly focused. The Buddhist principle of making friends with yourself, with our own mind, seems to have a parallel in the work that I do, where we need to make friends with the so-called enemy."

Fernando De Torrijos, an inner-city Mindfulness-Based Stress Reduction teacher, speaks to his experience helping others: "The thing I can do is to help people to allow their self-esteem to come back up, to lift—little by little—the deep depression that many of these patients have become accustomed to."

Mindful Environment

According to legend, just before the Buddha became awake, he touched the earth so the earth could serve as witness to this momentous event. What would he think if he touched the earth today?

> Thich Nhat Hanh warns, "If we continue to live as we have been living, consuming without a thought of the future, destroying our forests and emitting greenhouse gases, then devastating climate change is inevitable. Much of our ecosystem will be destroyed. Sea levels will rise and coastal cities will be inundated, forcing hundreds of millions of refugees from their homes, creating wars and outbreaks of infectious disease."

Stephanie Kaza teaches "a green practice path" and suggests taking action on the issues that are of most concern to you. You can't save the entire planet, so pick one cause and give that your energy. And you'll need your Buddhist training to do this difficult work of trying to ameliorate the suffering on this planet. She cautions, "This requires patience and equanimity in the face of disturbing realities—a clear cut forest reduced to stumps, a once-lush river deadened by chemical waste, a coral reef blasted by dynamite fishing. It is not easy to be clear-eyed at these troubling results of human activity." Kaza also explains, "The Buddhist systems-thinker involved in environmental controversy would ask as much about the human actors and their attitudes as about the affected trees and wildlife."

Mindfulness is integral to establishing this courage. She goes on to say that mindfulness provides an authenticity that can "provide a stable mental base from which to observe the whole catastrophe of human impact." The illusion of separation contributes to this catastrophe; so, too, do culturally conditioned ideas that look upon the environment as a resource for humans to exploit. The Buddha's concept of dependent origination can speak to environmental challenges. Everything is interconnected; actions in one place have ramifications on other places; something that affects one species will have an impact on many other species. In environmental science this is known as systems thinking.

If you want to devote your energies to the environment you can become an "ecosattva," a *bodhisattva* committed to ending environmental suffering. First, do no harm; second, do what you can to relieve suffering. It's bound to be a slow process and is part of what the Dalai Lama has called "ethics for a new millennium." Everyone must take responsibility for the well-being of the planet. This requires both compassion and restraint. Being *mindfully green* means to consider this question: "What is really important now, both in my own life and the world?"

Mindful Politics

Melvin McLeod edits the volume *Mindful Politics*: "Politics is really about how we live together as human beings, and all spiritual practices point to one simple but profound truth about human life—that only love leads to peace, hatred never does. This is as true for nations as it is for individuals."

McLeod's proposed Buddhist-inspired political platform is (that is, if the Buddha were a politician he might have based his politics on the Four Immeasurables):

May all beings enjoy happiness and the root of happiness.

May they be free from suffering and the root of suffering.

May they not be separated from the great happiness devoid of suffering.

May they dwell in the great equanimity free of passion, aggression, and ignorance.

Politics is emotions gone awry—vengeance, war, persecution of difference. As Buddhism, particularly through mindfulness, promotes emotional and social intelligences, it might have something to offer the world as an antidote to hostility, inequity, and damage. The dualistic and false sense of "us" versus "them" underlies much of the conflict. If everyone does not work together then there is the risk of being divided one against another. According to McLeod, the keys to change are: forgiveness, awareness, kindness, and selflessness. Politics is ultimately about relationships, and all relationships brook in power and conflict. How will these conflicts be resolved? Will they be resolved with mindful awareness or through the perpetuation of the Three Poisons?

Individual transformation is the prerequisite for societal transformation. The first step is not to save the world, but to save yourself. If each individual works to limit or even eliminate hatred, greed, and ignorance, the world will be a better place through the aggregation of this absence.

"When we talk about preservation of the environment, it is related to many other things. Ultimately, the decision must come from the human heart. The key point is to have a genuine sense of universal responsibility, based on love and compassion, and clear awareness."
—The Dalai Lama

Consider this statement from Buddhist monk and Vietnam veteran Claude Anshin Thomas, in his book *At Hell's Gate: A Soldier's Journey from War to Peace*. "Peace is not an idea. Peace is not a political movement, not a theory or a dogma. Peace is a way of life: living mindfully in the present moment… It is not a question of politics, but of actions. It is not a matter of improving a political system or even taking care of homeless people alone. These are valuable but will not alone end war and suffering. We must simply stop the endless wars that rage within . . . Imagine, if everyone stopped the war in themselves—there would be no seeds from which war could grow."

Engaged Buddhism in Action

Here are two examples of American Zen teachers who took their practice out of the Zendo to serve their communities and the *sangha*.

Bernard Tetsugen Glassman

Bernard Tetsugen Glassman is one of America's most provocative Zen teachers and promoters of engaged Buddhism. In 1982 he founded the

Greyston Bakery in New York City. His idea was to start a business that would employ the members of his *sangha*—allowing them to leave their day jobs—so they could concentrate more fully on their practice and contribute to the practice of engaged Buddhism. In 1993, The Greyston Foundation, a nonprofit corporation, was created to oversee social improvement programs. Profits from the bakery filter through the foundation, supporting its social development work for the poor and afflicted. Greyston helps the homeless, the jobless, provides childcare, health care, and living assistance for people with HIV/AIDS.

QUOTE

"So for me the question became, 'What are the forms in business, social action and peacemaking that can help us see the oneness in society, the interdependence in life?'"—Roshi Bernie Glassman

Once Greyston was established, Roshi Glassman (with Roshi Sandra Holmes) then went on to create an order of Zen practitioners devoted to the cause of peace; the Peacemakers Order subsequently emerged. The Peacemaker Community is now an international peacemaking group with members involving the world's five major religions, including organizations (Greyston Mandala in New York City; Prison Dharma Network in Rhode Island; Upaya Study Center in Sante Fe; StadtRaum in Germany; Mexico City Village, Mexico; La Rete d'Indra in Italy; and Shanti Relief Committee in Japan) and individuals worldwide.

Joan Jiko Halifax

Roshi Joan Jiko Halifax is a student of Thich Nhat Hanh, a founding member of the Zen Peacemaker Order, and founder and *roshi* of the Upaya Zen Center in Santa Fe, New Mexico. She is an author and activist, greatly respected for her work with the dying. Upaya programs include Being with Dying, the Partners Program, the Prison Project, and the Kailash Education Fund.

Being with Dying is a program aimed at helping caregivers work with dying people, to change their relationship to both the dying and living. A focus of the program is the training of health care professionals who take their work with the dying back to their own institutions where they can teach these practices to other health care professionals. The Partners Program matches dying people with caregivers they need, complementing the help of hospice workers and medical professionals. The Prison Project offers mindfulness training to inmates in the Mexico prison system, aiming to reduce stress in prison, and The Kailash Education Fund is aimed at providing educational opportunities to some of the poorest children in Nepal.

Mindful Leadership

If social change is going to occur, the people who are leading our institutions, corporations, and governments must embrace mindfulness. Janice Maturano, a VP at General Mills, put it this way: "Leaders today are faced with global economies, time measured in Internet seconds, and a future that is increasingly interdependent—challenges that require leaders to use all of their capabilities, including the innate abilities of mindfulness." Imagine if they actually trained these innate abilities with meditation? Companies like General Mills and Green Mountain Coffee Roasters (GMCR) have picked up this mantle and offer mindfulness meditation programs to their employees, and in the case of GMCR, to the wider community.

According to an October 2008 article on Bloomberg.com: "An increasing number of those hitting the cushion are players in corporate America, looking to more unconventional practices to calm frayed nerves at a time when the Dow Jones Industrial Average had its biggest drop since the Great Depression and financial institutions are declaring bankruptcy after the collapse of the U.S. subprime-mortgage market." Shinzen Young teaches the program at GMCR. He states, "If you don't have a meditation practice, you're going to suffer unnecessarily subjectively, and objectively you will make bad decisions; that sums up the story."

Buddha in Jail

The United States imprisons more of its citizens than any other country in the world. Buddhism has ventured into the prison system in the United

States and around the world. Shugen Sensei is the director of the National Buddhist Prison Sangha (NBPS) that started teaching inmates meditation in 1984 with John Daido Lori.

Prison can also provide the opportunity for awakening as portrayed in the compelling memoir *Razor Wire Dharma* by Calvin Malone. Here is an excerpt where he describes the mundane experience of eating an apple, an apple that stood out from the usual horrible prison food he was subjected to.

> *Breathing in I smelled apple, breathing out the universe. Everything there is or ever was was contained in this apple. I could see it with the wild exactness of shattered glass. The answer and the question were there in the apple. I was feeling an inexplicable joy, keenly aware. I never before felt better in my life. I realized this moment was as good as it gets.*

The Buddha's teachings offer this form of radical freedom. The happiest moment of your life could occur during a prison sentence. That true happiness could arise from the simple beauty of an apple, a living thing connected to everything else in the entire universe.

The pioneering work bringing Buddha into prison was conducted by S. N. Goenka at the Tihar jail in New Delhi, India. This prison was considered the most dangerous prison on earth. Before his work there, torture and murder were commonplace. A visionary warden, Kiran Bedi, embraced Goenka's aspirations to teach the inmates *vipassana* meditation. The Vipassana Prison Trust (VPT) teaches *vipassana* courses to Tihar inmates, a thousand at a time, and also teaches in prisons in Israel, New Zealand, Mongolia, Taiwan, Thailand, the United Kingdom, and the United States.

Mindfulness in Health Care

One of the most significant Buddhist influences in the West does not call itself Buddhist at all. This takes the form of mindfulness in health care, practiced every day in the United States and the rest of the Western world. Medical patients with chronic pain and other debilitating conditions engage in the same meditation that the Buddha did centuries ago, except that they are not practicing "Buddhism" at all; they are developing skills to get relief from their conditions.

The fulcrum for this worldwide movement resides in Worcester, Massachusetts, at the Center for Mindfulness in Medicine, Healthcare, and Society, founded by Jon Kabat-Zinn in 1979. Since that time, hundreds of thousands of people have been exposed to Buddha outside the context of formal Buddhism. Almost every major medical center in the United States has a mindfulness-based stress reduction program (MBSR), and there are hundreds or professionals worldwide who do this work. These include programs and professionals at prestigious university hospitals such as Harvard and Duke Medical Schools. This is, perhaps, the most widespread application of Buddhism in the world.

This practice helps people from all walks of life and from all religious traditions. Since MBSR patients are not being trained in Buddhism, they carry on with whatever beliefs and practices they have. What makes MBSR so special is that it has translated the Buddha's teaching into a practical and readily-learned eight-week format that is effective. Thirty years of research has confirmed its effectiveness in reducing stress and negative emotions, improving coping skills, and helping patients to get on with their lives.

Spiritual Revolution

Not all Buddhist teachers are about "making nice." Buddhism can be idealized, but it is a human institution, and like all human institutions, it can be dogmatic, reactionary, and ignorant of its blind spots. No one is immune from scandal or hypocrisy. The following authors take an honest and piercing look at Buddhism, and each goes back to the Buddha's fundamental teachings for guidance. The Buddha was a spiritual revolutionary and the revolution has some new legs.

The Revolutionary Manifesto

In his latest book *Against the Stream: A Buddhist Manual for Spiritual Revolutionaries*, Noah Levine, author of *Dharma Punx*, writes about how radical the Buddha's teachings are in a refreshing new way. He starts, "*Against the Stream* is more than just another book about Buddhist meditation.

It is a manifesto and field guide for the front lines of the revolution. It is the culmination of almost two decades of meditative dissonance from the next generation of Buddhists in the West. It is a call to awakening for the sleeping masses." This revolution began 2,500 years ago with Siddhartha, but Levine feels it is has gotten bogged down in dogmatism and corruption of the Buddha's original teachings. It's a "radical and subversive personal rebellion against the causes of suffering and confusion."

To wake up in our society is a radical act. To reject consumerism and the relentless pursuit of pleasure is downright un-American. There was something radical about the Buddha's insights in the Axial Age, and that radical spirit persists in the Information Age. His teachings went "against the stream."

Levine identifies four cries to action in his revolutionary manifesto:

- Defy the lies
- Serve the truth
- Beware of teachers
- Question everything

Levine cautions that "Human beings have created a deeply dysfunctional culture" and that "Buddhism" is not the solution. "I would reject so-called Buddhism along with the rest, because much of what masquerades as Buddhism today is in direct opposition to what the Buddha actually did and taught." The truth to serve is wisdom and compassion and the truth of reality. "The spiritual revolutionary practices nonviolence, generosity, and engagement to help others." And as a final note of advice, "Accept nothing as true until you have experienced it for yourself."

Hardcore Zen

Brad Warner is another contemporary Buddhist teacher. Like Levine, his teachings are raw, honest, and iconoclastic. Author of *Hardcore Zen: Punk Rock, Monster Movies, & the Truth About Reality*, and more recently, *Zen Wrapped in Karma, Dipped in Chocolate*, Warner issues similar warnings as Levine. He says, "Nothing is sacred. Doubt—in everything—is absolutely essential. Everything, no matter how great, how fundamental, how beautiful, or important it is must be questioned." And that includes Buddhism and

Buddhist teachers. Echoing the original teachings of the Buddha, he warns against holding any "beliefs." Rather, your direct experience must take precedence over belief. He goes on to say, "Some people think enlightenment is some kind of superspecial state without questions or doubts, some kind of absolute faith in your beliefs and the rightness of your perceptions. That's not enlightenment. In fact, that's the very worst kind of delusion."

As you contemplate taking action to make the world a better place, consider Warner's admonition: "You can't live in paradise—but you are living right here. Make this your paradise or make this your hell. The choice is entirely yours. Really."

Money, Sex, War, Karma

In his book, *Money, Sex, War, Karma*, Buddhist author, professor, and teacher David Loy presents essays on these topics to help to establish a "new vision of human possibility." Buddhist practitioners in the West are confronted with differentiating what needs to be retained from traditional Asian Buddhism and what needs to be unique to the West.

Like transplanting an exotic species to new soil, it may be helpful to retain some of the original soil. At the same time, he points out the irony that the Buddha was very flexible in his approach, "more flexible and open-minded than the institutions that developed to preserve his teachings." To save the planet, Buddhism will need to rediscover this flexibility.

To overcome the destructive influence of greed, hatred, and delusion, the self's sense of fundamental *lack* must be addressed. Westerners have constructed a sense of self that seeks to fill this sense of lack with money and material possessions, sex, and acts out through aggression, conflict, and warfare. "Awakening to our constructedness (that is, no self) is the only real solution to our most fundamental anxiety."

Loy states, "We live in a world radically different from anything that even Shakyamuni could have anticipated, which requires creative ways of adapting his profound insights to new challenges." Awakening is basically a personal affair, and while it may be tempting to think that Buddhism could provide enlightened solutions to political and economic problems, the translation from one domain to another may not be that seamless. Loy points out that Buddhism has more to say about the means of change rather than what to change. He recommends four components for the Buddhist revolution:

- Spiritual practice
- Commitment to nonviolence
- Awakening together
- Impermanence and emptiness

These four ingredients are unique to the Buddha's teachings. Maintaining a meditation practice will keep you from falling prey to greed, ignorance, and delusion. It will also help you to be nonviolent and approach change in that way. The path of the *bodhisattva* is a communal one where your awakening helps others to awaken. Finally, the recognition that things are always changing and empty of substantial reality will help change to be grounded in wisdom. Societies and cultures construct reality, and these constructions are always changing. Recognizing this and working to embody these four components can help to address collective *dukkha*—the pervasive suffering that has infected the world. Loy concludes that the "Buddhist emphasis on the liberation of our collective attention suggest that a socially awakened Buddhism might have a distinctive role to play in clarifying what the basic problem really is."

CHAPTER 20

Buddha in Daily Life

Meditation and all the Buddha's wisdom would not be of much value if it stayed on the cushion. Meditation trains you for living an awakened life. This chapter will take a closer look at mindfulness and how it gets applied in daily life, including when daily life happens in a meditation retreat.

Mindfulness

In *The Greater Discourse on the Foundations of Mindfulness*, the Buddha set forth the practice of mindfulness for his students:

> *There is, Monks, this one way to the purification of beings, for the overcoming of sorrow and distress, for the disappearance of pain and sadness, for the gaining of the right path, for the realization of Nirvana—that is to say the four foundations of mindfulness.*
>
> *What are the four? Here, monks, a monk abides contemplating body as a body, ardent, clearly aware and mindful, having put aside hankering and fretting for the world; he abides contemplating feelings as feelings;...he abides contemplating mind as mind;...he abides contemplating mind-objects as mind-objects, ardent, clearly aware and mindful, having put aside hankering and fretting for the world.*

Meditation practice helps you to be mindful in daily life; in other words, awake to what you experience and do as you move through life. It is easy to get caught up in stories about the future and the past, and sometimes these stories run to worry and regret. You may find yourself commenting, and more likely complaining, about the present, but not actually paying attention to it. To be awake is to be mindful; paying attention to the reality of this moment as it is happening without judgment or storytelling. To be mindful is to break the habit of automatic pilot and following every impulse that arises. To be mindful is to be awake in movement: in eating, eliminating, driving, working, loving, and whatever else you do during the course of your day.

To be mindful, try to give full attention to your lived experience. As William James said over 100 years ago, "The intellectual life of man consists almost wholly of his substitution of a conceptual order for the perceptual order in which his experience originally lives." To be mindful is to re-orient to the perceptual away from the conceptual, storytelling aspects of the mind. To be mindful, pay attention to what you see, hear, taste, smell, and most importantly, the sensations you feel in your body. Be aware how your mind generates thoughts in the form of stories, images, memories, and emotions (and all the possible combinations of these). The fruit of meditation practice on the cushion and all the techniques described so far is to facilitate this mindful awareness in daily life.

You should take your practice with you into everything you do. Vietnamese Zen Master Thich Nhat Hanh provides mindfulness exercises in his wonderful book, *The Miracle of Mindfulness.* Here are a few of his suggestions that you can use during the day:

- Measure your breath by your footsteps
- Count your breaths
- Set aside a day of mindfulness
- Half-smile
- Follow your breath while having a conversation

Strive to become mindful in every part of your life. When you are eating, eat. When you are walking, walk. When you are making love, make love. When you are cooking, cook. Be there in the moment each and every moment. The moment is all you have. *This* moment.

In *Zen and the Ways,* Trevor Leggett explains how meditation can push agitation away: "When in sitting meditation there is agitation of thought, then with that very agitated mind seek to find where the agitated thought came from, and who it is that is aware of it. In this way pressing forward as to the location of the disturbance further and further to the ultimate point, you will find that the agitation does not have any original location."

The art of meditation is a way to wake up to the world. You can learn new ways to see your troubles and your pain and bring true wisdom to your life. As American *vipassana* teacher Jack Kornfield relates in *A Path with Heart,* attention is like training a puppy. You sit the puppy down and tell him to stay, but the puppy immediately gets up and runs away. So you sit the puppy back down again and tell him to stay. And the puppy runs away. Sometimes he runs away and poops in the corner.

So it is with your mind. You tell your mind to sit still and it is off to the corner to make a mess and you have to start over and over again. With mindfulness, you can come back to the present moment in a matter of fact way, just picking up where you left off, or you can reproach yourself for attention having wandered. You wouldn't yell at the puppy, so try not to yell at yourself. All minds wander—that's what they do.

Anything worthwhile requires effort, and meditation practice is one of these worthwhile endeavors. Sometimes practice will flow fluently and at other times it will be a struggle. It is at those times that a community and a teacher are helpful to provide support and keep you on track. Once you have been practicing for a while, you will start to taste the fruits of your labor and have glimpses of something beyond the stories about yourself. You might even taste that sense of no-self the Buddha talked about as you experience yourself as a moment-to-moment process rather than a "thing" that needs to be protected and constantly convinced of its worth. Enjoy your practice and keep at it!

Diving In

The traditional way to learn Theravada-style meditation is a ten-day silent meditation retreat. If you go to one of these you will experience both *shamatha* and *vipassana*. The first three days are devoted to *shamatha*, focusing on the breath. Depending on the teacher's tradition, this focus may be very narrow; for example, just on the tip of your nose, or the focus may be broader on any aspect of the breathing process.

The instructions are clear and rather straightforward: Whenever you find your attention moving away from the sensations of your breathing, bring your attention back. This is what you should expect whenever you meditate. You will place your focus on your breathing, and within a few moments your focus will be somewhere else—into the future or past or engaged in a commentary about the present. Your mind will be engaged with talking thoughts, lost in images, or awash in emotions, or sights, sounds, or other bodily sensations may distract you. This is quite normal.

It can be a source of frustration if you think your mind should be perfectly behaved and never wander. The method is to keep repeating this process; noticing attention has moved away from the breath and bringing it back (and not adding any criticism of your mental focusing powers).

Breathing in the Retreat

In the retreat environment, this exclusive focus on breathing would be maintained for three days. You would arise early in the morning and engage in multiple meditation periods throughout the day. Depending on the tradition and the instructor, walking meditation may be interspersed with sitting meditation. Breaks are taken for meals, and these meals are a continuation of practice, the practice of mindful eating.

You may also have the opportunity to do work practice where you do a yogi job, such as sweeping floors or washing dishes, and the invitation is to be mindful as you do these activities. A typical retreat day may involve over ten hours of formal meditation practice with the remainder of the day engaged with informal practice.

In the Burmese tradition as taught by S. N. Goenka, only sitting meditation is practiced.

On breaks, you can walk, but this is not slow walking meditation practice. Goenka asks participants to give up all other practices for the ten days of the retreat so that you can intensify your experience of mindfulness. He will encourage you to, "Work diligently, ardently, patiently and persistently, and you will be bound to be successful."

After establishing a firm foundation of concentration (*shamatha*) through three days of breathing practice, the remainder of the retreat will be devoted to *vipassana,* exploring sensations arising in the body (Burmese tradition) or any arising of phenomena, especially bodily sensations (Thai tradition).

The Challenge of the Retreat

The ten-day retreat is an arduous undertaking. It might be one of the most difficult experiences of your life and also the most valuable. It's hard to sit for all those hours without physical discomfort and even pain. However, the retreat becomes a crucible for self-knowledge. Each time you practice mindfulness meditation you cultivate an intimacy with your own experience, and doing so intensively on retreat will give a very rare opportunity to get to know yourself. This is difficult to achieve in everyday life with all of its distractions. For this reason, the retreat environment employs what is called "Noble Silence." This means no talking (other than if you have to talk with a staff member, or some retreats have question and answer periods and interviews with teachers), so perhaps better stated as no unnecessary talking.

The goal is to disengage from typical discourse, and this includes eye contact and other non-verbal interactions with others. The retreat environment is an opportunity to, as the Buddha said, "become an island unto yourself." Also suspended for the duration of the retreat are writing, reading, and of course there are no televisions or telephones. In today's environment, there are no laptops, cell phones, iPods, or iPads. Imagine that—no texting, social media, emails—none of the usual distractions that you encumber your life with! The wisdom of Noble Silence is that it closes all of the escape routes and keeps your focus squarely on practice. After a while, even imagination gives up and you will find yourself dwelling in the present moment and experiencing the world in, perhaps, a way that you never have before. On retreat you can have a taste of monastic life without having to make those commitments.

Types of Retreats

Retreats come in many lengths and can be residential or non-residential. For example, at the Cambridge Insight Meditation Center in Cambridge, Massachusetts, retreats are non-residential and may be one or two days on a nine to five schedule. Other retreats can be three months, and in one tradition there is a three year, three month, and three days-long retreat! As mentioned earlier, a very common retreat length is ten days.

So again, concentration provides the foundation for insight. And morality provides the foundation for everything. In addition to becoming intimate with your experience, meditation also provides the means to change your internal landscape from one characterized by *dukkha* to one characterized by freedom. Mindfulness is an integral component to every Buddhist tradition and is, in fact, the method Siddhartha Gautama used to become the Buddha.

Contemplative Education

Mindfulness is not just beneficial for adults. Why not start with children when they are young? Why not bring mindfulness into the schools? The increasing popularity of mindfulness from healthcare is filtering into the education system. Linda Lantieri, founder of The Inner Resilience Program in New York

City, finds "students who engaged in mindfulness practice seem to experience reduced stress and acting-out behaviors and increased coping skills, as well as enhanced concentration and in increased sense that the classroom is a community." Other voices in contemplative education include David Forbes, author of Boyz 2 Buddhas, and Deborah Schoeberlein, author of *Mindful Teaching and Teaching Mindfulness: A Guide for Anyone Who Teaches Anything.*

Gardening

Gardening itself can be an act of meditation, as recently portrayed in the book *The Meditative Gardener* by Cheryl Wilfong. Dropping your preoccupation with the future and the past seems more possible with hands immersed in earth and your smile exposed to the sun.

When you garden, you connect with your environment in a powerful way. You become intimate with the cycle of life. You can notice the change in the seasons and how each season blends into the next—spring starts in winter with buds showing through the retreating snow, and the leaves start to fall in late summer. The insects have their own life cycles and agendas, and in watching the earthworms and the ants, you can see a larger pattern to life. You can see the interconnection of the roots and the soil, the creatures and rain. You can eat that which you have grown yourself and feel connected to the earth in a way you may have never known before. Gardening is a meditative act and an affirmation of life.

Try sitting in a garden and practicing breathing meditation. Moments of wakefulness may come as you drop your stories and notice the life around you. Lose yourself in the sound of the birds, the delicate tapping of the rain on leaves. Hear the movement of water and the flow of a gentle breeze. Anyone who spends time outdoors knows the connection between every living thing on earth.

Mindfulness in Sport and Exercise

All athletes have experienced a meditative state worthy of a Buddha. Sometimes athletic activities pull you into a natural state of mindfulness. Sport becomes a form of meditation when you engage it with your full attention.

Understanding mindfulness and mindfulness meditation can help to bring you closer to the experience of sport. This phenomenon can be called *sport-samadhi* (recall that *samadhi* is the Sanskrit term for "meditative concentration"). This type of focused and absorbed concentration is likely familiar to anyone who has slid down a snow-covered mountain at high speed, pushed the pain barrier on a long-distance run, felt at one with their kayak as it shot a set of rapids, or ripped a huge wave on a surfboard. The talking mind becomes quiet and fully absorbed in the action of the moment. You are not lost in thoughts about the past, worries, or planning for the future. You are not telling stories about the activity or anything else. You are present. There is a steady living presence in the fullness of the moment. This is the state of mindfulness. Mindfulness can be thrilling even if the activity is rather ordinary.

Non-gravity sports such as road running, road biking, and swimming offer a ready opportunity to full body awareness. Instead of a gravity-induced absorption, the immersion in the present moment includes the entire body. Take running, for instance, where you can experience a moment-to-moment connection with your total body experience, even when this experience includes pain and discomfort. The challenge is to stay with the experience at the level of sensation. That is, experiencing it as a pattern of gross and pointed sensations instead of labeling it "pain." However, the mind has a tendency to move you out of the moment of experiencing sensation and perception and to start evaluating and judging the experience. Ultimately, you start to tell stories about the experience: "I can't take this anymore." When you can be mindful of the present, the artificial distinctions between mind and body disappear and yield to an awareness of being.

Get on a surfboard to attain enlightenment! Jaimal Yogis suggests surfing as a spiritual path in his poignant and deep memoire, *Saltwater Buddha: A Surfer's Quest to Find Zen on the Sea*. He quotes Suzuki Roshi: "Waves are the practice of water. To speak of waves apart from water and water apart from waves is a delusion."

Mindfulness and *sport-samadhi* can also impact how you deal with exertion and the limits of your body. If you are running uphill and are engaged in a future-oriented conversation, you will be more apt to give up and not push through the pain and discomfort of that exertion. This future-oriented story may be mindless chatter, or it can also be focused on the activity itself. For instance, if you look up the hill and think, "my god, that's a long way up, I'll never be able to stomach that," it is very different than staying with the experience of embodiment at that moment. The running, when it becomes an experience lived in the moment, is a succession of moments. And as intense as they may be, because attention is focused on now instead of moments from now, the crush of the future is relieved.

You will get a lot more out of yourself by staying in the moment and feeling the sensations rather than thinking about them. This is not the same as brute gutting through the experience of what might be called pain. While exercising, you should listen to your body to extract any vital information out of the sensations and perceptions you are having. Pay attention, so you can know the difference between sensations that can be pushed through and those that should be respected.

Sport, like life, can be joyful, and some of this joy comes from the quality of attention you bring to the sport, in addition to the activity being fun.

Mindful Yoga

Siddhartha Gautama was an accomplished yogi before he became the Buddha. The word "yoga" derives from the verb *yuj*: "to yoke" or "to bind together." The yogi seeks to yoke body and mind and the future and past with the present moment. Yoga has become enormously popular in the United States with an emphasis on the physical postures or asanas. Yet, according to Frank Jude Boccio in his book *Mindfulness Yoga*, only three of Patanjali's 195 aphorisms deal with *asana*.

Like any activity, yoga can be done with our without mindfulness. However, when done with mindfulness, yoga can be a powerful practice for alleviating chronic pain and suffering. Yoga is an integral component in Mindfulness-Based Stress Reduction, where the emphasis is not on performing the postures correctly or getting a great workout. The emphasis, rather, is on bringing mindfulness to the postures where they are done very slowly. Mindful yoga provides you with an opportunity to take mindfulness into motion and facilitates its integration into daily life.

Awake at Work

If you are like most people, you spend at least forty hours or more each week at your job. You also spend time commuting back and forth to that job. The time devoted to work is roughly half of your waking life. How do you want to spend this time? If you live your life waiting for the weekends and vacations to "really live," then you are spending your life waiting and not living. The Buddha's message provides a way to be fully engaged with whatever you are doing, and this means, most of the time, your job. Being awake at work is one of the more challenging places to be awake. There are petty tyrant bosses, mindless colleagues, and not much evidence of the Noble Eight-Fold Path in action. If you are not awake at work, work will be stressful.

Stress is one of the most pervasive and insidious problems facing the workplace today. In fact, the Occupational Safety and Health Administration (OSHA) has declared stress a hazard of the workplace. It is estimated that stress costs American corporations $300 billion annually, or $7,500 per worker per year when lost hours due to absenteeism, reduced productivity, and workers' compensation benefits are considered.

"Human beings must, in a sense, always, in order to create meaning, in order to create an ecology of belonging around them, must bring the central questions of their life into whatever they are doing most of the time."—David Whyte

If you approach your work life as a necessity and an obligation, you might neglect its "soul" elements. The poet, corporate consultant, and Zen practitioner David Whyte suggests that connecting with your soul at work is a responsibility, not a luxury. In his three books on work life, *The Heart Aroused: The Preservation of Soul in Corporate America*, *Crossing the Unknown Sea: Work as Pilgrimage of Identity*, and *The Three Marriages: Reimaging Self, Work, and Relationship*, he identifies work as a place of sacred visibility. It is the expression of the public, community-serving self. It is the reflection of core values of competence, effectiveness, and accomplishment. If you are disconnected, dissatisfied, or disgruntled with your work experience, a significant portion of yourself may be compromised.

The workplace is the source of many conditioned reactions. Greed, hatred, and delusion are frequent visitors. Generosity, lovingkindness, and wisdom, perhaps less frequent. Today's workplace is also a place of great uncertainty. The Three Poisons have adversely impacted the economy. The financial collapse of 2008 revealed how the system was based on false assumptions and blind ignorance driven by greed. Each moment at work may be a reflection of impermanence. Mindfulness can help you to steel yourself against this uncertainty.

Work may be an unavoidable intrusion into life. For some, there is great joy in work. An October 2009 *New York Times* article, "How Mindfulness Can Make for Better Doctors," described one surgeon who said, "Time in the O.R. is not work; it's play." That's the Buddha at work!

Spiritual Materialism

Being in such a consumer culture, you may be at risk for consumerizing your spirituality. Is Buddhism immune from such consumption? Thubten Chodron warns, "When we turn to spirituality, we may think that we're leaving behind the corruption of the world for higher purposes. But our old ways of thinking do not disappear; they follow us, coloring the way we approach spiritual practice."

Chogyam Trungpa Rinpoche says in his classic *Cutting Through Spiritual Materialism*:

> *We have come here to learn about spirituality. I trust the genuine quality of this search but we must question its nature. The problem is that ego can convert anything to its own use, even spirituality. Ego is constantly attempting to acquire and apply the teachings of spirituality for its own benefit. We become skillful actors, and while playing deaf and dumb to the real meaning of the teachings, we find some comfort in pretending to follow the path. This rationalization of the spiritual path and one's actions must be cut through if true spirituality is to be realized.*

Buddhism is not exempt from such concerns. Just look at any issue of the *Shambhala Sun*. It is filled with beautiful and enticing ads for teachings and *dharma* paraphernalia—meditation cushions, bells, statues, you name it. If not careful, you can become attached to non-attachment. You can become identified with non-identification. You can get lost in spiritual materialism. A May 2005 cartoon in *The New Yorker* by Michael Crawford depicts a mother and her child exiting a burning house via an emergency ladder. The mother urges, "Simon, don't forget Mommy's yoga mat." Buddhist monks have been spotted wearing Gucci slippers and gold Rolexes. No one is immune to the allure of having things; the problem arises when your sense of contentment is dependent on having these things. Everyone must proceed with eternal vigilance in order to be free.

Cautions for Western Practices

Buddhism in America is inextricably entwined in marketing. Teachers must sell themselves and their services, and must raise money for their centers; they must sell their books and CDs. Spirituality is a product like any other product, right? You may also be looking for the "best" spiritual experiences—the highest states, the rarest teachings, the coolest teachers. Spiritual materialism may drive you to strive in a desire-laced way. You may get bored with following the breath because it is not as exotic as following some *terma* (secret teaching). The Buddha worked with his breath to awaken, and that practice can take you to awakening, too, if you can give yourself permission to do so and do the work necessary. And if you do so, fireworks won't accompany that awakening. It will be an ordinary moment of clarity. It has been said, "enlightenment is the ego's biggest disappointment."

The sheer abundance of teachings that are now available in the West may be both a blessing and curse. The blessing is the accessibility of the dharma in unprecedented ways, including the Internet. The curse is that such abundance may encourage consumerist attitudes. You may find yourself dining at the spiritual smorgasbord, taking a little of this and a little of that and creating a pastiche of teachings that serve your ego's needs and not the needs of true awakening. Instant gratification can be a trap.

In today's world, you don't have to work hard to get access to the teachings. You don't need to walk across a high Himalayan mountain pass; you don't need to sit waiting outside the gates of the Zen temple for days. You are a consumer with spiritual "dollars" to spend. In urban centers the choices can be dizzying, and the customer is always right. One danger is that if you don't like what you see in yourself working with one teacher, you'll just go down the street to another. Another danger is idealization. The honeymoon period can be ecstatic, expansive, and promising. But just like a good marriage, to get any spiritual attainment you need to stick around past the idealization once disillusionment sets in. All teachers, including the Buddha, are human.

Convenience is another consideration for spiritual materialism. Consumer culture is designed to make life more convenient or more of something (faster, cooler, healthier, et cetera). When you are in distress, you may recognize the increased need for practice, but can you sustain this commitment without a crisis? Meditation is hard. It takes time, and if you practice for prolonged periods, it can be physically uncomfortable and, mentally, may bring up things you'd rather not face. There is no quick fix and you need to be careful about seeking short cuts.

"Spiritual Olympics"

And if you do put in the effort, a final aspect of spiritual materialism to consider is what might be called "spiritual Olympics" or "The one with most spiritual toys wins." You can identify with how prodigious your sitting practice is, how many retreats you've been on, how many vows you've taken and teachings you've received. Is this any different than showing off your BMW to your neighbor? Is this any different than keeping up with the Jones's? Thoreau warned not to identify with the "clothes" of any new activity but to try to be different in how we engage with activity. He said, "Beware of any activity that requires new clothes, rather than a new wearer of clothes."

APPENDIX A

Glossary

Abhidharma: The philosophical section of the Pali Canon.

Anatta (Pali); Anatman (Sanskrit): No-soul, no-self, not self.

Anicca (Pali) Anitya (Sanskrit): Impermanence.

Arahat (Pali); Arhat (Sanskrit): "Worthy one." One who has attained enlightenment.

Ascetic: One who believes that spiritual growth can be obtained through extreme self-denial and the renunciation of worldly pleasures—ascetics often practice poverty, starvation, and self-mortification.

Bhikkunis: Buddhist nuns.

Bhikkus: Buddhist monks.

Bodhi Tree: Tree of Awakening; a fig tree; pipal tree.

Bodhisattva: A person who has already attained enlightenment, or is ready to attain enlightenment, but puts off his own final enlightenment in order to re-enter the cycle of *samsara* to benefit all sentient beings; the goal that a person taking the *bodhisattva* vows works towards.

Brahmin: The priests and the highest class of the hereditary caste system of India. The Brahmins controlled rituals.

Buddha: The Fully Awakened One. From the Sanskrit *budho*, which means "to be awake." Usually refers to Siddhartha Gautama unless otherwise noted but can refer to anyone who has attained full awakening.

Buddha-nature: True nature, original nature before you become a conditioned and constructed human being. *Buddha-nature* is the awakened nature that resides within you; your potential to become a *buddha*.

Chan: Literally, meditation. A school of Buddhism started in China in the sixth century by Bodhidharma. Known in Japan as Zen.

Daikensho: Enlightenment.

Dana: Acts of generosity.

Dharma (Sanskrit); dhamma (Pali): The teachings of the Buddha. Natural law; universal truth.

Dharma Wheel: The wheel symbolizes the Buddhist cycle of birth and rebirth. The wheel often has eight spokes, symbolizing the Eightfold Path.

Dhyana (Sanskrit); Jhana (Pali): Meditative states.

Dokusan: A private encounter with a Zen teacher.

Dukkha (Pali); Duhkha (Sanskrit): Dissatisfaction, suffering, disease, or anguish caused by attachment and desire.

Eightfold Path: The path to enlightenment outlined in the Four Noble Truths: right understanding, right thought, right speech, right action, right livelihood, right effort, right mindfulness, and right concentration.

Five Precepts (Silas): Buddhist guidelines for conduct and ethical living: 1. Do Not Destroy Life, 2. Do Not Steal, 3. Do Not Commit Sexual Misconduct, 4. Do Not Lie, and 5. Do Not Become Intoxicated.

Gassho: To place two palms together.

Kalpa: A unit of time for measuring the existence of worlds. One eon is said to be the amount of time it would take a seven-mile high mountain of granite to erode if it were brushed by a soft cloth every 100 years.

Karma (Sanskrit); kamma (Pali): The force generated by action and intention that affects one's quality of life. Good intentions and skillful actions lead to good outcomes for yourself and others. Negative intentions and unskillful actions lead to painful outcomes for yourself and others.

Kensho: "Self-realization" or seeing the nature of things, awakening. An initial enlightenment experience.

Kinhin: Walking meditation in Zen practice.

Koan: A verbal puzzle given to a Zen student by the Zen master designed to be contemplated and to bypass the rational mind. *Koans* transcend logic and are intended to be experienced.

Kshatriyas: According to the caste system of Hinduism and ancient India, Kshatriyas were rulers and warriors. This was the caste that the Buddha was born into.

Lotus Posture: A position used for meditation practice. Lotus posture entails sitting cross-legged with the top of your left foot on your right thigh and the top of your right foot on your left thigh.

Metta: Lovingkindness; lovingfriendliness.

Middle Way: The way between two extremes: neither excessive pleasure nor excessive pain. The Middle Way was the Buddha's path to enlightenment.

Mindfulness: Being aware of things as they are and as they happen. Living in the moment.

Mu: No-thing, no, nothingness; the most famous Zen *koan*.

Nirvana: The cessation of suffering by the elimination of desire. *Nirvana* is not a separate place or a destination. It is beyond all concepts and conditions.

Paranirvana: The continuation of *nirvana* after death. When the Buddha died, he reached *paranirvana*.

Prajna: Wisdom.

Prana: Breath, life force.

Pretas: Hungry ghosts. Frequently Anglicized as pretans.

Roshi: A title given to a Zen master, under whom a student must study if he or she hopes to reach enlightened mind. In Japanese it means "venerable master."

Samadhi: A profound meditative state with deep concentration.

Samsara: The infinite repetitions of birth, death, and suffering caused by *karma*.

Sangha: Community of Buddhists. Traditionally could be seen as the community of monks, but any Buddhist community of practitioners.

Sankharas (Pali); Samskaras (Sanskrit): Mental conditionings.

Satori: Enlightenment.

Sesshin: A Zen meditation retreat where intensive *zazen* practice takes place.

Shikantaza: "Just sitting." Sitting without breath practice or any other directed concentration.

Shunyata: Emptiness

Son: Korean for Zen/Chan.

Stupa: Burial monument that stands for the Buddha and his enlightenment. In India, Tibet, and Southeast Asian countries, *stupas* are usually dome shaped with a center spire. In China, Korea, and Japan, they are pagodas.

Sutta (Pali); Sutra (Sanskrit): The collected teachings of the Buddha.

Teisho: A presentation of insight from a teacher to students. Often the subject of a *teisho* will be a *koan*.

Three Jewels: *Buddha, dharma, sangha.*

Tipitaka (Pali); Tripitaka (Sanskrit): "Three Baskets" referring to the components of the Pali Canon: *Vinaya* (monastic code), *sutras* (discourses), and the Abhidharma.

Vipassana (Pali); vipashyana (Sanskrit): "Insight." The Buddha's method for meditation.

Zabuton: A rectangular cushion to place a *zafu* upon.

Zafu: A round cushion used for meditation.

Zazen: Seated meditation; total concentration of mind and body.

Zen: A school of Buddhism that emphasizes seated meditation and seeing directly into *buddha-nature*.

APPENDIX B

Periodicals and Websites

Barre Center for Buddhist Studies
"For the integration of scholarly understanding and meditative insight"
http://dharma.org/bcbs

Basic Mindfulness
Home Practice Program with Shinzen Young
http://basicmindfulness.org

Beliefnet: Buddhism
Buddhist practice, blogs, and inspiration
www.beliefnet.com/Faiths/Buddhism

Buddhadharma: The Practitioner's Quarterly.
Quarterly publication focused on dharma practice.
www.thebuddhadharma.com

BuddhaNet
Buddha Dharma Education Association
www.buddhanet.net

Buddhism Portal E-Sangha
Buddhist links
http://directory.e-sangha.com

Buddhist Directory
Buddha Centers in the Northeast
http://buddhist-directory.org

Center for Mindfulness in Medicine, Health Care, and Society
Founded by Jon Kabat-Zinn
www.umassmed.edu/content.aspx?id=41252

Dalai Lama
His Holiness the Fourteenth Dalai Lama of Tibet
www.dalailama.com

DharmaNet
"Worldwide net of study, practice and action"
www.dharmanet.org

Dharma Web
Includes worldwide directory of Buddhist Centers
www.dharmaweb.org

eMindful
Evidence Based Mind Body Wellness, Online Courses
www.emindful.com

Exquisite Mind Psychotherapy and Meditation Studio
Metaphors for Mindfulness and other mindfulness resources
www.exquisitemind.com

Greyston Bakery
Founded by Bernie Glassman
www.buycake.com

Inquiring Mind
Buddhist Periodical
www.inquiringmind.com

Insight Journal
Journal of the Barre Center for Buddhist Studies
www.dharma.org/bcbs/Pages/insight_journal.html

Mindfulness Matters: Tools for Living Now!
Daily Blog on mindfulness and Buddhism
http://blog.beliefnet.com/mindfulnessmatters

Sakyadhita
The International Association of Buddhist Women
www.sakyadhita.org

Shambhala Sun:
Bimonthly periodical on Buddhist topics.
www.shambhalasun.com

The Simple Living Network
Learning to do more with less.
www.simpleliving.net

Tricycle Magazine: The Buddhist Review.
Quarterly publication and online community.
www.tricycle.com

The Edicts of King Ashoka
Venerable S. Dhammika
www.cs.colostate.edu/~malaiya/ashoka.html

The Government of Tibet in Exile
Follow political developments.
www.tibet.com

In the Footsteps of the Buddha: Traveling in India and Nepal
A travel guide to pilgrimage destinations in India and Nepal.
www.buddhapath.com

WAiB (Women Active in Buddhism)
A website devoted to Buddhist women in society.
http://members.tripod.com/~Lhamo/13famou.htm

APPENDIX C

Book Resources

Armstrong, Karen. *Buddha.* (New York: Viking Press, 2001).

Aronson, Harvey. *Buddhist Practice on Western Ground: Reconciling Eastern Ideals and Western Psychology.* (Boston: Shambhala, 2004).

Batchelor, Stephen. *Buddhism Without Beliefs.* (New York: Riverhead Books).

Batchelor, Stephen. *Confession of a Buddhist Atheist.* (New York: Spiegel & Grau, 2010).

Batchelor, Stephen. *Verses from the Center.* (New York: Riverhead Books, 2000).

Bien, Thomas. *Mindful Therapy.* (Boston: Wisdom, 2006).

Bikkhu, Thanissaro. *The Paradox of Becoming.* (Barre, MA: Dhamma Dana, 2008).

Bikkhu, Thanissaro. *The Wings to Awakening.* (Barre, MA: Dhamma Dana, 1996).

Boccio, Frank Jude. *Mindfulness Yoga.* (Boston: Wisdom, 2004).

Brach, Tara. *Radical Acceptance: Embracing Your Life with the Heart of a Buddha.* (New York: Bantam, 2004).

Chödrön, Pema. *The Places That Scare You.* (Boston: Shambhala, 2002).

Chödrön, Pema. *Uncomfortable with Uncertainty: 108 Teachings on Cultivating Fearlessness and Compassion.* (Boston: Shambhala, 2003).

Chödrön, Pema. *When Things Fall Apart.* (Boston: Shambhala, 2000).

Dalai Lama, His Holiness. *The Art of Happiness.* (New York: Hodder, 1998).

Dalai Lama. *Ethics for the New Millennium.* (New York: Riverhead Books, 1999).

Dalai Lama, His Holiness. *The Universe in a Single Atom: The Convergence of Science and Spirituality.* (New York: Morgan Road, 2005).

Epstein, Mark. *Going to Pieces Without Falling Apart.* (New York: Broadway, 1998).

Epstein, Mark. *Thoughts Without a Thinker.* (New York: Basic Books, 1995).

Fischer-Schreiber, Ingrid, Franz-Karl Ehrhard, and Michael S. Diener. *The Shambhala Dictionary of Buddhism and Zen.* (Boston: Shambhala, 1991).

Forbes, David. *Boyz 2 Buddhas: Counseling Urban High School Male Athletes in the Zone.* (Peter Lang, 2004).

Fronsdal, Gil. *The Dhammapada.* (Boston: Shambhala, 2005).

Gethin, Rupert. *Foundations of Buddhism.* (New York: Oxford University Press, 1998).

Glassman, Bernie. *Infinite Circle: Teachings in Zen.* (Boston: Shambhala, 2003).

Goldstein, Joseph. *One Dharma.* (San Francisco: Harper, 2002).

Gross, Eric. *Liberation from the Lie: Cutting the Roots of Fear Once and for All.* (Book Surge, 2009).

Gunaratana, Bhante Henepola. *Beyond Mindfulness in Plain English.* (Boston: Wisdom, 2010).

Gunaratana, Bhante Henepola. *Mindfulness in Plain English.* (Boston: Wisdom, 1996).

Hanh, Thich Nhat. *Living Buddha, Living Christ.* (New York: Riverhead Books, 1995).

Hanh, Thich Nhat. *The Miracle of Mindfulness.* (Boston: Beacon Press, 1976).

Hanson, Rick. *Buddha's Brain: Happiness, Love, and Wisdom.* (Oakland: New Harbinger, 2009).

Harvey, Peter. *An Introduction to Buddhism.* (Cambridge: Cambridge University Press, 1990).

Kabat-Zinn, Jon. *Coming to our Senses.* (New York: Hyperion, 2005).

Kabat-Zinn, Jon. *Full Catastrophe Living.* (New York: Hyperion, 1990).

Kabat-Zinn, Jon. *Wherever You Go, There You Are.* (New York: Hyperion, 1995).

Kakuzo, Okakura. *The Book of Tea.* (Philadelphia: Running Press, 2002).

Kapleau, Philip. *Awakening to Zen.* (New York: Scribner, 1997).

Kapleau, Philip. *The Three Pillars of Zen.* (New York: Anchor Books, 2000).

Kaza, Stephanie. *Hooked: Buddhist Writings on Greed, Desire and the Urge to Consume.* (Boston: Shambhala, 2005).

Kaza, Stephanie. *Mindfully Green: A Personal and Spiritual Guide to Whole Earth Living.* (Boston: Shambhala, 2008).

Kerouac, Jack. *Wake Up: A Life of the Buddha.* (New York: Viking, 2008).

Khema, Ayya. *When the Iron Eagle Flies.* (Boston: Wisdom Publications, 2000).

Khyentse, Dongzer Jamyang. *What Makes You Not a Buddhist.* (Boston: Shambhala, 2007).

Kornfield, Jack. *A Still Forest Pool: The Insight Meditation of Achaan Chah.* (New York: Quest, 1985).

Kornfield, Jack. *After the Ecstasy, the Laundry.* (New York: Quest, 1985).

Kornfield, Jack. *The Inner Art of Meditation.* (Boulder, CO: Sounds True, 1998).

Kozak, Arnie. *Wild Chickens and Petty Tyrants: 108 Metaphors for Mindfulness.* (Boston: Wisdom, 2009).

Levine, Noah. *Against the Stream: A Buddhist Manual for Spiritual Revolutionaries.* (San Francisco: HarperOne, 2007).

Levine, Noah. *Dharma Punx: A Memoire.* (San Francisco: HarperOne, 2003).

Loori, John Daido. *The Eight Gates of Zen.* (New York: Dharma Communications, 1992).

Loy, Davd. *Money, Sex, War, Karma: Notes for a Buddhist Revolution.* (Boston: Wisdom, 2008).

Magid, Barry. *Ordinary Mind: Exploring the Common Ground of Zen and Psychotherapy.* (Boston: Wisdom, 2002).

Maguire, Jack. *Essential Buddhism: A Complete Guide to Beliefs and Practices.* (New York: Pocket Books, 2001).

McLeod, Melvin. *Mindful Politics: A Buddhist Guide to Making the World a Better Place.* (Boston: Wisdom, 2006).

Mipham, Sakyong. *Ruling Your World: Ancient Strategies for Modern Life.* (New York: Broadway, 2006).

Mipham, Sakyong. *Turning the Mind into an Ally.* (New York: Riverhead Trade, 2004).

Olendzki, Andrew. *Unlimiting Mind: The Radically Experiential Psychology of Buddhism.* (Boston: Wisdom, 2010).

Rahula, Walpola. *What the Buddha Taught.* (New York: Grove Press, 1959).

Rinpoche, Sogyal. *Glimpse after Glimpse.* (San Francisco: Harper, 1995).

Robinson, Richard, Johnson, Willard, & Bikkhu, Thanissaro. *Buddhist Religions: A Historical Introduction.* (New York: Wadsworth, 2004).

Roemer, Elizabeth. *Mindfulness and Acceptance-Based Behavioral Therapies in Practice.* (New York: Guilford, 2008).

Rosenbaum, Elana. *Here for Now: Living Well with Cancer Through Mindfulness.* (Satya House, 2007).

Rosenberg, Larry. *Breath by Breath: The Liberating Practice of Insight Meditation.* (Boston: Shambhala, 1998).

Rosenberg, Larry. *Living in the Light of Death.* (Boston: Shambhala, 1998).

Schireson, Grace. *Zen Women: Beyond Tea Ladies, Iron Maidens, and Macho Masters.* (Boston: Wisdom, 2010).

Schoeberlein, Deborah. *Mindful Teaching and Teaching Mindfulness: A Guide for Anyone Who Teaches Anything.* (Boston: Wisdom, 2009).

Segal, Zindal V., J. Mark G. Williams, and John D. Teasdale. *Mindfulness-based cognitive therapy for depression.* (New York: Guilford. 2003).

Shantideva, Acharya. *A Guide to the Bodhisattva's Way of Life.* (Dharamsala: Library of Tibetan Works & Archives, 1979).

Siegel, Daniel J. *The Mindful Brain.* (New York: Norton, 2007).

Siegel, Daniel J. *The Mindful Therapist: A Clinician's Guide to Mindsight and Neural Integration.* (New York: Norton, 2010).

Siegel, Daniel J. 2007. *Mindsight: The New Science of Personal Transformation.* (New York: Bantam, 2010).

Smith, Jean. *Breath Sweeps Mind.* (New York: Riverhead Books, 1998).

Snelling, John. *The Buddhist Handbook.* (Vermont: Inner Traditions, 1991).

Soeng, Mu. *The Diamond Sutra: Transforming the Way We Perceive the World.* (Boston: Wisdom, 2000).

Soeng, Mu. *The Heart of the Universe: Exploring the Heart Sutra.* (Boston: Wisdom, 2010).

Soeng, Mu. *Trust in Mind: The Rebellion of Chinese Zen.* (Boston: Wisdom, 2004).

Suzuki, Shunryu. *Zen Mind, Beginner's Mind.* (Boston: Weatherhill, 1970).

Tart, Charles. *Living the Mindful Life.* (Boston: Shambhala, 1994).

Thurman, Robert. *Essential Tibetan Buddhism.* (New York: Harper Collins Books, 1995).

Thurman, Robert. *The Tibetan Book of the Dead.* (New York: Bantam Books, 1994).

Trainor, Kevin. *Buddhism: The Illustrated Guide.* (New York: Oxford University Press, 2004).

Trungpa, Chogyam. *Cutting Through Spiritual Materialism.* (Boston: Shambhala, 1973).

Trungpa, Chogyam. *Meditation in Action.* (Boston: Shambhala, 1996).

Warner, Brad. *Hardcore Zen: Punk Rock, Monster Movies and the Truth About Reality.* (Boston: Wisdom, 2003).

Warner, Brad. *Zen Wrapped in Karma Dipped in Chocolate.* (Navato: New World Library, 2009).

Watts, Alan. *The Way of Zen.* (New York: Vintage, 1957).

Whyte, David. *Clear Mind Wild Heart.* (Boulder: Sounds True, 2002).

Whyte, David. *Crossing the Unknown Sea: Work as a Pilgrimage of Identity.* (New York: Riverhead, 2002).

Whyte, David. *The Heart Aroused: Poetry and the Preservation of Soul in Corporate America.* (New York: Crown Business, 1996).

Whyte, David. *The Three Marriages: Reimaging Work, Self, and Relationship.*

Wilfong, Cheryl. *The Meditative Gardener.* (Putney, Vermont: Heart Path Press, 2010).

Yogis, Jaimal. *Saltwater Buddha: A Surfer's Quest to Find Zen on the Sea.* (Boston: Wisdom, 2009).

Young, Shinzen. *Break Through Pain: A Step-By-Step Mindfulness Meditation Program for Transforming Chronic and Acute Pain.* (Boulder, CO: Sounds True, 2005).

Young-Eisendrath, Polly. *Awakening and Insight: Zen Buddhism and Psychotherapy.* (New York: Routledge, 2002).

Young-Eisendrath, Polly. *The Psychology of Mature Spirituality.* (New York: Routledge, 2000).

Young-Eisendrath, Polly. *The Self-Esteem Trap: Raising Confident Kids in an Age of Self-Importance.* (New York: Routledge, 2008).

APPENDIX D

Buddhist Monasteries and Practice Centers in the United States

National Organizations

BodhiPath Buddhist Center
www.bodhipath.org/centers
Tibetan Buddhism

Buddhist Directory
Buddha Centers in the Northeast
http://buddhist-directory.org

Buddhist Society for Compassionate Wisdom
www.zenbuddhisttemple.org
Zen Buddhism

Chagdud Gonpa
www.snowcrest.net/chagdud
Tibetan Buddhism

Community of Mindful Living
www.iamhome.org
Zen Buddhism

DharmaNet
"Worldwide net of study, practice and action"
www.dharmanet.org

Dharma Realm Buddhist Association
www.drba.org
Zen Buddhism

Dharma Web
Includes worldwide directory of Buddhist Centers
www.dharmaweb.org

Diamond Way Buddhist Center
www.diamondway.org
Tibetan Buddhism

Foundation for the Preservation of the Mahayana Tradition
www.fpmt.org
Tibetan Buddhism

Jewel Heart
http://jewelheart.org
Tibetan Buddhism

Karma Triyana Dharmachakra
www.kagyu.org
Tibetan Buddhism

Nalandabodhi
www.nalandabodhi.org
Tibetan Buddhism

Padmasambhava Buddhist Center
http://padmasambhava.org
Tibetan Buddhism

Palyul Ling International
www.palyul.org
Tibetan Buddhism

Shambhala Center
www.shambhala.org/centers
Shambala Tibetan Buddhism

Vipassana Mediation Centers
www.dhamma.org
S. N. Goenka

Alabama

The Fairhope Tibetan Society
Fairhope, AL
www.angelfire.com/yt/fairtibet

Green Mountain Zen Center
Huntsville, AL
www.gmzc.us

Alaska

Anchorage Zen Community
Anchorage, AK
www.alaska.net/~zen

Arizona

Bodhi Heart
Phoenix, AZ
www.bodhiheart.org

Desert Lotus Zen Sangha
Chandler, AZ
www.desertlotuszen.org

The Garchen Buddhist Institute
Chino Valley, AZ
www.garchen.net

Zen Desert Sangha
Tucson, AZ
www.zendesertsangha.org

Arkansas

The Ecumenical Buddhist Society of Little Rock
Little Rock, AR
www.ebslr.org

California

Deep Streams Zen Institute
San Francisco
www.deepstreams.org

Dharma Zen Center
Los Angeles, CA
www.dharmazen.com

Dzogchen Community
Berkeley, CA
www.dzogchencommunitywest.org

Empty Gate Zen Center
Berkeley, CA
www.emptygatezen.com

Empty Nest Zendo
Central Valley & Sierra Foothills
http://emptynestzendo.org

Gyalwa Gyatso Buddhist Center
Campbell, CA
www.gyalwagyatso.org

Hazy Moon Zen Center
Los Angeles, CA
www.hazymoon.com

Jikoji Zen Mountain Retreat Center
Los Gatos, CA
www.jikoji.org

Kadampa Buddhist Centers
Various locations
www.kadampas.org

Kagyu Droden Kunchab
San Francisco, CA
www.kdk.org

Land of Compassion Buddha
West Covina, CA
www.compassionbuddha.org

Mahayana Zengong
El Monte, CA
www.zengong.org

Mt. Baldy Zen Center
Mt. Baldy, CA
www.mbzc.org

Nyingma Institute
Berkeley, CA
www.nyingmainstitute.com

Odiyan Buddhist Retreat Center
Berkeley, CA
www.odiyan.org

Shasta Abbey Buddhist Monastery
Mount Shasta, CA
www.shastaabbey.org

Sonoma Mountain Zen Center
Sonoma, CA
www.smzc.net

Spirit Rock Meditation Center
Woodacre, CA
www.spiritrock.org

Thubten Dhargye Ling
Long Beach, CA
www.tdling.com

Vajrapani Institute
Boulder Creek, CA
www.vajrapani.org

Vajrayana Foundation
Watsonville, CA
www.vajrayana.org

Zen Center of Los Angeles
Los Angeles, CA
www.zencenter.org

Colorado

Crestone Mountain Zen Center
http://dharmasangha.org

Denver Zen Center
Denver, CO
www.zencenterofdenver.org

Great Mountain Zen Center
Lafayette, CO
www.gmzc.org

Tara Mandala Retreat Center
Pagosa Springs, CO
www.taramandala.org

Thubten Shedrup Ling
Colorado Springs, CO
www.tsling.org

Connecticut

The Center for Dzogchen Studies
New Haven, CT
www.dzogchenstudies.com

Chenrezig Tibetan Buddhist Center
Middletown, CT
www.chenrezigcenter.com

Delaware

Delaware Valley Zen Center
Delaware Valley, DE
www.dvzc.com

Insight Meditation Community
Lewes, DE
www.imc-lewes.org

Florida

Cypress Tree Zen Group
Tallahassee, FL
http://webdharma.com/ctzg

Palm Beach Dharma Center
Palm Beach, FL
www.pbdc.net

Southern Palm Zen Group
Boca Raton, FL
www.floridazen.com

Tubten Kunga Center
Palm Beach, Broward, and Dade Counties, FL
www.tubtenkunga.org

Georgia

Atlanta Soto Zen Center
Atlanta, GA
www.aszc.org

Drepung Loseling Monastery, Inc.
Atlanta, GA
www.drepung.org

Hawaii

Diamond Sangha
Honolulu, HI
www.diamondsangha.org

Idaho

Golden Blue Lotus Tara Tibetan Buddhist Meditation Center
Moscow, ID
http://community.palouse.net/lotus

Illinois

Ancient Dragon Zen Gate
Chicago, IL
www.ancientdragon.org

Blue Lotus Buddhist Temple
Chicago, IL
www.bluelotustemple.org

Buddhist Temple of Chicago
Chicago, IL
www.budtempchi.org

Chicago Zen Center
Chicago, IL
www.chicagozen.org

Rimé Foundation
Chicago, IL
www.rimefoundation.org

Indiana

Cedar Rapids Zen Center
Cedar Rapids, IA
www.cedarrapidszencenter.org

Gaden KhachoeShing
Bloomington, IN
www.ganden.org

Indianapolis Zen Center
Indianapolis, IN
www.indyzen.org

Sanshin Zen Community
Bloomington, IN
http://sanshinji.org

Tibetan Mongolian Buddhist Cultural Center
Bloomington, IN
www.tibetancc.com

Louisiana

Blue Iris Sangha
New Orleans, LA
www.blueirissangha.org

Dhongak Tharling Dharma Center
New Orleans, LA
http://quietmountain.com/dharmacenters/dhongak_tharling/dhongak1.htm

New Orleans Zen Temple
www.nozt.org

Maine

The Morgan Bay Zendo
Surrey, ME
www.morganbayzendo.org

Maryland

Sakya Phuntsok Ling
Silver Spring, MD
www.sakyatemple.org/spl

Tibetan Meditation Center
Frederick, MD
www.drikungtmc.org

Massachusetts

Barre Center for Buddhist Studies
Barre, MA
www.dharma.org/bcbs

Cambridge Insight Meditation Center
Cambridge, MA 02139
www.cimc.info

Cambridge Zen Center
Cambridge, MA
www.cambridgezen.com

Insight Meditation Society
Barre, MA
www.dharma.org

Kurukulla Center for Tibetan Buddhist Studies
Boston, MA
www.kurukulla.org

Sakya Institute for Buddhist Studies
Shrewsbury, MA
http://home.earthlink.net/~sakyacenter

Single Flower Sangha
Cambridge, MA
www.singleflowersangha.org

Michigan

Buddhist Society for Compassionate Wisdom
Ann Arbor, MI
www.zenbuddhisttemple.org

Lama Tsong Khapa Center
Kalamazoo, MI
http://vajra.us

Minnesota

Clouds in Water Zen Center
St. Paul, MN
www.cloudsinwater.org

Minnesota Compassionate Ocean Dharma Center
Minneapolis, MN
www.oceandharma.org

Missouri

Boonville One Drop Zendo
Boonville, MO
http://zen.columbia.missouri.org

Rime Buddhist Center
Kansas City, MO
www.rimecenter.org

Nebraska

Nebraska Zen Center
Omaha, NE
www.prairiewindzen.org

New Jersey

Olna Gazur
Howell, NJ
www.olnagazur.org

Pine Wind Zen Community
Cinnaminson, NJ
www.jizo-an.org

New Mexico

Albuquerque Zen Center
Albuquerque, NM
www.azc.org

New York

Dharma Drum Mountain
Elmhurst, NY
www.chan1.org

Empty Hand Zen Center
New Rochelle, NY
www.emptyhandzen.org

Kagyu Thubten Chöling
Wappingers Falls, NY
www.kagyu.com

Namgyal Monastery
Ithaca, NY
www.namgyal.org

Pine Hill Zendo
Katonah, NY

Rochester Zen Center
Rochester, NY
www.rzc.org

Zen Center of New York City
Fire Lotus Temple
New York, NY
www.mro.org/firelotus

Zen Mountain Monastery
Mt. Tremper, NY
www.mro.org/zmm

North Carolina

Chapel Hill Zen Center
Chapel Hill, NC
www.intrex.net/chzg

Charlotte Community of Mindfulness
Charlotte, NC
www.charlottemindfulness.org

Kadampa Center
Raleigh, NC
www.kadampa-center.org

Southern Dharma Retreat Center
Near Asheville and Hot Springs, NC
www.southerndharma.org

Ohio

Cloud Water Zendo
Cleveland, OH
www.cloudwater.org

Oregon

Dharma Rain Zen Center
Portland, OR
www.dharma-rain.org

Kagyu Changchub Chuling
Portland, OR
www.kcc.org

Zen Community of Oregon
Portland, OR
www.zendust.org

Pennsylvania

The Philadelphia Meditation Center
Havertown, PA
http://philadelphiameditation.org

Three Rivers Dharma Center
Buddhist Society of Pittsburgh
Pittsburgh, PA
www.threeriversdharma.org

Rhode Island

The Kwan Um School of Zen
Cumberland, RI
www.kwanumzen.com

The Skyflower Dharma Center
Pelion, SC

Tennessee

Losel Shedrup Ling
Knoxville, TN
www.lslk.org

Nashville Zen Center
Nashville, TN
www.nashvillezencenter.org

Padmasambhava Buddhist Center of Tenessee
Nashville, TN
www.pbc-tn.org

Texas

Dawn Mountain Tibetan Temple
Houston, TX
www.dawnmountain.org

Maria Kannon Zen Center
Dallas, TX
www.mkzc.org

Utah

Big Mind Zen Center
Salt Lake City, UT
www.bigmind.org

Vermont

Anadaire Celtic Buddhist Center
Putney, VT
www.celticbuddhism.org

Exquisite Mind Psychotherapy and Meditation Studio
Burlington, VT 05401
www.exquisitemind.com

Karmê Chöling Buddhist Meditation Center
Barnet, VT
www.karmecholing.org

Mindfulness Practice Center, University of Vermont
Burlington, VT
www.uvm.edu/~chwb/counseling/mindfulness

Shao Shan Spiritual Practice Center
East Calais, Vermont, 05650
www.shaoshantemple.org

Sky Meadow Retreat
Greensboro Bend, VT
www.skymeadowretreat.com

Vajra Dakini Nunnery
Lincoln, VT
www.vajradakininunnery.org

Vermont Zen Center
Shelburne, VT
http://vermontzen.org

Virginia

Ekoji Buddhist Sangha
Richmond, VA
www.ekojirichmond.org

Washington

Blue Heron Zen
Seattle, WA
www.blueheronzen.org

Cloud Mountain Zen Center
Castle Rock, WA
www.cloudmountain.org

Dai Bai Zan Cho Bo Zen Ji Temple
Seattle, WA
www.choboji.org

Dharma Friendship Foundation
Seattle, WA
http://dharmafriendship.org

Sakya Kachöd Chöling Retreat Center
San Juan Island, WA
www.sakya-retreat.net

Sakya Monastery of Tibetan Buddhism
Seattle, WA
www.sakya.org

Washington, D.C.

Insight Meditation Community of Washington
Cabin John, MD
www.imcw.org

Washington Mindfulness Community
Washington, D.C.
www.mindfulnessdc.org

West Virginia

Bhavana Society
High View, WV
www.bhavanasociety.org

Wisconsin

Deer Park Buddhist Center
Oregon, WI
www.deerparkcenter.org

Dragon Flower Ch'an Temple
Rhinelander, WI
www.dragonflower.org

Mahayana Dharma Center
Spring Green, WI
http://mahadharma.org

Zen River Sangha
Oshkosh, Neenah, and Appleton, Wisconsin
www.zenriver.org

Index